Red Nails, Black Skates

Red Nails, Black Skates

GENDER, CASH, AND PLEASURE ON AND OFF THE ICE

ERICA RAND

DUKE UNIVERSITY PRESS   DURHAM & LONDON   2012

IN MEMORY OF

NADINE McGANN

*The black skates were
really for you*

© 2012 Duke University Press
All rights reserved
Printed in the United States of
America on acid-free paper ♾
Designed by Amy Ruth Buchanan
Typeset in Scala by Tseng
Information Systems, Inc.
Library of Congress Cataloging-in-
Publication Data appear on the last
printed page of this book.

CONTENTS

Acknowledgments vii

Introduction. Skate to Write, Write to Skate 1

I. SEEING AND GETTING: NOTES ON FIELDWORK

Introduction. *Being in Deep* 17

1. Seeing and Getting 20
2. Sandbagging, or Grown-Ups Do This? 26
3. Score 32

II. SKATING IS LIKE SEX, EXCEPT WHEN IT ISN'T

Introduction. *Pleasure Points* 43

4. Skating Is Like Sex, Except When It Isn't 46
5. The End of Me, or My Brief Life in Hockey 52
6. When God Gets Involved 60

III. HOOKS

Introduction. *Redoing the Laces* 71

7. White Skates Become You 73
8. Form-Fitting: The Bra in Three Stories 79
9. My Grandmother's Shoes 85
10. Black Skates, or the Stake in Wanting 89

IV. LADIES

Introduction. *Athletic, Artistic, or Just Plain Perverse* 97

11. Skank or Ballerina: Codes of the Crotch Shot 103
12. Cracking the Normative 111
13. Oh, Right, Policing Femininity: Nine Inch Nails at Adult Nationals 117
14. Booty Block: Raced Femininity 128

V. MASCULINE WILES

Introduction. Masculinity with Teeth 139

   15. "I Stand beside Him with an Axe!": Hockey Guys Together 144

   16. Quads Make the Man, or What's too Gay for Men's Figure Skating 153

   17. The Girl who Fooled My Butchdar 160

VI. HAVING THE WHEREWITHAL

Introduction. Up from the Bottom 169

   18. Buy-In: Some Notes on Cost 174

   19. So You Think You Can Train, or Why Can Joshua Dance? 180

   20. Gifts of Nature, Freaks of Culture 186

VII. BLADE SCARS/BIOPSY SCARS: RETHINKING RISK AND CHOICE

Introduction. Blade Scars/Biopsy Scars 199

   21. Parsing Perilicious 204

   22. Telling the Mrs. 210

   23. What Sticks Out 215

   24. Losing her Manhood 219

VIII. THE POLITICS OF PLEASURE

   25. Pleasure on Its Face 227

   26. Politics at Hand 235

   27. Getting the Goods 242

Conclusion. If I Ruled the Rink, or Make the Rink by Skating 249

Notes 263

Bibliography 285

Index 297

ACKNOWLEDGMENTS

As this book details, one result of a decade increasingly immersed in adult figure skating is that I often think of myself as "a skater who," bumping teacher and writer down on the list. So I begin within my skating communities. At my home rink, the Portland Ice Arena (PIA) in Portland, Maine, Lynda Hathaway runs one of the most welcoming programs for adult skaters that I have encountered, and she helped bring a new dimension to my research by inviting me to become a volunteer coaching assistant. Thanks to everyone on Sunday night adult ice whom I've gotten to coach, skate with, and be coached by, and to so many others on public ice, freestyle ice, and club ice there and at Family Ice Center down the road. I could hardly begin to name them, but the adult skaters, and former kid skaters who turned into adults, include Mark Bettney, Dave Brook, Judy Fisher (accessorizing entourage extraordinaire), Teresa Henderson, Kathleen Janick, Allison Johnston, Amy Kaplan, Jennifer Lenardson, Dave Leonard, James Light, Laura Smith Martineau, Heather McGrath (who explained to me, among so many helpful tidbits to a new skater, that a fancy guy needed to sharpen my skates), Joe McGrath, Ed Morin, Elena Morrow-Spitzer, Diane Nugent, Janet O'Toole, Caroline Allam Paras, Lori Sheldon, Val Smith-Punsky and Anna Welch (the other two members of the Fab Femme Fatales competition team), Molly Spindler, Norma Ware (who found me at public skating and helped me relearn some basics), and Glenda Winn. Our skating lives are diminished without John Walker, Tom Beckman, and Dave Brook, who died over the last several years. Thanks to the kids I have had the chance to (stop being scared to) skate with, to the parents I got to know, who occasionally stepped in when I needed a skating mom myself, and to the staff and volunteers at both (and all) rinks who make skating possible, whether in the office, on the Zamboni, or during late nights at the computer, including Sharon Ingalls, D. J. Whitten, Rob Carrier, Mike Blanck, Anthony Reynolds, Luane

Howard, Josh Brainard, Dennis Patenaude, and Kevin Sackville, as well as Alan Wolf and many others in the North Atlantic Figure Skating Club.

I first ventured into skating beyond southern Maine at the 2006 Gay Games in Chicago. Jason Goldman generously came along as friend, research assistant, and not-since-junior-high competitive bowler; Jim Neal was a great fellow traveler. Three skaters I met there, Johnny Manzon-Santos, Sara Shley, and Mary Squires, have immensely enhanced my life, skating, and project. I thank them for sharing friendship, insights, and ice time, and for, on occasion, "putting me on the ice." From the Gay Games and Adult Nationals, I also thank Amy Entwistle, Cindy Crouse, Debbie Leung, Bradley Erickson, Burton Powley, and the "Ladies" in my competition group, Ladies Bronze IV (IV meaning ages fifty-one to sixty). I thought I'd have to stick it out in hockey to experience that locker-room camaraderie I'd heard about, but not when competitors cheer each other on. To Category V ("sixty-one-till-death") skaters, I aspire to live up to you. Massive volunteer labor goes into putting on Adult Skating events; my wish for some changes does not diminish my profound respect and gratitude for the work of all involved.

You know you're a serious skater when you've skated to "All That Jazz" (2011 PIA adult-skater group number, check), had a sponsor (Sheila and Shonë at Epiphany, now Salon Paragon, thanks!), and heard a coach tell you, even just that once, to "attack" your jumps. Ann Hanson has been a truly wonderful coach and friend. I hope she keeps telling me to "try one more" (meaning possibly sixteen more) for years to come. Thanks also to my first coach, Mathea Daunheimer, and to my frequent ISI Freestyle Five and sometimes bonus coach, Kristin Andrews.

On skates without toe picks: Dorothy Diggs and Denise Tanguay hooked me up with Greater Portland Women's Ice Hockey, where the players, and those in Falmouth, generously shared their locker rooms and enthusiasm. Maine Roller Derby also graciously let me hang out, watch, listen in, and ask questions. Killer Quick, Patty O'Mean, Vexacious D, Punchy O'Guts, and Jacked Rabbit provided extensive time for interviews.

Off skates (almost) entirely: At Bates College, where I teach, I received financial support in pursuing this research from the Bates Faculty Development Fund, and I owe thanks as well to the students in my courses; my colleagues in Art and Visual Culture; those in Women and Gender Studies (WGS), who offered extremely helpful discussion on a chunk of the manuscript; the Committee on Athletics, which has been my privilege to chair; Bates Athletics; the people connected to the Multicultural Center and Outfront; and everyone at the ready for emergency actions and other aspects of working toward an environment where people of diverse genders, sexualities, races, ethnicities, and economic status can thrive. Sawyer Stone, Jordan Williams, Meagan Doyle, and Jarrett Freedman, in order of appearance, were invaluable research assistants, sometimes continuing to offer interest and insights after they graduated. Lorelei Purrington, Anne Odom, Jessie Govindasamy, and Denise Begin have provided great administrative support. So, too, has Lauren Webster at University of Southern Maine, the school where people only think I teach, and where the WGS faculty, among other faculty, staff, and students, have provided another home.

I received very helpful feedback when I presented skating material in progress at the University of Wisconsin; the University of Southern Maine; the Boston Atheneum; the 2008 Flow TV conference; the 2009 Sport, Sexuality, and Culture conference at Ithaca College; and the 2011 Cultural Studies conference. At Duke University Press, Ken Wissoker's way with ooh, yes, or hmmm, maybe not, as I worked my way to the short-essay format and content of this book is just one reason that I have loved working with him. He also sent the book to two anonymous readers whose suggestions really sparked my thinking. Mandy Earley worked with me through the first rounds of the book process. Jade Brooks and Mark Mastromarino then helped make the book happen. I'm grateful, just to start, for Jade's ability to make daunting endeavors seem, and be, manageable and for Mark's graciousness in letting me grab the files back more than a few times without reminding me of my aspiration to be the lowest-maintenance writer he'd ever dealt with. Thanks also to Amy Ruth Buchanan for designing the book; to Katie Courtland, Dafina Blacksher Diabate, Helena Knox, Michael McCullough, Laura Sell, Amanda Sharp, H. Lee Willoughby-Harris, and Emily Young in Marketing; to Chris Dahlin for meticulous copyediting; and to Scott Smiley for the index.

For diverse forms and combinations of collaboration, sports talk, queer sex and gender community, intimacies, political work, family, friendship, pleasure, insight, manuscript reading, and help with hair, music, costumes, photography, and more, I thank, besides those already mentioned: Shana Agid; Cynthia, Ron, Rebecca, Jacob, and Sophie Barabas;

Toby Beauchamp; Jed Bell; Courtney Berger; Sheila Bourassa; Deborah Bright; Anna Campbell; Lorrayne Carroll; Yee Won Chong; Laurie Beth Clark; Ryan Conrad; Scott Cooke; John Corrie; Ra Criscitiello; kt Crossman; Craig and Kurt Daunheimer; Gabriel Demaine; Katie Diamond; Jennifer Doyle; Michel Droge; Jonathan English; Jonathan Flatley; Soon Flynn; Stephanie Foote; Judy Frank; Keelin Godsey; Debbie Gould; Stretch Graton; Gary Gurney; Sage Hayes; Rebecca Herzig; Jen Hodson; Lise Kildegaard and Luther, Kaj, and Axel Snow; Katharine Kittredge; Gwen Lexow; Paqui Lopez; Alexis Lyon; Roger Mayo; Kevin McHugh; Dorn McMahon; Joe Medley; Scott, Vera, and Gary Miller; Meaghan and Fili Monaghan; Jackie Parker; Spencer, Liz, Ellie, and Isaac Rand; Lydia Savage; Anna Schwartz; Annie Sprinkle; Beth Stephens; everyone at Outright/Lewiston-Auburn and Trans, Genderqueer, and Allies Yoga; the Portland Y; Words with Friends; the "Battle of the Sexes" game and other joys of morning drive-time radio; and the editorial boards of *Radical Teacher* and *Salacious*.

My mother, Marilyn Graton, has offered open-spirited engagement with some not-so-usual features of my life in more ways than attending the recitals of her hardly recital-age kid. I thank her also for the insights about education, class, and movement that have honed my thinking here, just as the mix of guts and garters that I associate with my three late grandmothers, Sophie Chananie, Adele Rand, and Iola Graton, has animated my passions. Sarah Holmes has attended virtually every Portland Ice Show I've skated in since 2002; her enthusiasm at the beginning encouraged me to imagine performing on ice, one small element of her friendship throughout. Wendy Chapkis has long been an amazing friend to share projects, among so much more, with; I am grateful that she kept reading even when I decided to write about sports. Finally, I thank Quinn Miller for the early-morning launches into writing, for so many generative discussions, and for the extravagant response to "I need skating music" that wound up producing more sparkle than any ice extravaganza.

Fresh Ice

In 2002, at age forty-three, I bought a pair of figure skates. It was almost on a whim although they weren't my first pair. I'd figure skated for a few years as a kid, enough to learn beginning jumps and spins. Despite a family income that was far too limited to pursue the sport seriously, I had even acquired one pair of skates with a key marker of goals beyond occasional recreation: The boots and blades came separately. After I quit skating in 1973, I kept the skates for decades. Mostly, they hung on a hook like a pair of idled toe shoes, except for a few ventures in the 1990s on a pond next to my office. Finally, during a 2001 move, by which time they were incredibly stiff, decrepit-looking, and, I had to admit, too small, I got rid of them, imagining they'd be my last pair. Even if I wanted to skate again, I reasoned, I wouldn't know which boots and blades to buy.

Maybe tossing my old skates initiated a tiny, percolating "no, wait!" Maybe it freed up a bit of longing that my nostalgic attachment to "good" skates had actually squashed, because my feet hurt merely putting them on. Whatever the reason, a few months later, on the lookout for a workout activity in my new neighborhood, it occurred to me that I hardly needed "boots and blades" anymore, just skates. I suddenly wanted to find some. I went to the local Play It Again Sports, bought low-end figure skates, learned that I lived four blocks from an indoor rink, and took myself to a public-skating session. All I could do at first was skate shakily around the edge of the rink, but I really enjoyed it. When I saw that the rink offered classes for adults only, I signed up, started back at the beginning, and was increasingly drawn in. I knew I was hooked after I fell on a turn six months later, badly spraining my writing wrist, and heard myself in the emergency room asking, "when can I skate again?" before almost anything else.

I was back on the ice three weeks later, on the way to becoming an "adult figure skater," which, in skating culture, is both a colloquial and official term for people like me. While "adult" as a common euphemism for "sexual" may invoke thoughts of a xxx movie, "adult skater" refers, among skaters and within the skating organizations that regulate training, testing, and competition, to people skating after an age when they might reasonably expect to become the next Brian Boitano or Peggy Fleming. The term also refers to a skater who never figure skated as a child or had insufficient childhood training to make a serious run at national competition. Brian Boitano, then, is not an adult skater but a figure skater who still skates. Some people classified as adult skaters, however, can be recognized from certain skills and their ease on the ice as having quite significant childhood training; they occupy a slightly different conceptual category.

I had expected that buying skates would help me switch up my workouts a little. Instead, over the next few years, skating changed my life dramatically. It transformed my athletic life, my work life, my social life, and, less directly, my erotic life. It increasingly determined my long-range plans as well as my daily and weekly schedules, which I came to arrange around available ice time and other physical activities, like ballet and cardio, that I newly thought of as cross training. It changed how I use and think about my body, about bodies in general, and about interconnected matters regarding gender, sexuality, sports, movement, resources, risk, age, race, economics, politics, pain, and pleasure.

Gay Games, Queer Paths

This book emerged from my skating. But it began with an opposite intention: to get more skating out of a book project. In 2005, at dinner with a few friends, the group started talking about a road trip to the Gay Games in Chicago the following summer. An international athletic competition for adults, the Gay Games, echoing the Olympics, takes place every four years. With "participation, inclusion, personal best" as its motto—in deliberate opposition to the Olympics' "faster, higher, stronger"—it offers competition in a wide range of sports, including track, soccer, rowing, bowling, DanceSport (competitive ballroom dancing), ice hockey, and figure skating. People can compete at diverse levels, divided in some sports according to age and ability, and sometimes with options for a queer twist. Figure skating includes "same-sex" pair competitions, which several of us at dinner thought would be fun to try.

Our group plans didn't get too far. Yet the idea stayed with me after the realities of expense, time, and other obstacles had taken out everyone else. I didn't really understand why I wanted to do it. I still don't. Yes, by that point, I was pretty deep into skating. I skated three or four times a week. I had a lot of skating friends. I was back to boots and blades. I still took group classes but also private lessons from a coach. I skated in the adult-skater production numbers in the rink's annual recital, which I loved. It fulfilled a certain hankering to be a backup dancer, a hankering big enough to embolden me in my first year past a lot of shyness as well as self-consciousness about a relatively low skill set.

But that didn't mean I wanted to perform solo programs, which are the routines set to music used for testing, exhibition, or competition. I'd only had test programs up to then and I could hardly handle skating them on practice ice. Sometimes other skaters just stop and watch. Because I have stage fright about certain performances—although not, for some reason, about teaching, presenting at conferences, or being a guest speaker—I dreaded those moments. During work on my first, beginning-level test program, I'd managed to avoid the situation because it had been choreographed to allow skaters to succeed somewhat independently of musical particulars that otherwise would require such-and-such a move on such-and-such a beat. So I'd go to public-skating sessions and practice the Freestyle I program, which was set to music from the movie *Titanic*, to Van Morrison's *Tupelo Honey* instead. *Tupelo Honey* was compatible enough in tempo and in heavy rotation at the time on the "classics of yesterday, best of today" radio station playing over the loudspeakers. In general, while I love movement to music, and the challenges of mastering a program's tricks and choreography, I'd never seriously even considered doing a solo in our ice show and certainly not for competition. I'm not much of a competitive type anyway, so that whole idea largely seemed alien to me.

So what was up? Probably an impending fiftieth birthday contributed a certain now-or-never impulse. I'm hardly the only person to toss physical and emotional challenges at advancing age. W. Hodding Carter IV recounts trying to qualify for the 2008 Olympic trials at forty-five in a book that is subtitled *The Probably Insane Idea that I Could Swim My Way through a Midlife Crisis—and Qualify for the Olympics*.[1] Dara Torres, praised in the press for showing what a "middle-aged mom" can do (with a training staff of seven), took on Olympic swimming more famously and successfully that year, medaling at age forty-one. Stories of related effort, if not matching glory, abound. Indeed, while figure skating at my age often strikes people as unusual, it situates me alongside many people I have little else in common with. Narratives about fear-conquering feats appear frequently in women's magazines for my age demographic, such as *More*, that often have little to say to queer dykes like me. Nor, I presume, do they speak to the comedian Adam Carolla, who offered a similar perspective, getting "philosophical for one second," upon being booted off *Dancing with the Stars* (DWTS). Carolla, famous for being unabashedly boorish and sexist on shows like *Loveline* and *The Man Show*, was Marie Osmond's successor in the DWTS role of representing for the mid-lifers. He sounded a bit like her, too, when he told viewers, apparently channeling Eleanor Roosevelt: "There's something that scares you. There's something that is *your Dancing with the Stars*. Don't run from it, embrace it, do it."[2]

In any case, while moving back and forth between the inexplicable lure and very explicable terror of competing in the Gay Games, I got an idea: Maybe I'd be brave enough to do it if I wrote a book about it. A book project would give me a second purpose to take my mind off competing and a stake to keep me from backing down. I'd have a reason to approach other skaters once I was there, thus mitigating the shyness that sometimes makes me experience social events as a series of would-be conversations turned into tortured internal struggles. Best of all, I'd get to skate more. Practicing would be research, my job. I wrote a little grant proposal, describing a plan to use the method called participant observation—that is, studying something by doing it—and a research question: How would the gender traditionalism and sexuality stereotypes that dominate figure skating be transformed in a queer context? I got funded to attend, signed up, and talked a former student, Jason Goldman, into reprising his role as a research assistant. He agreed to compete in bowling, so that he could participate and observe, too.

Pretty and Witty but Not Quite a Book Project

The project was on, and I was now skating toward a book, if not quite this one. The question I had proposed about gender and sexuality, a serious one despite its opportunistic genesis, turned out to be a bit of a bust, at least in terms of my preliminary expectations. I thought that the Gay

Games might offer a queerer rink culture in terms of sex and gender than the ones I was coming to know. In some ways, it did. Two women did a pairs routine that was kind of a punk butch/femme romance. A male pair acted out *Brokeback Mountain*, then newly released, complete with the beloved shirt that the heartbroken Heath Ledger character cradles at the end. Other programs invoked topics that had resonance for queer audiences, including one related to mourning that used a square from the AIDS Quilt and the group number, in which I participated. Set to Christina Aguilera's song "Beautiful" ("you are beautiful no matter what they say"), it challenged hate language. Still more competitors drew on camp and drag traditions. One male skater used an instrumental version of "I Feel Pretty" from *West Side Story*, a staple of gay entertainment. The audience response when the skater visibly punctuated the point at which a singer would have announced feeling "pretty, and witty, and *gay*" made the moment an insider love fest.[3]

Yet in many ways, sexuality and gender at the Gay Games ice rink were just the same as I'd come to expect at home. Who thinks of men's figure-skating competitions as the straight games anyway? Who thinks dykes figure skate? The much smaller number of women skaters accorded with the common lore about who participates in the sport, and the dykes I met there who frequently competed at the annual U.S. Adult National Figure Skating Championships, or "Adult Nationals," told me that I had met most of the out dykes who might be there, too. Meanwhile, the stereotype that feminine women figure skate while butches play hockey, hardly the whole truth anywhere, did not seem much differently related to truth at the Gay Games. In the femme/butch pair, the femme, not the butch, was the seasoned skater, and with a few notable exceptions, women's figure skating—note that one had to compete as either male or female—simply was not the Gay Games event for spectators in search of butch eye candy.

In addition, I didn't see much "queer" in the sense of deviating from mainstream, white-dominated, gay cultures. It was fitting that we ended the group number, "Beautiful," wrapped up together in a giant rainbow ribbon, one of the most palatable, popular, and marketed queer symbols, generally taken to reference a celebration of diversity rather than liberation struggles. Relatedly, surveying the program, the skaters, and the audience, I didn't see much that would make me expect a very queer reading of the line in "I Feel Pretty" about a "girl" who is "loved by a pretty wonderful boy." It alluded to gay men referring to each other as "girl," sure, but I suspected that probably few viewers would call up the boy as trans, the girl as genderqueer, or the pair as fag and dyke (in either direction). Nor did it seem likely that the number after the *West Side Story* program would be, say, to Queen Pen's "Girlfriend," the pronoun-switching cover of Meshell Ndegeocello's "If That's Your Boyfriend (He Wasn't Last Night)."[4] Queer hip-hop stands to the side of the white-dominated gay canon.

I Needed New Choreography

What next? A lot. To begin with, I knew that surveying the scene and some beginning interactions with other skaters did not really tell me enough about gender as lived or imagined by the participants. I wanted to know more about what I couldn't see yet, more about the normativity that prevailed on the surface, and more about the people who apparently fit cultural clichés. Consider two gay male skaters I met there. One started skating after he "blew out [his] elbows during the first Gulf War" (as a result of abusive push-up drills, not in combat as the phrasing might imply). The other began to skate as a meditative practice during a period when an ex-lover he was still close to was dying with AIDS. How people come to inhabit unsurprising categories like "gay male figure skater" may not be simple.

Nor do apparently simple categories always have simple criteria. What exactly, for instance, is that crazy combination of balletic aristocrat and child-beauty-pageant trampiness that characterizes many figure-skating costumes for girls and women? Why is it acceptable, while decked out in this careful, if confusing, production of highly stylized femininity, for female skaters to readjust their skating panties in front of judges and audiences, or to perform spirals (skating arabesques) that seem virtually designed for crotch display? What are the racial dimensions of acceptable femininity in a sport dominated by white people in which, as I will discuss later, skate-color conventions, rewarded body types, and the occasional harem-girl costume combine to suggest that Avoiding Racism 101 isn't part of the skating curriculum? These were just some of my questions that did not fold into the simpler "how queer will the Gay Games be?" formulation I started with.

I began to pursue them further, through various research strategies. Many, happily, involved me skating. I explored diverse skating scenes more mindfully than when I had started out: public-skating sessions versus figure-skating practice sessions; the municipal rink versus the skating club; whatever sessions I could join at places I visited. These included a rink in suburban Philadelphia owned by the oldest figure skating club in the U.S.; a rink in San Francisco with a far more ethnically and racially diverse population than most; a rink in the rebuilt, relocated version of a Portland, Oregon, shopping mall where the notorious Tonya Harding had skated; and the rink at Rockefeller Center in New York City, much smaller than it looks on the *Today* show, where my mother had skated once about sixty years earlier.

As I skated, I cultivated people I met through skating as informants, negotiating along the way how many of them began also and importantly to enter into the "friend" category. I worked as a volunteer coaching assistant for adult beginning skating classes, which enabled me to witness interactively how gender-encoded movements are taught and received as well as some aspects of skating that can fade from view: the long, slow process of learning basic moves that may come to feel like second nature; the huge difference that good equipment makes as opposed to skating on rentals. I competed at Adult Nationals, the competition around which many serious adult skaters organize their skating. In 2008, Adult Nationals took place at Lake Placid, where, despite skating in the lowest freestyle category there, I competed on the rink where the 1980 U.S. Olympic hockey team beat the U.S.S.R. in what is known in the annals of athletic and nationalistic glory as the "Miracle on Ice." In 2011, I competed at the Salt Lake City Sports Complex, an "official training venue," as a sign at center ice reminded us, for the 2002 Olympics, which is famous in the history of skating for a vote-trading scandal that led to the still controversial overhaul of the judging system, including the demise of the perfect 6.0.

Besides studying skating activities and events in which I participated myself, I studied skating that occurred in other contexts. I watched skating on TV as well as many of the competitions covered by IceNetwork. com. Among other materials, including TV skating specials, the website offers archived video streaming, which stays up until the next season, for all the major competitions under the auspices of U.S. Figure Skating (USFS), the association that presides over the competition system within the United States that feeds into international competitions like the World Championships and Olympics. I attended local competitions for kids and adults and two of the regional competitions that function as a qualifying event for the U.S. Figure Skating Championships, or "Nationals." (Unlike the Adult Nationals, which requires only passing requisite tests to participate in most events there, the regular Nationals requires most competitors to secure eligibility in tiered competitions along the way.) I went to holiday and end-of-season ice shows at local rinks, besides the ones I skated in, and in 2007 I attended the tenth annual spring show, "A Gift from Africa," for the group Figure Skating in Harlem, a nonprofit organization that combines figure-skating instruction for girls with tutoring and life coaching.

I also followed two local organizations of women skaters in other skate sports, attending practices, contests, and events: the Greater Portland Women's Ice Hockey League and the Maine Roller Derby (MRD). The first offers training and playing opportunities both to women starting hockey as adults and the increasing number who played on, or occasionally still play, on teams in school. The MRD is part of the reemergence of roller derby, as, in this recent incarnation, a women-run, women-played sport that, while still often engaged with sexiness, emphasizes athletic contest instead of staged brawling.[5] In turn, some of my observation led to participation. I never tried roller derby, which, I saw immediately, was beyond what my body could handle. But I let some hockey players convince me that playing was the best way to learn about why they loved it. I did learn more, but not with the effect that some of them expected.

Sidetracks to the Center

Meanwhile, as I read, skated, watched, and interviewed in systematic pursuit of research goals, several influences outside of skating worked to shape and reshape the project. These included a voracious appetite for TV talent contests like *So You Think You Can Dance, Project Runway, America's Best Dance Crew, Top Chef, America's Next Top Model*, and *America's Got Talent*. Among the biggest narrative makers these days about talent, money, training, and dreams of glory, they helped me bring into focus what I was also learning on practice ice: the extent to which money for training, far more than any talent that carries the implicit adjective "raw," is the key factor in how far people may advance. The shows also involve repeated encounters with the kind of benevolence scenario famously satirized in the cheerleader movie *Bring It On*, in which an Oprah-like figure provides the funds for an "inner-city" squad to attend the national championships. As I learned to itemize what undercapitalized skaters might want Oprah to pay for, I wanted to think more about the largesse economics that increasingly fund both pleasure and survival—and the effects of the likelihood that Oprah won't show up.

A breast cancer scare that required several biopsies affected my work, too. Most simply, it made me realize how central skating had become to my life. When the technician administering what had started as a "routine" mammogram told me that I might need a biopsy, I responded, "This isn't the right time for bad news. I'm skating in an ice show this weekend and my mother is coming to watch; I can't get through the show if she knows." Obviously, I was deflecting panic about deeper-order possible consequences, but it was true. Then, I went straight to the rink to tell Ann, my coach. I remember marveling as I was driving, when fear or forced calm put me into survey-your-life mode, that having barely (and not always) passed gym class, I now not only had a coach but also considered her integral, as both a coach and good friend, to figuring out how to get through the next few days. Once using autopilot was the clear solution, I didn't tell other skaters until after the show, but skaters figured in every subsequent stage of opening up about it.

Biopsies also started to shift my thinking about risk, age, and choice. Retraining my body to do a backbend so that I could pull my leg up by my blade into a catch-foot spiral had felt somewhat age defying in ways that now seemed delusional against the age-appropriate mutation of my cells. As people kept telling me, that's why women over forty need mammograms: Cells are more likely to go bad now. (Mine turned out to be nonmalignant "atypical hyperplasia.") Picking a dangerous sport that risked expense-incurring injuries also had different implications and consequences now that my body was generating trouble by itself, given the hefty-out-of-pocket expenses under privatized medicine even with good health insurance. This juxtaposition of risk-related body troubles was also marked for me physically because many skate blade accidents and biopsies leave, essentially, knife marks on the body. I felt like I'd been handed a compare-contrast assignment that I couldn't stop looking at and could never drop or finish.

In addition, and much less gravely, I took a new turn in the area of gender and the absurd when I learned that while marketers were asking me, as a member of USA Hockey, if I had titanium in my shaft (the long handle of the hockey stick),[6] the titanium clip inserted in my breast during my first biopsy was shaped like a breast cancer awareness ribbon, a contested token of corporatized and pink-ified approaches to the disease. These breast and "shaft" titanium products fed my interest in how gender becomes transformed and embedded, in the ribbon's case literally, through materials and technologies, a subject that had already grabbed me regarding figure skates, which are rigidly gendered by color (skates for females are white, for males, black). I was also struck, regarding the hockey-stick ads, by another contrast: between recent cultural products that seem to parody over-the-top displays of masculinity, like the figure skating comedy *Blades of Glory*, and persistent evidence that vaunted awareness about sexist foolishness did not translate into antisexist attitudes or practices.

Hooked

Finally, as I skated, researched, shared my work, and lived other facets of the life that skating increasingly dominated, I became increasingly focused for various reasons on the topic of pleasure. Adults who love skating often do so intensely. They evince their passion in the costs and risks they undertake to pursue it, in the accommodations they make for it, and in the ways they describe it—often through some widely common habits of reference that reflect, I think, both a desire to express huge and vast dimensions of pleasures and a culture in which extreme pleasure is often considered suspect. Possession, addiction, lunacy, compulsion, disease, or dementia, hence also humorous terms like "adult-onset skating." As I said earlier about myself, people get hooked.

My research put me in the middle of both pleasures I could apprehend intimately and those that eluded me personally, like the thrill some people find in competition or just about anything people love about playing hockey. These experiences made me want to do more, know more, and think more about pleasures. What sensual, emotional, and mental treats (or just the right trials) may bring someone back day after day and fall after fall? Intellectual interests mixed with political, activist ones, because I could already see how much skating pleasures depend on and illuminate numerous issues that call for thoughtful action on diverse fronts. Some I have mentioned already, like access to time, money, and health care. Besides, if an anti-oppression vision of a just and good world includes pleasure, then pleasure as an end, not just as a route to knowledge, matters, too.

I Wrote This Book a Lot Like I Skate

It was two rich girls who took my mother, Marilyn Graton, skating. She met them in 1943 when, due to a complicated circumstance related to the war, she transferred from P.S. 86, a New York public school full of poor kids, to P.S. 6, a school outside her district that was full of rich kids from Park Avenue. While she still lived in a tiny apartment with only a screen between her parents' bed and her own, her new classmates might dine at home on food borne on silver trays by maids who could be summoned by a button under the dinner table. (Their educational paths, my mother emphasized, would later diverge from hers again. They were destined for expensive private schools like Dalton; she, like other smart but poor kids, went to magnet schools like Hunter or, in her case, Bronx Science.)

As Mary Louise Adams points out in *Artistic Impressions: Figure Skating, Masculinity, and the Limits of Sport*, "Rich people and poor people . . . learn to move their bodies in different ways" through "cultural and economic practices" that can make them look like innately "different kinds of people."[7] The students at P.S. 86, my mother remembers, learned to sit with their hands folded, in front if students behaved, behind if even one of them didn't—"being trained to be good workers, I think." At P.S. 6, students learned to "speak out, work in committees, and write reports." Her new classmates also benefited from having disposable cash for special outfits and lessons, including for skating. Once on the ice at Rockefeller Center, my mother, in skates that hurt her feet, clutched the barrier while her friends, wearing little skating dresses, did tricks in the center. Then as now and as before—always, as Adams details, in changing, historically specific ways—ice rinks were places to display social status and to clock likely class differences.[8]

I owe both this book and my skating, with my own tricks in the center, to similarly intertwined conditions of economic and educational privilege. Like my mother's, my history includes some educational opportunities developed for children more affluent than I, kids who didn't, I was sure, hear "OK, but don't forget that it costs $25 to have the repair man even *look* at the electric typewriter" every time they wanted to use it. Schools focused on developing independent thinking more than docile behavior eventually brought me to a teaching position that includes intellectual endeavors in my job description. Partly because it, too, functions with money for teaching rich kids—with some cushion missing from public institutions being devastated by tanked government budgets—it provides me with both the flexible scheduling and cash that permit me to skate.

I also wrote this book like I skate in ways that extend beyond the conditions of doing both. In some ways, that doesn't make my writing different than before. Like anyone's writing, my writing is both a physical and mental practice. As my colleague Rebecca Herzig, who pointed out the writing-skating connection, rightly emphasizes, everything that might be labeled brainwork is always embodied labor. I have strains and remnants of overuse to show for both skating and writing. I'm also one of those skaters who can hardly avoid adapting to other people's music when I'm practicing. With similar habits of ear, I edit my writing for rhythm and cadence—at least the sort of writing that engages my attention to creative form. ("This paragraph needs a topic sentence" or "Don't forget our Athletics Committee meeting at 11:10 on Tuesday" gets no such attention.) In both writing of the former sort and skating, I rework even small bits over and over with the goal of having the product appear unlabored—but accomplished. In both I take risks, and not only physical risks in skating, in the ways I put myself out there.

But other connections to skating are specific to this book. In the same way that assembling a footwork sequence, program, or repertoire of skills happens one turn, one edge, one trick at a time, I wrote each of book's eight sections as a series of short essays or connected lingerings that I came to think were the best ways to get at the topics of the book. For in the details of pleasure—details weird, surprising, and mundane; details physical, emotional, or material; details delicious, repelling, or both or neither—I found that three things resided at the same time: important information about the intimate workings of pleasure, power, and politics; a call for democratized access to pleasures; and the enticing prospect of making pleasures better still. I hope in this book to contribute to advancing work in these three areas, including a sense of their connectedness. The *Red Nails* and *Black Skates* in the title stand in for the juicy, revealing details. Because red nails and black skates can mess with each other and might well generate rich ideas and associations in readers, I find them well suited for that purpose.

I also chose to write short pieces, and to avoid as much as possible academic language, with the goal to offer the pleasure of a good read. Ideally, it will be like a good skating show, carefully ordered yet easy to pick up anywhere, providing small satisfactions and a taste for more: more reading, more thinking, and more pleasure on and off the ice.

A Note about Naming the People I Talk About

I tell stories in this book based on observations, encounters, discussions, and interviews. I refer to people by full name or first name if I've received their permission (or request) to do so. To adhere to the derby code whereby players choose whether to divulge private identities to the public, I offered derby girls willing to be named the option of having me use their derby name, their civilian name, or both. Sometimes I asked permission to name someone after the fact if a casual conversation yielded an insight I wanted to credit or if disguising the identity of the person would be virtually impossible given the details I wanted to relate. I also followed the principle that I was authorized to name people who spoke to me from an official position, but I often chose not to do so. While insiders may deduce those names, I chose not to aid the process; my purpose is not to point fingers. Mostly, however, I refer to people anonymously or by pseudonyms, occasionally omitting or altering demographic, geographic, and other details, along with dates of encounter, to keep people's identities private. Some will recognize themselves anyway — or think they do — without, I hope, dismay.

I

Seeing and Getting

"Wow. You're really deep into this," my editor remarked as we talked about my skating venture earlier that day at the mall that was attached to our conference site in Dallas. I'd been thinking that myself, but for totally different reasons than his. When Ken had told me about noticing the rink, I was certain I'd never skate on it. I hadn't packed my skates and didn't want to skate on rentals. "Luxuries unfit us for returning to hardships easily endured before." That's what Hans Brinker finds in the nineteenth-century classic children's novel bearing his name when, to raise money for his family, he sells the skates that he'd received as a gift and returns to traveling Holland's frozen waterways on his old creaky handmade wooden runners.[1] It's true. Though I happily rented bowling shoes, I was too accustomed to my own figure skates: worn by me alone, remolded by my use, with good boot support and a nicely sharpened blade. Besides, I needed a break. Two months before the 2008 Adult Nationals, skating-as-training dominated my ice time. I worked almost exclusively on the spins, jumps, and footwork elements in the program, doing double run-throughs to build stamina. The feeling of having to practice had started to trump loving to skate, even on days when both were true, which occurred less frequently. Sometimes I skated when I was exhausted, a little injured, kind of sick, or just not in the mood; after all, working through the bad days is part of training anyway. A few days off sounded great. When I saw the rink myself, I was doubly sure. It sat in the middle of a food court. Skating for an audience, including maybe a bunch of my colleagues, did not appeal to me.

That was then, which lasted a day. By my second day off the ice, I couldn't look at the rink without longing to be on it. The champion skater Maribel Vinson Owen wrote in 1938 that figure skating has "siren charms."[2] It does for me. I couldn't resist.

What motivated Ken's comment, however, was not evidence that I was in thrall, but my explanation of why blade technology made skating on rentals so challenging. While blades may look from a distance like a flat knife on the ice, I told him, they have two edges, with a hollow in between, and a curve toward the front of the blade called a rocker, which skaters can use to rock to the front or back. Every move on skates, starting with tentative first steps, negotiates rockers, edges, and, on figure skates, toe picks. Spinning, for instance, requires finding the "sweet spot," the part of the blade best suited to spin on. Skaters, or their coaches, often choose a blade partly for its particular rocker and toe pick. Skating on rentals offered a brutal reminder of how much skaters depend on familiarity with their blades (and boots). On my rented skates, it took me a while just to skate forward somewhat comfortably. Eventually, I could execute some basic turns from front to back and a spiral. But they felt scary rather than taken for granted (although any skater can tell you that the most rote move, even standing still, can send you sprawling one day). I wouldn't have dared trying to jump.

Yet it wasn't my knowledge about blade technology that I associated most with insider knowledge. Instead, it was my experiences with skate sharpening. Figure skaters do not hand their skates over to any rink employee. Instead, for two to three times the price, plus the possible extra expenses of travel or shipping, they pay an expert who sharpens skates according to a person's type and level of skating. I get a pretty standard ".5" sharpening (here, the insider terminology) from someone in Massachusetts. He serves a substantial number of Portland area skaters despite being based at least ninety minutes farther south than the rinks we ordinarily skate at. I switched to him, several years into expensive sharpenings, from someone equally far away, after I experienced for myself something that I had skeptically heard other skaters describe: the ability to discriminate between different sharpeners' work, and the accompanying likelihood of strongly preferring one.

Over time, I increasingly went out of my way for his sharpenings, despite having previously deemed other skaters pretentious or self-inflated for similar behavior, and despite being able to see external influences beyond the actual sharpening that feed into an "I would only let so and so sharpen my skates" mystique and market. One is that some sharpeners let you know when they recognize someone else's work and then explain its patent inferiority. But by the time several sharpeners had made me feel like a faithless or undiscerning lover—"Who sharpened your skates?!"—I had resituated the bar for extreme measures that only top skaters could justify: Well, it's not like I'm not overnighting my skates to California or New York. By then I also knew that my tales of reprimand, which I'd correctly judged as an ooh-aah generator for my dinner companion, held little novelty to experienced skaters. They generally responded, "Oh, yeah, they're all like that."

The essays in this section concern being deep into something: what you can, and cannot, learn; how deep you can, and cannot, get; and how hard it can be to discern, remember, or keep in focus what constitutes insider information and where you stand in relation to it. In the essay named "Seeing and Getting," I talk about the research method called participant observation in the particular context of my research on skating. The next essays, "Sandbagging, or, Grown-Ups Do This?" and "Score," discuss two topics that grabbed me once I was deep into skating in ways that both extended my thinking about participant observation and made me realize that, on some matters, I would never stop thinking, in bemusement, anger, or befuddlement, what a messaging acronym expresses so succinctly: WTF.[3]

Seeing and Getting

Imagine yourself in the stands at one of the U.S. Figure Skating (USFS) regional championships, or "Regionals," watching a group of young skaters compete in the category "Juvenile Girls." What can you discern about them and how? If you ordinarily pay no attention to skating but have a schedule or program, you can probably tell that Juvenile Girls compete at the lowest level offered there. The exact order of the levels—Juvenile, Intermediate, Novice, Junior, and Senior—doesn't make obvious sense. But Juvenile definitely sounds young, even a bit nastily like those hockey categories for kids: Mite, Squirt, Peewee, Bantam (small chicken?), and Midget. Besides, competitors at all the other levels skate as "Ladies" and "Men" rather than "Girls" and "Boys."

Looking around can be informative, too. Dresses for Juvenile Girls, for instance, may suggest a general consensus about the standards of femininity deemed to suit "Girls" aspiring to be "Ladies," although even from a distance contradictions may emerge. Rhinestones can appear to betoken custom tailoring or mall-chic Bedazzling gone amok. Dresses and makeup geared at upscale elegance can instead look like déclassé, age-inappropriate oversexualizing, especially if you don't know that plunging necklines and backlines only fictionally bare skin. Flesh-colored "illusion fabric" covers much that more visible material doesn't.

Prior understandings gleaned elsewhere can make the scene look different still. Pop skating movies, for instance, almost universally portray figure skating competitors as bitchy, backstabbing girls, sometimes with bitchy, backstabbing parents, whom unsophisticated skaters encounter at their peril. In the 2005 Disney movie *Ice Princess*, Casey, the protagonist, is a brainiac high school student new to skating whose science skills propel her to rapid skating success. Not knowing yet that high-performance skates must be broken in, she mistakes an act of sabotage for sportsmanly, aristocratic generosity when her competitor's evil mother buys Casey new skates at a competition. Bloody feet, falls, and an overall bad performance result. In the 1978 cult classic *Ice Castles*, Lexie comes from rural isolation to compete at Regionals in a clunky, handmade skating dress, with her name clumsily embroidered on its hopelessly dorky Peter Pan collar. The dress symbolizes her fate as she loses to girls with less talent but more sophistication. From a perspective shaped by movies like this—even given their obvious melodramatic license (Lexie later loses her eyesight in a freak accident and triumphs anyway)—a person might be prompted to wonder about the personalities behind the scenes as well as the function of the outfits. Is the right skating dress a component of victory rather than simply a marker of athletic fashion?

Prior viewing of competitions or skating shows, in person or on TV, can also be a source of illumination or of confusion. Why do some of the Juvenile Girls seem so advanced? Well, in a common practice that is known, at least to people who question its ethics, as sandbagging, skaters may improve their odds of winning by deferring tests that would move them into a higher level of competition. One might expect skating regulators to frown on sandbagging, which seems far from good sporting practice. But USFS actually acknowledges, allows, and tacitly supports this practice by giving skaters a lot of leeway about what they can include in their programs. Juvenile Girls, for example, need only single jumps to compete in their category. Yet the guidelines found on the Well-Balanced Program (WBP) charts allow all doubles, forbidding only triples. As a result, Juvenile skaters who win regional championships, and many who don't, can do more and score higher than many skaters competing several levels up. In the 2009 New England Regional Championships, the winner, with seven double jumps in her program, received 50.66 points, outscoring half of the Junior Ladies. Scoring, too, then, is no simple indicator of level—or, actually, of anything. It's hard to figure out exactly what a 50.66 means, even if you know that each trick or element has a base value (e.g., 3.60 for a double flip-double loop jump combination in the 2010–11 season), with other marks for qualities like "choreography" and "interpretation" factored into the total score.

What You See, What You Get

I sometimes think of participant-observation fieldwork as a series of activities pursued systematically to facilitate doing something that people do all the time in diverse ways: try to move from seeing to getting, to make sense of what we perceive. I use "seeing" metaphorically; a key feature of participant observation is embodied study that uses all the senses. Participant observation isn't fully distinct from other forms of serious attention, although certain features separated my research, I think, from other forms of being engaged in skating. I had a responsibility to avoid violating the institutional codes of academic practice, known as Institutional Review Board (IRB) rules, that govern research involving "human subjects," or, in other words, studying living people by interacting with them.[4] I pursued some endeavors for research that I probably wouldn't have done otherwise, like competing and playing hockey. I thought about my behavior and appearance partly in terms of what might aid or thwart productive interaction, and I undertook some pursuits more systematically than I would have otherwise, like skating at several rinks in an area I visited even if I loved the first one I found there. I sometimes took numeric stock of certain skating staples, such as the percentage of female competitors wearing ballet buns at the 2009 Synchronized Skating championships: nearly 100 percent, setting aside the skaters whose whole teams were pony-tailed.

Yet the fruits of fieldwork do not always come from the systematic parts of it. For example, I got hooked into the local women's hockey scene, which dramatically transformed my project, through a coach I met at a party who knew the host as her former neighbor. Meanwhile, as common descriptions testify, people often pursue information systematically for reasons other than academic. They read or watch everything they can get their hands on; religiously follow certain blogs; memorize sports statistics; or pursue objects of fandom across media, tabloids, and water coolers.[5]

Besides, even though the goal of moving from seeing to getting is a good description of the overall project of fieldwork, seeing and getting relate to each other in more ways than the idea of traveling from one to the other conveys. Illuminations can be sudden or fleeting. They can redirect me immediately back to what I don't know, forgot, or now see differently. For example, one former Juvenile Girl I know is now an adult male. If he had once skated as a "Juvenile Girl," then who's to say that any group of such skaters presents the array of female-identified people that it appears to? I know full well that many people do not comfortably inhabit, or continue to live in, the sex they were assigned at birth, or the clothes considered proper to that sex in particular situations. Yet encountering him offered an important reminder: Even among a group of kids whom one might imagine to self-select into a sport with such regimented femininity, a number may be ill-represented to varying extents by the outfit.

But they are not necessarily totally ill served. The skater I just mentioned remembers being increasingly miserable as the dissonance grew between the femininity he was admonished to refine for the sport and the male identity he was coming to recognize. Another former Juvenile Girl, however, who has always identified as female but is far from feminine, found in girly skating attire, paradoxically, a way to escape some restrictive perceptions, including her mother's, about what was proper for girls. She happily made the trade-off. She'd wear the dress, the makeup, the bun, anything asked of her, as long as she could go out on the ice and jump.

Sometimes getting is not about solving a mystery but figuring out later what I didn't get in the first place, sometimes by discovering what others don't know. A cousin's outrage at the skimpiness of skating dresses she'd seen on TV shifted when I told her about the illusion fabric. The conversation helped me figure out that knowing about it can affect people's perceptions of how risqué the outfits are. It was an interesting finding that people might interpret pretend bared skin differently than actual bared skin. Our interchange also reminded me about how easily you can forget acquiring knowledge that transforms your perceptions. Once you know about illusion fabric, its faint necklines and slight deviations from a skater's skin color often come readily into view.

Similarly, I remember being stunned at my first Adult Nationals to discover that almost all the women competitors competed in some version of the traditional skating dress, although I'd grown accustomed enough to seeing adult women in matching show-number costumes. By 2007, I could recognize (because I had formerly had it) the reaction of a student research assistant when he came to take some field notes at the Portland rink's annual show: Eww, he thought, the girls are dolled up like women and the women are trying to look like girls. But I'd presumed that adults would choose differently for their own programs. Now I'm so accustomed to seeing those skating dresses in competition, if not to wearing them, that the sight doesn't look odd, and the category of dress that signals to me "trying to look decades younger" has shrunk significantly.

Similarly, if what awaits getting becomes clearer in the process of getting it, so, too, I think, does the process of getting. A few weeks after attending the New England Regionals in 2007, I told a local skating friend that I had been struck by the sophistication and material trappings, in excess of what some of our local skaters display, that placing well seemed to demand. Yes, my friend replied adamantly, that's exactly why many girls don't make it past one trip to Regionals. She told me about an acquaintance's daughter, a "home-grown skater," from a nice but not fancy skating environment. When she encountered the girls coming from powerhouse training centers, she wilted. That was the end, right there. The regimen, accomplishments, and accoutrements that had made her feel like a serious skater made it obvious to her that she could never be a contender.

This was echoes of *Ice Castles* minus the fairy tale, but I find a better source of comparison in another friend's story about playing basketball as a teenager on an all-city team in Kuala Lumpur. Accustomed to being star players, the kids got trounced by a team from an affluent international school after the shock of seeing the school's facilities when they arrived to play. The school had an indoor gym, locker rooms, and a pool, far outclassing the visitors' well-worn outdoor courts. The visiting team, my friend remembers, felt humiliated and intimidated. Feeling out of their league socially, they played as if they were out of their league athletically.

Nice venues or upscale costumes, then, do not merely satisfy judges or reflect disposable cash for training, although, of course, they do that, too. The same people who can afford expensive training are the ones who can pay to have just the right glassy stones affixed to their skating dresses by precisely those dressmakers who know the codes of tasteful sparkling. Yet these stories also suggest that the very spectacle of means—especially delivered as stinging new evidence about lack and ignorance—contributes to performance along with the amenities that cash can deliver.

So much, then, is in the mix to figure out about understanding, even concerning this one issue. What in particular was so daunting in these panoramas of affluence? Dresses that look expensive or highly polished arm movements? A gym that has new bleachers or one that is simply indoors? From what angle, with what details, for whom exactly, and with what consequences do these spectacles emerge? While the idea of moving from seeing to getting may conjure a path laid with increasing information, what lies between often seems to me more like a hole or gap that's far from empty, filled with issues and sources of information that are more or less tangled, more or less knotty, more or less murky.

One other matter concerning seeing and getting: the fact or feeling of getting, not getting, being gotten, or not being gotten has politics, effects, and emotional content. Not getting, for instance, can hinder or reflect power. As Eve Sedgwick points out, the cliché that power is knowledge obscures the way that power confers the right not to know, as when political leaders from the United States can count on having their international interactions conducted in English.[6] Not getting can annoy or enrage. It can barely register, bemuse, panic, or hurt like hell. Think about the many possible intonations and implications of "Wow, you really like that?": Who cares? How interesting. Stay away from me. No, bring me in. Wait, can't you want this, or that, or me, instead?

Get This, or Don't

Fieldwork can reveal various relations to seeing and getting. For me, every day of working in the gap between seeing and getting meets, thwarts, leads to, and engenders moments of insight and connection. Sometimes getting and not getting are like flipping an on and off switch. Sometimes I want to climb into messy knots and just live there. Sometimes I want to untangle them. Sometimes I want to bust them open in the mythified fashion of storming the Bastille. That's the case with the topics I take up next.

2

Sandbagging, or Grown-Ups Do This?

I had a big clue several months after the Gay Games that some adults take actions in the quest for medals that might seem over the top when several people pointed out to me that the results posted online indicated a change in rankings for one event. There was one likely explanation: that the competitor whose placement rose, and who had been visibly and vocally angry about the outcome at the time, had contested the results. I was surprised. I'd learned of this grievance procedure at the on-site skaters meeting preceding the events. But I'd paid more attention to a rule suggesting a different relative value of winning. Skaters who find themselves alone in their category can agree to "compete up" against people whose age (younger) or tests passed (harder) puts them at an advantage, at least on paper. I'm sure my limited experience with competitors and competition contributed to my surprise. But others were confused, too: "At the Gay Games—really?"

Several years of skating and fieldwork later, my shock and confusion had been rerouted to curiosity about when and why grown-ups sandbag, that is, skate below their level, by deferring proficiency tests to increase their odds of winning. In USFS, the Adult skating levels are Pre-Bronze, Bronze, Silver, and Gold—named semiconfusingly after competition hardware. In addition, there are higher "Masters" levels based on tests that most Masters skaters passed as kids. Each level has two tests: the Free Skate test, with mandatory jumps, spins, and footwork; and Moves in the Field, which includes elements like edges, crossovers, and turns.

At Adult Nationals (or AN), sandbagging clearly abounds. Yet when and why people sandbag are not always clear. Competitors at my level, Bronze, often demonstrate that they can easily perform all of the jumps and spins on the Silver Free Skate test, often with a speed and comfort suggesting that they tested Bronze years earlier. Yet their programs may camouflage other limits. A skater may have the jumps and spins, which get all the attention, but not the back inside 3 turns that the Silver Moves test requires. In addition, certain skill levels involve age-related likely ceilings. Passing the Gold test, for instance, entails mastering an axel, a one-and-a-half revolution jump that requires a skater to jump from forward to backward, assume a backspin position, and then rotate one more time, all before coming down. A skating friend in his forties calls the axel the Holy Grail of adult skating. Unless you "had" an axel when you were a child, it's really hard to land one later—"land" is the skating term for successfully completing a jump, and "having" a trick means being able to execute it consistently—especially after one's (twenties or) thirties, even for adults who continue to advance in spins, footwork, flow, and jump combinations. Even the top Silver skaters may never be able to advance beyond their level.

Discerning when skaters are sandbagging, then, requires more than seeing their competition programs. Discerning why involves even more. People's relation to competition can be idiosyncratic or common, casual or intense, and more or less accessible to consciousness, as my own weirdnesses may begin to illustrate. I started to notice them at the Gay Games, where, accidentally, I competed up myself. Here's how. The figure skating events there did not occur under the auspices of USFS, apparently because USFS refused to accord same-sex pairs and dance events the same status as those on standard offer. Instead the Ice Skating Institute (ISI) sanctioned the event. ISI is known as the organization for recreational versus competitive skaters, although it also offers tests and competitions. When I decided to go to the Gay Games, I had only passed ISI Freestyle 3, which enables a skater to compete in that category, but I really wanted to compete in Freestyle 4. The Freestyle 4 programs could be thirty seconds longer than the Freestyle 3 programs lasted then (1:40, now 1:50). I thought 2:10 would give me a less hurried program. I could do more than rush from one jump or spin to another, and I would have more time for footwork, which I felt more confident about than the other tricks. So I really pushed myself to pass the Freestyle 4 test before the Gay Games' testing deadline. With a bit of generosity from the tester, I did. I didn't learn until I got to Chicago that an observation about my small-pond sample of southern Maine actually characterized adult skating in general. Women in my age group rarely pass Freestyle 5, which has the same barrier as the USFS Gold test: the axel. Thus, I had unknowingly squeaked

into what turned out to be, at that competition, the highest level represented by women in my age group, otherwise occupied by skaters much
better than I.

Competing up actually helped me a lot psychologically. Seeing myself
as the warm-up act for the real competitors (not totally correctly, as it happened) greatly diminished my stress. That surprised me, because I hadn't
recognized any pressures or desires that not being a contender would
take off the table. What I've seen since is that it makes me incredibly
miserable to frame competing in terms of trying to beat other people.
I'm not immune to the desire—which I usually frame as not wanting to
be last—but if a well-wisher says something cheerful about my chances,
my visceral distress is immediate. I'm nervous, seminauseous, and depressed, in debilitating ways; my skating tanks. This is something I've
had to learn about myself and teach people trying their best to support
me, especially in a context where, logically, competing to win is the focus
of many people around me.

Me, Too! Me, Too!

Yet even people clear about wanting to win have divergent understandings of meaningful victory and reasonable ways to accomplish it. Kids
sandbag for an obvious reason: Everyone else is doing it. That excuse
is the standard parental eyebrow raiser, except that now parents green-
light it. Young skaters can only forego sandbagging if they, or the adults
in charge of them, decide that their dreams or prospects do not include
national championships.[7] But an adult skater will never be the next
Michelle Kwan. So what gives?

For some adults, doing what the kids do is part of the appeal. When I
first heard "the kids do it" as an explanation, it seemed like the flimsiest
excuse. But I came to see that, sometimes, a desire to emulate ambitious
kid skaters may reflect, signal, and invite taking your skating seriously.
Maybe you can fend off some of that pat-on-the-head, isn't-that-special
condescension, which gets harder to escape the older you get. My friend
Rayne's basketball team went to the 2009 Senior Games, a biannual
event for athletes fifty and over. She came back enraged about the "you're
inspirational" speeches. Many, adding to the gag-me effect, were delivered by big pharma reps whose omnipresence—as at the "Celebration of

Athletes, presented by AstraZeneca"—also worked to frame the athletes as having decaying bodies ripe for heavy reliance on pharmaceuticals.[8]

This condescension happens in skating, too. I attended a practice at AN 2008 in the friend-as-informal-coach role, when a professional coach standing next to me, mistaking me for a professional, too, said, "Aren't they cute!" gesturing to some ice dancers. What a scumbag. His comment made me understand the possible appeal of the abusive jerk I'd seen coaching the day before. I'd wondered why his skater put up with him—we're grown-ups, no one can force us to take this. But at least he barked high expectations.

But Still

Sandbagging never affects merely the sandbagger, and maybe here is where the ethical disconnect mystifies me most. A Bronze sandbagger in a different age group than mine whom I had met at a competition commented after one AN that she had been more optimistic than I about my prospects for advancing beyond my qualifying round. I responded that if only five or six people in my group did what she did—skate in Bronze years after they could have passed into Silver—it made qualifying for any other skaters virtually impossible. She looked at me in some surprise and said, "But the kids do it. And I really wanted to medal." Her own actions and desires seemed to register in a different mental sphere than their effect on her competitors.

Maybe that's partly because she hadn't medaled anyway and had been outdone at emulating the kids in at least one significant way. Skaters who medaled in her event, she said, had each brought a coach to "put them on the ice." That's the figure skating expression for a particular set of partly ritualized support activities performed at tests and competitions: standing "at the boards," behind the barrier circling the ice, to offer assistance, directions, advice, and encouragement; holding your skate guards and a backup CD with your music; dealing with your particular craziness as much as it is recognizable (hug, no hug; say this, but never that); helping you deal with the aftermath. Obviously, familiarity helps; thus that is the huge benefit of having your coach put you on the ice. My coach, for instance, can immediately answer my inevitable, frantic question "where did my sit spin go?" because she knows what I usually forget. But skating friends make great substitutes. At competitions with tight restrictions, we can't always get right to the boards. But we can often diagnose each other's problems, understand requests like "remind me to curve my entry edge," and use our experience to forge workable dynamics.

A skater I met at AN 2009, Robin Johnson, marveled that adult skaters make ourselves so vulnerable by totally putting ourselves in the hands of coaches. The vulnerability piece, I think, for skaters at any age, is what makes sense of the phrase "put on the ice," which conjures a skater being plopped down by external forces rather than forcefully entering a competition space to demonstrate athletic accomplishment. Not surprisingly, and as I've learned from putting people on the ice myself, skaters relate in varied ways to that model. Personally, I relish yielding control in that situation (while also being anxious to avoid diva behavior).

Even Then?

Sandbagging is hardly the only method for securing advantage. Significantly, it's one of the rare free ones. Regardless of sandbagging, any notion of a level skating rink or playing field is a joke anyway, given skaters' divergent resources and a legion of obstacles built into the testing and judging structures. A few are particular to adult skating, like the continuing premium on jumps, the tricks least amenable to aging, and the inability to test down. Some adult hockey organizations, for instance, recognize that former college hockey players will not be in the A league at seventy or perhaps even at thirty. In USFS, you remain at the highest level you attained, even if you got there fifty years ago. Thus, while competing against skaters who have tricks two levels above mine, I may also compete with the same repertoire as skaters four levels ahead of me and twenty years older.[9] But I won't have the same finesse. Another antileveler, impossible to counter, is the duration of one's skating history. People who skated seriously at a young, or younger, age are often easy to pick out. They have diverse advantages, as a conversation with two skaters at AN 2010 emphasized. Both competed in the category affectionately known as "sixty-one till death," and they had started skating in their forties or fifties. One noted that, until recently, having less wear and tear than people who started younger, even a little younger, gave her an edge in jumping. The other one noted, however, that they competed against some women at a permanent advantage because they had once been show skaters. Coming late to skating also meant coming late to pizzazz; it was hard to beat ingrained stage presence.

A level skating rink would also require common access to deciphering what's going on around you—again, there is that relationship between seeing and getting. No one ever has it all figured out. The snotty coach ensconced in his insider status mistook me for his elite peer. The idea that a friend could put you on the ice, which other skaters had taught me to ask for, was still a bit foreign to the Bronze sandbagger, despite her greater experience with competitions. She punctuated her comment about bringing coaches by exclaiming that some of her competitors had "even brought an entourage." She could easily create one for herself, I told her. I had. That's one of the great pleasures in adult skating, I think: the mutual, rotating-star entourage.

That I could do this at my first AN partly through connections made during an expensive trip to the Gay Games—with a faculty research grant that I'd turned into a weapon against shyness—suggests how far from "free" are the resources that don't get filed under "expenses." It also sets off sandbagging, again, as probably the cheapest method around for getting an edge. I still don't get it, however, and I certainly don't get behind it. Sandbagging still dwells in my WTF category, although its lowercase variation may seem more appropriate in comparison to my next topic: the crazy obfuscations of scoring.

3

Score

Unfuckingbelievable

Rules of sport should be accessible and understandable. Yet in USFS, some rules for competition are so opaque and convoluted, even at the lowest levels, that coaches, skaters, and judges don't always know what they are supposed to mean. Sometimes I think that even the word *unfucking-believable* only begins to describe the situation. Diligent research and decades of experience can be inadequate to the task. I offer as an example my sad tale of trying to clarify spin guidelines for skaters competing at my level, which requires a detour into scoring rules to explain.

Something New, Something Old

In 2005 the International Skating Union (ISU) instituted the new International Judging System (IJS). Under the old 6.0 system, judges awarded each competitor a technical and an artistic mark, up to the "perfect" 6.0. In contrast, the IJS Code of Points accords each element a specific point value, with a Grade of Execution (GOE) that raises or lowers the base value, depending on how well it is executed. Spins and footwork sequences are also "leveled," or assigned a level ranging from 1 to 4, according to difficulty, variations, and novelties; spirals were leveled until the 2011 season. There are overall program marks, too, for five other criteria: skating skills; transitions, including footwork between elements (as opposed to in a footwork sequence); performance and execution; choreography and composition; and interpretation. In addition, various offenses, including falls and costume violations, receive standard deductions. (figure 1).

The International Judging System offers a fascinating example of how intention may utterly fail to determine effect or theory to anticipate practice. For one thing, while it was supposed to make scoring less subjective, IJS is far from objective. The same footwork sequence may be leveled

Short Program
Final

Free Skate
Final

Start time: Jan 29, 6:35 PM Eastern Standard Time   Venue: Greensboro Coliseum Complex   Judge detail scores

Place	Start No.	Name	Short Program Place	Short Program Score	Free Skate Place	Free Skate Score	Total Score
1	21	Alissa Czisny, Detroit SC	2	62.50	1	128.74	191.24

Free Skate Score	Executed Elements	Factored Program Components	Deductions
128.74	64.19	64.55	0.00

Planned Elements	Executed Elements	Base Value	GOE	Score
Triple Lutz+Double Toeloop	Triple Lutz + Double Toeloop	7.40	0.70	8.10
Triple Flip+Double Toeloop	Triple Flip	5.30	0.40	5.70
Triple Toeloop	Triple Toeloop + Double Toeloop + Double Loop	7.30	0.50	7.80
Flying Camel Spin	Flying Camel Spin 4	3.20	0.86	4.06
Triple Loop	Triple Loop (under-rotated)	3.96	-0.90	3.06
Choreo Spirals	Choreo Spirals 1	2.00	2.00	4.00
Triple Flip	Triple Lutz + Double Toeloop	8.14	0.40	8.54
Double Axel	Double Axel	3.63	0.29	3.92
Triple Toeloop+Double Toeloop+Double Toeloop	Triple Toeloop	4.51	0.20	4.71
Change Foot Combination Spin	Change Foot Combination Spin 4	3.50	1.43	4.93
Circular Step Sequence	Circular Step Sequence 4	3.90	1.57	5.47
Layback Spin	Layback Spin 3	2.40	1.50	3.90
	Totals	55.24		64.19

Program Components	Unfactored Score	Factor	Deductions	Value
Skating Skills	7.89	1.00	Costume/Prop violation	0.00
Transitions	7.46	1.00	Time violation	0.00
Performance/Execution	8.21	1.00	Music violation	0.00
Choreography	8.32	1.00	Illegal element/movement	0.00
Interpretation	8.46	1.00	Falls	0.00
			Interruption in excess	0.00
Total Factored Program Components	64.55		Total Deductions	0.00

1. Competition scoring made (somewhat) legible, if no less opaque, for fans keeping track on Icenetwork.com. Skaters receive a printout with codes like CCoSp4 (Level Four Combination Spin with Change of Foot) instead. Scores for Alissa Czisny's long program at the 2011 U.S. Figure Skating National Championships, http://www.usfigureskating.org.

differently at different competitions. Mistakes may be downgraded or not. After attending a seminar for would-be technical specialists, who are the people at competitions who identify and level elements for judges, a friend suggested a combination of problems built into the system: pressure to "call" the elements in a short time; the way under-rotation is hard to see from certain angles; how "grumpy or rigid" a person is feeling on a particular day; political complications like rivalries; and a reaction to stylistic elements possibly bleeding into the call. A double lutz might more likely look cheated (short on revolution) if you hate the skater's dress or music.

In addition, ıjs has had unintended effects that dismay or enrage numerous fans, critics, skaters, and coaches. Skating programs have developed a certain sameness in a quest to rack up points because creativity may not mesh with goals like executing numerous different turns at high speed in both directions for a Level 4 footwork sequence. Similarly, tricks like one gorgeous long-held spin in a single position have given way to hasty and, by now rote, point-getting variations, some none too flattering. In many people's estimations, these developments have contributed to numerous other ills, including more injury for top skaters preparing jump-heavy, body-contorting, no-rest programs, and declining ratings for televised skating, which critics attribute to monotonous programs and the scoring system's opaqueness to the casual or even engaged viewer. A scoreboard popping up a line of unanimous 6.0s for "artistic impression" after Jane Torville and Christopher Dean's legendary ice dance to Ravel's "Bolero" at the 1984 Olympics offers an easily legible thrill. Not so for the single 162.72 posted after averaging the judges' scores (which are no longer displayed separately) for Evan Lysacek's free skate program at the Nationals in 2008, even if he bested Johnny Weir's 161.37 by the tiniest margin.

At the Adult Nationals, IJS is used for the Gold and Masters levels of competition, while the old 6.0 system remains for Bronze and Silver levels, apparently for reasons related to expense and skill. IJS requires more technology and judging personnel. It also incorporates execution standards that some people think would unduly penalize adult skaters at lower levels. The older you get, for instance, the harder it is to get a sit spin low enough to count as one under IJS, with the thigh on the skating leg parallel to the ice.[10] The 6.0 system, allegedly, allows judges more discretion to reward effort.

Spinning into Hell

So here is the problem that my tale concerns. I've tried to explain it without generating a brain ache but if you feel one coming on, take the underlying point that some regulations make no sense and skip the next three paragraphs. The WBP Chart identifies the hardest tricks that skaters will get credit for at their level—thus offering a modicum of control against sandbagging—as well as the mix of elements that a program should contain. For the Adult Bronze singles program, the chart indicates that skaters can do three spins at most. It lists several guidelines for the spins, including the following: "Spins must be of different nature (e.g. spin combinations with/without change of foot and/or change of position, spins with only 1 position, etc.)." The spin descriptions for all levels actually have largely the same wording, although all higher levels include the "flying entry" as an option.

What does this requirement mean exactly? From the construction of the sentence, the material inside the parentheses seems to elucidate "different nature." Thus, all spins with only one position, such as a camel spin or a sit spin, are spins of the same nature. A spin combination that changes positions, like a camel/sit, is of another nature, which is differentiated, too, from spins that change the standing foot. So, to do three spins of a different nature a person would have to do a single-position spin, a change-foot spin, and one that changes position but not feet.

But within the context of skating culture, it's not clear at all for the following connected reasons. First, the phrase "spins of different nature," or "a different nature" as fully written out in the guidebook, comes from IJS, which offers a clear marker of "different nature." In IJS, spins are of a different nature if they have different codes. Working from that definition, it would seem that, despite syntax to the contrary, a person could fulfill the "different nature" requirement with different single-position spins because those have different codes, like an USp for upright spin and a CSp for camel spin. Second, the rule thus interpreted makes a lot more sense for Bronze-level skaters, because the Bronze test requires only single-position spins. Even if USFS allows elements beyond those tested, does it really want to forbid more than one spin to skaters who cannot yet do combination spins? It would be more logical if the rule basically means, "Just don't do three sit spins," which is how many people interpret it. But then again, that pesky syntax suggests that "different" is explicated within the parentheses. So, what is it?

Inquiry Can Be Overrated

In early 2008, after continuing debate among coaches and skaters at my rink, I decided to investigate. I e-mailed the USFS contact person listed on the AN announcement, who forwarded it to someone high up in USFS whose position title suggested she knew the answer. She responded to me, explaining that IJS codes determine spins of a different nature, adding the extremely helpful clarification that codes do not differentiate back spins from forward spins. Because spinning backward is a hard-won accomplishment taught at higher levels than a simple forward spin, this point might also be far from obvious to a Bronze competitor. I thanked her, saying that she was "especially helpful . . . in confirming that the definition of 'spins of a different nature' conforms to the ɪJS system even if the judging is under the old 6.0." I received a brief, friendly response about the "understandable" confusion.[11]

Taking her response to be authoritative, thoughtful, and generously thorough, I shared this information with people at my rink. Some remained skeptical. I then discussed the issue with many skaters at AN a month later. Not surprisingly, a lot of them expressed confusion and different interpretations about what the requirement meant. A Silver skater told me a related story about the jump requirement that "each jump may be repeated once but only as part of a combo or sequence." (A combo is two jumps where the second takes off right from the landing of the first; a sequence has more.) Under that rule could a skater do the maximum two of a particular jump in one jump combination or sequence? She and her friend, both veterans of Adult competitions, had recently gotten different answers. Also, one answer had come from a technical specialist and the other from a skating judge, two people responsible for deciding whether skaters get credit for their jumps!

Fast forward to a few months later when someone high up on the USFS Adult Skating Committee asked me in an e-mail if I had any items to suggest for the new quarterly Adult Skaters e-newsletter. Yes, I responded, excited about the chance to share the fruits of my research: How about clarifying the spin rules, and maybe the jump rules, on the WBP charts? I recounted what I had learned about how many people were confused as well as my own search for clarification, copying into my e-mail the helpful e-mail response about spins that I had earlier received. To my surprise, I got the following response:

> In Bronze and Silver, ["]spins of a different nature["] refers to the contents within the parentheses for the explanation. In ɪJS it means something different based on codes and points. I have been a part of creating the rules and WBP charts for six years, so [the person who responded to you] is correct, but not for 6.0 categories.
>
> In regard to the jump combos/sequences, there are countless hours that go into establishing the best possible verbiage for the WBP charts. After a jump is performed in a combo or a sequence, it may only be repeated if it is done alone. How is this not clear?[12]

Here is one of those WTF moments that shaped my understanding of fieldwork. Part of the WTF concerned the apparent spin and jump requirements in this latest e-mail. Could it really be true that the same spin directive had different meanings on a single page of instructions—that is, for 6.0 and IJS skaters?—or that Bronze skaters without a combination spin could only do one spin? Plus, I knew that her explanation of the jump requirement was wrong. Due to limits involving the particular edges that jumps take off and land on, it is common for programs to include two loops or two toe-loops performed in combination.[13] I could generously attribute this mistake—and the dismissive, rather mean, implications of "how is this not clear?"—to an annoyance-induced transposition of the actual restriction, which is that a jump once performed as a solo cannot be repeated except in combination or sequence. Yet I was still taken aback by what was missing: the slightest concern or apology that I'd been handed allegedly incorrect information despite following appropriate channels, or a pretense of interest in the evidence that the valiant work to articulate clear guidelines had not yet paid off.

Open Mouth, Insert Skate

I probably shouldn't have expected any such thing, given the history of my e-mail interaction with this woman. She had first contacted me four months earlier to tell me that research that someone else at USFS had agreed to share about the demographics of adult skating was actually "proprietary data," available only, subsequent e-mails explained, to clubs bidding to host competitions. I hastened to assure her that I had no desire to scam USFS out of proprietary data and little chance anyway, as an academic writer, to cash in on her information. To the contrary, I wrote, I was eager to fulfill a basic principle of ethical fieldwork: not to take from your informants without giving back. Might she let me write up an article about the information in exchange for the chance to see it? In any case, I said, I'd love to offer my writing services.

It was all to no avail. She offered to answer more specific questions, but I couldn't craft any that she'd answer. Nor could I talk my way out of being an object of suspicion, and I can't defer all the blame. I blew it. In trying to avoid looking like a smarmy suck-up, I omitted some niceties that I couldn't introduce later without looking like an even smarmier, now back-pedaling suck-up. I meant every word, however. I did look forward to the writing about adult skaters already in *Skating* magazine. I hadn't meant to imply any disregard or superiority. In retrospect, it's almost laughable to have imagined that she'd welcome my e-newsletter suggestion or that I could deliver it without yet another inadvertent gaffe. Our interaction ended when she specified what she would accept from me for the e-newsletter: "100 words is sufficient. Something upbeat from the perspective of a new adult bronze skater."[14] Two or three sentences on an assigned topic with an assigned point of view—that's equivalent to being told "you're dismissed."

Who Wants to Know?

People share or withhold information for reasons ranging from attitudes toward the seeker to claims upon ownership of the information. Part of my fieldwork entailed learning what might be taken as cheeky to ask, which I never quite managed to do. For instance, why decline my request for data about changing trends in the ages of competing adult skaters? It's hardly the secret formula for Classic Coke, or, exactly, "in the vault." I could have figured it out myself by making tally sheets from archived competition programs. But I'd potentially have to spend hundreds of dollars in travel costs and tens of labor hours to acquire it. Thus, while not exactly proprietary information, it functions as such. It belongs to people who can pay for it.

A lot of figure skating information functions as proprietary in just the same way. I don't suspect nefarious plots behind confusing Adult Bronze wbp charts. But certain people clearly do benefit from confusing rules in advanced ijs skating. Numerous "clarifications" and changing criteria for getting the most points have led to in-crowd advantages. One year a skater can earn two level-of-difficulty credits on a back-camel/back-sit spin by changing positions within the camel and then within the sit; the next year, only one change counts if you haven't changed the standing foot. Who can access all these picky, sometimes seemingly pointless, little changes? Coaches at big training centers, with skaters medaling nationally, and income for travel to professional education venues—on top of what it now costs to acquire usfs coaching credentials—have easier, sometimes earlier access to information. People in smaller programs operate at a disadvantage, being later to "get the memo," literally and conceptually, about judging details.

Some people benefit from hoarding information; others have a stake in failing to receive it, especially when revelations can hurt one's self-image or reveal that the fruits of diligent efforts are less than hoped. I've avoided plenty of information myself because of an emotional stake in believing the opposite. So I had no reason to be certain that my USFS contact, even with no prior rocky relationship, would receive my suggestion in the spirit in which I'd proffered it: as the gift of free road-testing that USFS Adult Skating didn't even have to ask for.

. . . . .

As I said above, a cardinal rule of fieldwork is to give back to the communities you study. I thought I could offer a bit of free labor for the people who work so hard to put on Adult Skating events. Maybe I could even help USFS articulate clearer WBP rules for skaters, given my bit of insight into what people found confusing. Sadly, all I can offer instead is that participant-observation research needs the same warning found at every rink and beside bodies of water that beckon with glassy smoothness before the ice is thick enough to skate on: Danger. Proceed at your own risk.

Skating Is Like Sex,
Except When It Isn't

While pleasure is a central topic of this book, my goal isn't to define it. A relatively satisfying definition circulates widely online: "Agreeable sensations or emotions; the excitement, relish, or happiness produced by the expectation or the enjoyment of something good, delightful, or satisfying."[1] I want to pull the judgmental "good" out of the mix, however, partly for a reason related to my disinclination to define pleasure further. I believe that thinking and acting about pleasure—politically, critically, in innumerable situations large and small—benefit from a certain leap-of-faith openness to accepting accounts of other people's pleasures that might seem alien or inexplicable. Fieldwork, activism, and other activities of research and living have also made me wary about relations between judging, naming, and policing where pleasure is concerned: Because you love x, thus you are a y, so now you can or can't do z.

I prefer to follow the example of Kate Bornstein in *Hello, Cruel World: 101 Alternatives to Suicide for Teens, Freaks, and Other Outlaws*. Bornstein exemplifies a wonderful open-mindedness about what might work for other people and a healthy disrespect for some questionable boundaries delineating the legal. She also has only one overarching criterion: If satisfying a desire entails "being mean to someone else," don't do it.[2] Like Bornstein, I understand the parameters of pleasure to be a matter for collective, expansive, and malleable definition.

Smells Like Team Spirit

Yet if, and because, *Hello, Cruel World* models expansive thinking, it also illustrates that every single person sometimes needs help to conjure other people's pleasures or make that leap of faith. Consider Bornstein's alternative to suicide #26: "Join a group that wants you as a member, or start your own group." The list of suggested groups illustrates the impressive array of depression-busting, life-choosing, and hanging-in-there possibilities on offer throughout the book. It includes gangs, unions, and bands; volunteer firefighting organizations; convents, community centers, and political campaigns; health, book, sex, and auto clubs; "The Party" and the mile-high club. Bornstein also offers a sidebar on why it's OK to "go stealth" if "there's something about you that disqualifies you" from a group you want to join.³ As she elaborates under #66 ("Go Stealth"), "Every outlaw, freak, or outsider dreams at one time or another of passing for normal, and not having to deal with the staring and the questions and the laughing and the harassment. Moments of stealth are moments free from all that." You can maintain your integrity if you "work at being the same you, no matter what else you're being."⁴ While she doesn't offer examples of going stealth, I envision someone participating in the Boy Scouts, whose national organization maintains an anti-gay policy, or in a religion-based social group whose stated beliefs don't accord with yours. Sometimes such groups are the only game in town or the most likely source of decent social interaction. Yet even having embraced the notion that people might benefit from joining groups that are less than fully welcoming or satisfying, Bornstein neglects to mention one type of group that scads of people join and that many people understand as a source of great pleasure and identity: a sports team.

From one angle, her omission is totally understandable. Teams function in some people's lives primarily as sources of great humiliation and misery whether they're on teams or off teams or waiting to be picked last for them in gym—or in my case usually second to last and ashamed of feeling relieved to beat out that one girl. Sports teams often represent everything that an "outlaw, freak, or outsider" can't get away from fast enough. Thus, the 2009 pilot of the TV show *Glee* could economically establish a key theme—misfits in high school—by showing football players perform a daily ritual of putting Kurt, the well-dressed, femmy queer kid, in the dumpster. The scene reads just as clearly as in the 1990 pilot of *Beverly Hills, 90210*, with shots of transfer students pulling into the parking lot at West Beverly High, looking wide-eyed at fancy cars that they hadn't seen back in Minnesota. On *Glee*, Kurt and the football players are not only antagonists—they contribute to defining each other. Bullying the queer kid and having the jock-tossed dumpster destination identify jocks and gay boys in popular cliché, and as mutually exclusive categories—although *Glee* later complicates that cliché with another one about how homophobes often turn out to be queer.

But then again, there's also the cliché that girls' and women's teams are filled with lesbians. Yes, it's a stereotype, and yes, lesbians on those teams have too often experienced soul-chilling antigay policing.[5] Still, stories abound of lesbians, proto-lesbians, and other queer people of various genders who found joy or haven, if perhaps imperfect, on sports teams. Without doubt Bornstein knows some of them; I doubt anyone queer doesn't. But something far from what moves you is easy to forget about and hard to envision recommending.

About Yes

Pleasures are diverse and diversely accessible. They can be physical, mental, spiritual, and/or emotional. They can be enjoyable at the time and—or only, differently, or not at all—enjoyable in retrospect. Their causes and content can be obvious or mysterious to people who experience them. They can be easy to articulate or impossible to put into words.

The essays in this section work to bring words and generosity of spirit to people's pleasures. Ice rinks offer numerous occasions to consider the intimate alongside the alien because many people find both there: sports they love to do and sports they'd never want to try (but might love to spectate); people who share a taste for the same sport but find different pleasures in it. "Skating Is Like Sex, Except When It Isn't" brings together diverse accounts of figure skating's intense appeal. I hope to convey the payoffs of attending to other people's pleasures, including maybe even a contact high. "The End of Me, or My Brief Life in Hockey" considers the barriers to that contact high, recounting one of the most informative and distressing features of my research for this book: a brief attempt to play hockey. Finally, "When God Gets Involved" dwells on the pleasures of an unlikely friendship, the possibilities of reaching across seeming chasms, and the movement of the spirit in the life of the body.

4

Skating Is Like Sex, Except When It Isn't

The pleasures I get from figure skating are enormous, despite frustrations, discomfort, injury, the cold, stress before an upcoming event, the occasional imposition of bad outfits, and other bothers. (Skaters, however, might add an imagined smiley-face emoticon, a knowing gesture to a certain pleasure in what we're willing to put up with.) For me, skating is a lot like sex. It's at once hot, intense, smooth, and sweet. It involves control, in ways that mix taking and yielding it. It's rhythmic, you can improve with practice, little things can make all the difference, it can feel like flying, and when it really works it's intensely in-body and out-of-body at the same time. While sex, skating, and pleasure are hardly coextensive, for me, they overlap a lot.

Speed Glide

I didn't interview anyone who described figure skating in terms of sex. Yet no matter how few figure skaters compare their skating to sex, which I don't presume to know, figure skating and sex have a number of characteristics in common, including the way that similar pleasures may be variously come by, interpreted, and prized. The feeling of wind on skin is a great example. It can be enjoyed as soft or stinging, cool or cold. It can come from moving through still air or from wind blowing outdoors. Consequently, wind on skin can signal "the outdoors" both actually in the outdoors and indoors, sometimes with a nostalgic tinge for makeshift rinks, local ponds, winding rivers, or distant pasts.

It can also signal and evidence "going fast," especially when speed is a key component of skating's appeal. A few people I taught to skate were impatient to go fast right away even if it meant tripping over their feet. They looked at me scornfully when I suggested a brief lesson in stopping, and they looked at me skeptically when I suggested slowing down to learn a few techniques that could ultimately help them generate speed.

Personally, I like speed after I've gotten some ease in movement under control and, if it's cold out, I prefer that indoor breeze, although the exhilaration of skating under the sun at Rockefeller Center made me rethink my absolutes on the topic.

Transcend, Dig in, and Smell the Popcorn

I also love the spaciousness of indoor rinks. But I didn't figure that out, despite my tendency to claustrophobia, until another adult skater mentioned it. She prized that feature partly from having had young children, making big outdoor excursions hard. Like many adult skaters, she'd gotten involved with skating lessons after signing up her kids. What she liked about skating was bound up with them, too. "I love being at the rink," she said, "everything about it: the combined smell of ice and popcorn, the energy of the kids' teachers," how the kids were safe there but independent, gaining mastery. At the same time, regarding her own skating, she loved how it took her away from everything else going on in her life. Unlike swimming, she said, where your mind drifts to other matters, skating is "totally engaging" because you have to have your mind on what your body is doing. "It's almost transcendent," she said. "You really escape into the moment."

Adult skaters often mention escaping life outside the rink. At first, I thought the meaning of such statements was self-evident. I don't anymore. One of my favorite interactions on group-lesson ice occurred when I was teaching a lawyer who had lauded skating as a totally different way to use your mind and body. One day she said to me sternly, "We usually learn, like with crossovers, to keep the skating leg [the one the skater stands on] bent. Yet this other coach told us today that when we stroke [i.e., skate forward] we should let the skating leg straighten after we push off. Can you account for this discrepancy?" When I pointed out the lawyerly formulation of that question, we both laughed.

The criteria for totally different can be very specific and, from the outside, difficult to see, especially because familiar mental processes, like analogies rooted in familiar realms, can help people accomplish physical activities that feel like moving and thinking in a totally different way. For that reason, I've found coaching skaters to be a lot like teaching college students, or the teaching that I aspire to do. At best, both involve back-and-forths that abet trying diverse strategies, although coaching involves a different arsenal for its focus on training in physical movement presented as such—as opposed to the physical training implicit in expectations that students sit during class, don't fidget too much, and, in some standard classroom architectures, literally look up to the teacher. My own coach mentioned that people may respond best to hearing, watching, hands-on guidance, or to particular combinations of those. By now, she can merely touch a place on my back to convey the following reminder: "Instead of letting your shoulders or back roll forward, your back needs to be straight or arched, concentrating exactly right there from entrance to exit."

Without question, that's true. At the same time, it represents a bit of wishful thinking to suggest that I think through my body to my brain. Like the lawyer, maybe, I have a stake in seeing skating as a world apart. My coach also sometimes asks me to stop (over)analyzing, telling me just to go out there and feel it. I always want to protest that I'm not thinking as much as she thinks I am. Even though I'm paid to think and think about issues in skating that crop up in all my research and teaching, having my coach tell me that I think too much is a sad dose of delusion-busting reality.

The lawyer's satisfactions in skating also depended on her changing ideas about it. For instance, she came to think that while the gendering of figure skating is "obvious on its face," figure skating also transcends both gender and gender stereotypes, including her own prejudices. Until she watched advanced skaters from closer up, and tried skating herself, the feminine aspects of skating that she had seen from a distance, like on TV, prevented her from understanding how much strength and difficulty were involved. The difficulty appealed to her and, she thought, would put feminine flourish beyond her reach anyway. She was happy enough about that, although femininity on ice was not beyond her reach to the extent that she implied. It takes no skating skills to show up at the rink decked out in a dress or pink sparkles, and just a few skills to add some gestures that commonly signal femininity (or effeminacy to some when men do it). She was absolutely right, however, that a lot of what is read as feminine in skating—to some people arguably all of figure skating—requires muscles, skill, and training to accomplish. Even placing your arms exactly where you want them to be is, in several senses, a production.

Something Old, Something New

In an essay involving training as a runner, subtitled "When My Cells Trained My Body-Mind," Deborah Gambs writes, "I had seen it on television. Close-up slow-motion shots of athletes at the end of the race. An image transmitted from my quadriceps through to my brain. Made a picture in the brain. Slow motion."[6] The image moves muscles, the muscles make images, the brain sees them, and the brain makes the body act on them. Gambs's account gets at something that I've marveled at with skating and wondered about: the many ways that external sources of influence seem to emerge from or inhabit a deep inside. Once in a while, like Gambs, I perceive images to have inhabited my body and directed its operation. I watch a more skilled skater do a camel spin and later perceive my own body to be executing that skater's technique—suddenly I can hook the spin!—without having consciously itemized what I saw. Or I sense having picked up a gesture or style of move from someone else, which I experience, in a way, as inhabitation. People commonly talk about the feeling of watching themselves as if from the outside. It's a little like that except that both watching and doing are foreign and familiar. As myself somehow outside of myself, I can watch and feel myself move, both as myself and as myself with someone else inside of me. Of course, I know by now how delusional can be our perceptions of what our bodies do and look like, whether those perceptions seem like dispassionate self-surveys or uncanny habitations.

I think that there's something key to the practice and pleasures of skating in the various feelings of deep-insideness that skating can engender, feelings that can be heightened when they mask, or conversely highlight, patently external sources of instruction and inspiration. Skating has the interesting feature of involving arduously learned ways to move that may come to feel natural. That's not unique to skating, although I wonder sometimes if the thrill of gliding on ice amplifies it. Skaters frequently mention gliding, often rapturously described, as key to skating's appeal, sometimes with further specification. A ninety-something skater, slowed but not fully deterred by advancing equilibrium problems, told me enthusiastically on the ice that nothing beats catching a great outside edge.

One magical facet of gliding is that, once you can propel yourself forward and maintain enough balance to feel confident that (most likely) your feet won't slip out from under you, gliding can seem effortless even if evidence to the contrary exists all over skating: on the ice at beginner lessons, where gliding is a taught skill that every skater has to fight for, at least a little; in the never-distant history of all skaters who regularly replace their skates. Because gliding, like everything else in figure skating, depends on the shape of the blade, new blades can temporarily return gliding to being a precarious activity, even if the new blades merely replace the same model that have been slightly reshaped by sharpening.

Insides Out

Feelings of deep-insideness can be fleeting instances of a palpable thrill at something that is so right. Or they can be durable, a "that's me" truth about the self that may be experienced as inherent even if the content of that truth is discovered by looking at other people and the expression of that self belongs in a future that one might not ever expect to have. Mary Gray suggests something similar in *Out in the Country* about identity in general. The book studies queer rural teens, who often came to understand their gender and sexuality partly by finding people they considered similar to themselves in various forms of media, ranging from old TV documentaries to Internet chat rooms. Gray argues that one component of their discoveries, which they rarely recognized as a find, was the idea that identity is primarily an inherent truth to be uncovered—something inside that, in popular language, "comes out." She proposes that we look at identity, instead, as "a highly social, contextual, and collective achievement," a perspective that the very involvement of other people's narratives supports.[7]

Gray's work on identity helps me look at the pleasures of skating, partly as they sometimes involve the pleasures of identity. Skating can illuminate, confirm, and feed identity, helping you "find yourself" or "be yourself." I like a particular kind of skating because I'm a particular kind of girl—or because it turns out that I don't have to be, as my knee-bend-investigating lawyer determined. But Gray also reminds me that what seems most deeply inside is bound to time, culture, and context. This point seems patently obvious when I see girls and much younger women tucking girly hair into hockey helmets or expressing some bemusement at gender or sexuality stereotypes newly encountered after moving to a different geographic region. But it was frequently inaccessible to me, at least emotionally, when I tried to play hockey myself. Encased in form-hiding padding, in dread of every approaching puck, I couldn't get beyond the miserable certainty that I was betraying an identity that, like those rural teens, I'd worked hard to uncover.

5

The End of Me, or My Brief Life in Hockey

The whole time I was writing this book, I used a photo for my computer desktop that, I think, perfectly captures why playing hockey, in terms of gender and sexuality, felt like the death of me (figure 2). The photograph was actually taken after I quit. I wanted a document of what I looked like dressed for hockey. But when I had suited up to get on the ice, soliciting a photograph was more than I could handle largely for reasons related to my identity as a queer femme dyke. *Femme*, like *butch*, is a term popularized in nonheterosexual contexts. The terms convey femininity and masculinity manifested by people whose assigned sex may or may not correspond to them. While some people consider butch and femme to be "lesbian genders," pointing to their erotic dimension for some lesbians, not all lesbians identify themselves erotically through those terms, and many people who do, me included, do not call ourselves "lesbian," even if we consider ourselves female and not heterosexual.

While femme identities and expressions, like butch ones, may take many forms, a key feature of my identity involves largely avoiding androgynous or masculine clothes. Having lived through a period where, among some lesbians, such clothing had seemed almost required, I never lost the thrill of realizing I could chuck it all—even that stupid pink tie. So I dreaded wearing hockey garb, even more so because almost everyone I told of my plans to try hockey responded, from various combinations of curiosity, disbelief, levity, and lechery, "Ooh, can I watch?" or, when erotic dismay was mixed in, "Oh, no, I can't bear to imagine it." The result was a feeling of humiliation, a dread of being seen that was so intense that I had to shame myself into putting the hockey gear on by reciting a list of imagined research benefits in my head. I also kept reminding myself about what I knew I had accessed a mere sliver of: the trial that some people face daily, and hardly just for recreational activities, when forced to submit to clothing that violates their sex or gender identities. It is the privilege of gender normativity that I hadn't felt so terrible for a clothes-

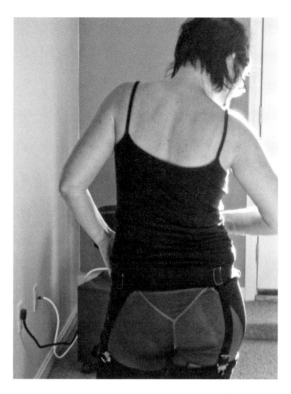

2. Hockey stealing my gender. Photograph by Yee Won
Chong, 2007. Courtesy of the author.

related reason since the class humiliation I experienced in elementary
school when I was ridiculed for a fake-fur winter coat that my mother had
neither the sympathy nor the cash to help me replace.

After I quit hockey, I couldn't bring myself to wear hockey gear again
in public, so I asked someone to photograph me in hockey gear in private. Yee Won suggested shooting the cumbersome process of putting
on hockey gear, which involves many separate pieces—including shin
guards, shoulder pads, hockey pants, wrist guards, and helmet—that
need variously to be pulled on, strapped on, carefully situated, or taped
in place.

The photograph, taken from the back, picture number 24 in a series
of approximately 170, represents the last moment in the process, not very
far into it, before the possibility of being photographed in my own gender expression became buried by gear. By that point, I had already put

on shin guards, which also cover the knee, and hockey socks, the knit leggings that go over the shin guards. From the back, however, the bulky guards aren't visible. Nor is the fact that I had not yet inserted the "pelvic protector" into my spandex "jill shorts," so-called because they offer a female version of the cups that athletes with flesh penises wear in sports that involve hurtling objects. Jock and Jill. The shorts also have Velcro at the bottom of the legs to secure the hockey socks, but I didn't use that. Instead, I used a designed-for-hockey garter belt, the method usually employed by players who wear boxer-type shorts instead of the shorts that I chose. The garter belt was the one piece of hockey attire that appealed to me. I felt comfortable, expert, and at ease using it. I associate garters with femininity, sexiness, and feminine lineage. Even though I almost never wear stockings that require a garter belt, my grandmothers did. But while I wanted the garter, I couldn't bring myself to wear boxer shorts or, I have to admit, the pelvic protector. Despite being shaped for pussy, the protector made me feel like I had an appendage where I didn't want to have one, flesh or artificial. I decided that my intense aversion to using it made it worth risking going without, hoping that if I got hit there, the padding in my hockey pants would suffice.

Still I felt unsexed in the outfit, in every possible use of the term *sex*— degendered, unsexy, desexualized, unable to recognize myself as desired or desirable. This remained true even after an ex, Annette Dragon, who had clearly liked me in my own gender, shared both a different displeasure with hockey garb and a highly more elastic erotic taste.

> I too hate hockey uniforms. If someone gets smashed into, I want to see the pain on his/her face; if someone scores, I want to see the elation. I'm not surprised that you hate the "outfit"—but a hot fantasy came to mind the minute I pictured you in one. Imagine that you get body-checked by a whole gang of women. You're lying on the ice, dazed, while they all gather 'round you. One of them starts removing your gear, piece by piece. She yells, "Stand back—give her some air!" But they only move in closer, waiting to see what's under that last item of protection . . .

While that fantasy didn't transform my view of wearing the gear, the idea that she could conjure it was comforting.

Oh, Puck

Annette was responding to an e-mail plea for advice that I sent to a bunch of people—in the overlapping categories of friend, colleague, relative, athlete, intimate, acquaintance, and comrade in the enjoyment of gendered pleasures that fit just right. I sent it when I realized how desperately I wanted to quit hockey after a month. The prospect of quitting made my heart race with delight. Yet I also felt cowardly, rigid, closed-minded, unadventurous, too quick to judge, and possibly deficient as a researcher, although hockey had been a late addition to the participant portion of my participant-observation research plan. Some of the local women players had talked me into it. Their description of playing didn't entice me in the least; neither did watching. But players kept inviting me to try. Why not, they argued; I already knew how to skate and would finally, unlike in figure skating, be wearing gear to protect me from injury. They didn't buy my certainty that I just wasn't the kind of girl who played hockey. They thought that hating the hockey outfit—which someone finally told me players never called an outfit—was a flimsy excuse. After a while it seemed flimsy to me, too. I decided to give it a minimum of six months, which I thought would be long enough to get a feel for the game, and maybe the kind of belonging that teams seemed, from outside, to offer. I wanted to hang around in the locker room as a player (in training) rather than a generously tolerated interloper, go out for a beer after practice, maybe even get invited to a holiday party.

But hockey made me miserable. This was not just because of the outfit, although the outfit contributed to my misery in a way I hadn't anticipated. Probably because I felt so alien to myself in it, I also felt, against any logic or fact, less safe from injury than in my figure skating practice clothes. In addition, once on the ice, I recognized that I had been deploying a preferred family coping device: to displace worry about an upcoming nerve-fest onto the question of what to wear. Now I had to face other unpleasant features of hockey: having to chase, receive, aim, and strike a moving object, all with minimal hand-eye coordination that decreases under stress, and the likelihood of crashing into other players. That last one should have been screamingly obvious far in advance. Secondary sources, my own interviews, and watching these same women play offered ample evidence that I'd probably had to suppress for long enough to talk myself into trying the game. I missed the evidence also, I'm sure, because I don't place crashes under the rubric of enjoyable rough contact, even though that is far from an empty category for me. So I misconstrued the rule in women's and girls' hockey against body checking, using one's body intentionally to knock someone down or into the boards. I thought it signaled that players valued avoiding collision. Now I couldn't avoid learning that some players love it.

Nor could I avoid learning that some distastes transcended the causes I initially ascribed to them, like a deep resonance with gym class that marked my first few times on the ice. I'd signed up for two hockey activities: the Tuesday night sessions offered by the Greater Portland Women's Ice Hockey League (GPWIH) for new and still early-along players; and a clinic, also for newer players, that a woman who plays and coaches with GPWIH strongly recommended. It started a few weeks earlier. When I got to the first clinic session, I learned that due to low enrollment, it had been readvertised as an opportunity for more advanced players to hone skills. Only a few of us were new to hockey, which amplified every gym-class horror. We lined up for drills, where everyone else had to wait and watch those who were struggling to complete the task. We had scrimmages — game simulations — before I even knew what a "wing," my assigned position, did. A coach held "chalk talks" during the "break" in which he described strategies for game situations; I had no clue what he was talking about. If I took off my helmet for the chalk talks, I then had to re-perform a challenging task that epitomized the nerd-among-jocks abjection that characterized my childhood if no longer my adulthood: securing the helmet without skewing my eyeglasses. That was more crucial to do correctly with progressive lenses, a little reminder of aging added into the mix.

On the ice with GPWIH, however, the differences from gym class were just as striking. In gym class I had been pulled from play one way or another: rotated out all the time (basketball) or instructed to step away from approaching flying objects to let someone else cover my position (volleyball, badminton, softball). Here, people really wanted to help me learn to play and to enjoy it. They kept passing me the puck in a way I could manage to receive. They were encouraging no matter what I did with it, which was rarely good. Despite all the generosity and goodwill, I just wanted to get it away from me. In fact, the best thing separating Portland women's hockey from gym class was that participation was voluntary. When it came time to scrimmage, I just said no.

Ooh, Can I Watch? Revisited

I don't regret trying hockey, or failing to stick it out, although players had indeed talked to me differently in the locker room when I was dressing to join them. One woman relegated me afterwards to a category of gross cluelessness that she hadn't put me in beforehand. Earlier quite willing to entertain questions, she started responding that I simply wouldn't understand. "Try me" wouldn't budge her; it was like she'd booted me in her mind from exactly the environment of shared knowledge that I imagined the locker room to offer. But other players seemed just as happy to relate to me in my role as an enthusiastic fan. They'd seen me in the stands before. Given the few people who came to their games, my presence was notable, if perhaps not as memorable as the people I saw at one game, when the Breakaways, the more advanced GPWIH team, played a team of middle-aged men visiting from Japan. Twelve Japanese women, presumably partnered with the male players, sat close together several rows in front of me. Once, after the men scored, one of the women gestured the others to stop their quiet clapping and murmuring. Then, at her signal, they did the Wave, to the immense delight of all, themselves included.[8] Eventually, after one game I attended, I did get invited along for beer after a game. I knew it wouldn't feel the same as having played together, but at least I got to hang out.

I also got to dwell on other people's enjoyment, which I highly recommend as a pleasure in itself. I remember a conversation with one of the few other beginners in my hockey clinic, who was new to skating altogether. We'd commiserated about wishing for some coaching on actual beginner skills. Yet when I asked her later how she was doing, her eyes lit up. She loved it just like she expected to. I, meanwhile, just wanted to get back to being me: the kind of girl who, as I sometimes shorthanded it to female hockey players, would rather be twirling around. Some of them were mystified until I asked them if they'd ever considered figure skating. "Of course not," said one of the women who had been most adamant that I should try hockey. Her tone suggested that she found the question ridiculous and the prospect horrifying. "That's like when my mother tried to make me take ballet." Exactly.

I think that many players my age, older, or even substantially younger, had another reason besides loving hockey themselves for presuming that I would. They expected hockey to liberate me from constraints imposed in childhood regarding what physical activity and aggression is considered appropriate for girls. They were like a friend who described as "amazing" the new "permission to hit" she found when she took up boxing at twenty-eight. With hockey, I discerned this factor in retrospect during an illuminating interchange in a locker room several years later with a player just off the ice as I laced up to get on. After she said something friendly like "we have to get you out there with us," I supplemented my usual comment about preferring to twirl around. I told her that I had chosen to try figure skating as a kid and listed other activities I had enjoyed: hula hooping, jacks, and, indeed, ballet. The information that I had actively pursued all these feminine-coded activities reoriented her perspective.

I don't mean to imply here that I had an innate gender identity that impelled me toward only activities that could be correctly identified as appropriate for girls. For one thing, I was also the girl who pursued being "good at math" despite enduring daily sexual harassment for it in fifth grade (including what I now recognize as low-level assault), and, in high school, I schemed my way past the sexist gatekeeper to get into calculus junior year.

More importantly, I know that affinities and genderings that may seem natural generally aren't, despite a phenomenon I've noticed when teaching beginning adult skaters. They often show up with a clear idea of how they want to move, of what they were meant to do on skates if only they could learn how. Despite all my talk about figure skating and hockey, I think especially of a woman I encountered at a public-skating session after having taught her in a class. She told me, in a tone stereotypically associated with gushing over a dreamy boy, how badly she wanted not to have the speed skater she pointed at, but to *be* him. With new recreational options available after losing one hundred pounds, it was seeing speed skaters that drew her to the ice; she couldn't care less about other kinds of skating.

I have more questions than answers when I think about what makes beginning adult skaters envision in their fantasy futures a sit spin, a puck, or a speed skating oval. What's in the culture, the training, the equipment, and the movements that contributes to ideas about what is or will be exactly right? Kathleen Stewart suggests that intricate concoctions of power, values, and identity are often characterized by the way they seem to just occur: "Ideologies happen. Power snaps into place.

Structures grow entrenched. Identities take place. Ways of knowing become habitual at the drop of a hat."[9] The smooth moves, the embodied sense of just-right-for-me: Skating exemplifies and can emblematize how hard-won those can be.

Yet I don't dismiss the idea of affinity either. A friend who read my e-mail about wanting to quit hockey told me gleefully about her own "blood lust: the desire to smack someone really hard," the "kind of physicality that so many of us dig about contact sports, find so pleasurable." For her there was an "entanglement . . . of violence, pleasure and sociality" or "relationality," so that "smacking isn't just about building connections with one's teammates, but also (more importantly?) with the people trying to hit me/not be hit by me." Her comments reminded me of the "intimacy in exchange" that the boxer described, of various interviews with derby girls who did, or didn't, relish blocking, and of my own fondness for rough contact in other contexts. Intimacy, physicality, exchange—a certain portion of pain and violence with parameters created by negotiation, common understanding, or a history of practice—all of that I can relate to. But not on the ice, where bodies coming together for a kick-line seem immensely more appealing.

In other words, is there an inner "animal," as one player put it, hanging out with my inner backup dancer? Sure, but not one that wants to play hockey. It does, however, love to watch.

6

When God Gets Involved

I first got to know Teresa Henderson during the summer of 2005 when we wound up sharing a hotel room in Hackensack, New Jersey. Six of us had come from Maine to the Ice House in Hackensack to attend the Adult Training Camp Weekend, two days of classes with famous coaches and skaters. Teresa and I paired up because the other four fell into obvious duos. We hardly knew each other. She lived an hour farther north than the rest of us, and she ordinarily skated closer to home. We'd spoken a bit when she skated in Falmouth or Portland. Nothing memorable. I'd taken more notice of the clothes she skated in, which seemed a bit odd. They didn't conform to the usual practice gear, even broadly described to include the double-duty clothes that adult skaters may wear to facilitate squeezing in some ice time around work. Teresa wore long, loose skirts or dresses that might suggest something of a hippie or thrift-shop aesthetic, but I could tell that neither was quite her deal. I didn't know what her deal was until we were all at dinner the night we arrived in Hackensack. I overheard Teresa responding to someone, "My faith tells me that. . . ." I don't remember what her faith was telling her, just my bit of alarm. "What faith is that?" I asked. "Pentecostal." She was a minister, too. Aha. Pentecostal explained the clothes. I now saw the loose fit as piously unclinging, rather than unconstricting, and the fabric as importantly antidiaphanous rather than thick due to the semi-happenstance of resale finds.

My immediate preoccupation, however, was the semi-happenstance of roommate finds. Little did she know that she was about to spend two nights with a Jewish dyke. I probably would have been laughing hysterically if my delight in the cosmic hilarity hadn't been outmatched by dread. What if Teresa wanted to spend the weekend trying to convert me from carnal sins and heathen ways? True, I didn't have to divulge them, but I wouldn't evade. It had been drilled into me growing up that it was acceptable to deny one's identity only in dire circumstances, and then only maybe. "Your plane is hijacked by anti-Semites who say, 'All the Jews step forward.' Do you?" With dinner-table assignments like that behind me, fun at skating camp hardly qualified. Plus, my researcher's curiosity had already started to overtake wanting to avoid annoying or hurtful conversations.

As it turned out, I didn't have any such conversations to avoid. We got along great, even as we learned more about each other. Of course, we had to let a few things slide by. When I told Teresa I was Jewish, she responded cheerfully that Pentecostals had a certain affinity to Jews because, basically, Pentecostals had succeeded Jews as God's chosen people. I didn't revel in the idea that we'd been demoted or even that God has favorites. But I took the comment as the point of connection she intended it to offer. Teresa, in turn, didn't comment when I emerged from the bathroom in a towel and proceeded to dress in the room; it was her discrete look elsewhere that reminded me that the display of nudity among roommates might better be seen as a consensual practice.

But avoiding conflict wasn't our primary key to harmony. Maybe it helped to discover that we differed on so many levels besides the hot-button ones that it started to seem funny. Teresa hates getting up in the morning; I'm an early riser. (Wait, I teased her when I knew her better, isn't sunrise God's glorious wake-up call?) I'd spent most of my childhood wanting to be a grown-up; Teresa had been reluctant to become one. Then again, our differences often functioned to help us identify compatibilities. We each saw our (for different reasons) missing fathers as key to our dissatisfactions with the duration of childhood, just as we easily identified clear benefits of being an early riser and late riser duo, at least for a short hotel stay.

By the end of the weekend, we seemed a little like the title characters from the 1965 children's book *How Joe the Bear and Sam the Mouse Got Together*. Joe and Sam feared that their divergent tastes might prevent them from being friends until they discovered they both liked ice cream. Teresa and I both liked skating, and each other, so much so that, to the great bemusement of curious fellow skaters, we started planning ways to hang out. We returned to the Hackensack weekend a few years later, this time as deliberate travel companions and roommates. We traveled together to the 2008 Adult Nationals, even after USFS refused to let Teresa compete because a postage mistake delayed her entry form the tiniest bit past the postmark due date. She came to Lake Placid with me anyway and attended every practice. I went to cheer her on when she tested her Silver Moves in the Field, and I attended two community theater performances for which she served as the music director. Who knew that I would love *Joseph and the Amazing Technicolor Dreamcoat* or could call up from childhood the lyrics from *Once Upon a Mattress* about being "in Love with a Girl Named Fred"? We did what we could to attend each other's ice shows, grab ice time together, and have the occasional lunch. We shared our time, joys, challenges, and sadnesses to a greater extent than I'm sure either of us imagined possible.

Gliding Spirit

In the process, I learned a lot about Teresa's skating history, fleshing out the answer to a question I had asked back on our first weekend together. Skating camp took place on a weekend, requiring someone to run Sunday worship in her absence. Why, I wanted to know, does God let you skate on Sunday, the Sabbath? God wouldn't want Orthodox Jews to skate on Saturday, at least if cash or driving were involved. I also wondered how a life devoted to ministry allowed for the bigger luxuries of skating at all, including a weekend that couldn't be pulled off for much less than $500 even with a shared room and modest meals.

The answer to most such questions boiled down to this: Teresa knew that God wanted her to skate. How did she know? Over the years, I learned from Teresa that people do not always correctly discern when God is communicating with them or what exactly God is saying. You have to evaluate whether you heard right. In her ministry, she frequently dealt with people who got it wrong and needed to "pray on it" again. Is God really telling you to skip work on the day that the Portland Sea Dogs baseball team has a home game? Is doing badly in school part of God's message to drop out, or might God be helping you develop the very strength and character to resist the temptation to give up?

Teresa knew God wanted her to skate partly because of skating's compelling first appearance in her adult life. During a long stretch in a hospital's psychiatric ward after a dramatic mental breakdown, she dreamed that she was skating, gliding peacefully over the ice. After she got out of the hospital, which was a turning point toward mental and spiritual health, the vision of skating and gliding stuck with her, and she started taking lessons a few years later. She skated once a week at first, then gradually more, then a lot. Here, her story matches up with mine and that of so many other skaters, who find ourselves far more engrossed than we ever anticipated, whether we find explanations in pleasure, the spirit, competitive drive, or a combination of those and more. In Teresa's case, the relation between her skating and her faith was so central that she categorized telling her skating story within the religious practice of testifying. For that reason, while many people spoke to me on the promise of anonymity, Teresa's condition was the opposite: Because her skating story was part of witnessing, she wanted me to use her real name.

My discussions with Teresa about faith and skating led us in all sorts of directions, including my persistent interest in clothing and appearance. Teresa's practice clothes reflected a religious dictum to wear gender-appropriate clothes as well as a requirement for modesty. Her competition costumes were a bit less so, but still modest in the context (figure 3). Teresa's long hair, too, reflected a religious requirement that we surveyed against related but conflicting interpretations in other faiths. Teresa told me about a fight she had with an annoying Mennonite who interpreted a text in the Bible's Book of Corinthians to mean that a woman's head required three coverings, which the Mennonite fulfilled by wearing long hair (#1), bundled on the head (#2), and placed under a cap (#3). Teresa strongly disagreed; long hair was enough. She was interested to learn from me that Orthodox Jewish women sometimes covered their heads differently and for different reasons, if also in a display of modesty. They wear wigs after marriage to prevent the display of natural hair, presumed to be sexier, lest they tempt, or indicate a desire to tempt, men other than their husbands. In this discussion also lay clues about why we get along, in the odd ways that our interests and histories resonate. I had enough interested familiarity with religious lives and texts, including what Christians call the New Testament, to carry on a conversation. She had a life history sound-tracked in earlier years by singers like Janis Joplin, as she shared after learning that I had decided to skate to "Piece of My Heart" when our local show had the theme "I ♥ Skating."

Offerings

Then there was the topic of how a good relationship with God might contribute to one's skating. Regarding a Christian god, a number of sources supply answers to this question. In her 1996 memoir, *My Sergei: A Love*

3. Teresa Henderson competing at the Worcester Open figure skating competition in Worcester, Massachusetts, 2005. Photograph by TimDoiron Photography, Inc. Courtesy of Teresa Henderson.

Story, which describes life with her skating and romantic partner Sergei Grinkov until his early tragic death, former Russian pairs skater Ekaterina Gordeeva describes the guidance of Father Nikolai, their priest, before they departed for the 1994 Olympics in Lillehammer: Skate for your loved ones, don't pray to win—"better ask that He give you a chance to be happy when you skate"—and thank God for giving you the chance to do something you love. "The very idea of beating someone in competition doesn't go very well with religious thinking," Gordeeva reflected, although she credits God's guidance for helping them win by offering a calming focus.[10]

Brigitte Gitta Laskowski, a Canadian adult skater, founded a website named "Figure Skaters for Christ." In the "about me" section, however,

4. Skirts fly up, and siblings hold hands on the covers of Christian skating novels for children from the late 1990s. Photograph by Paul Heroux, 2011.

which offers something like a journal recounting "skating news from 2004 to 2006," religion guides her choices of music more than anything, although the site's "Online Figure Skating Prayer Chain" states that the Canadian skater Jeff Buttle "needs prayer for his back and to get a quad toe and quad flip." She also invites, alongside prayer for victims of war and natural disaster, prayer for "fair play in judging" and for the judges themselves, especially given the challenges of the new scoring system.[11]

Christian figure skating novels for children (figure 4), which had a tiny publishing boom in the late 1990s, offer another set of perspectives about what God offers skating. They include appropriate scripture prioritizing spiritual crowns over athletic ones (I Corinthians 9:24–25),[12] the lesson that you'll skate better if you obey your coaches, and the evidence that good things may come to you after you get your relationship with Jesus just right. In *A Perfect Landing*, Amy desperately needs but can't afford new skates. Almost immediately after asking Jesus to be her Savior, she receives a barely used pair just her size from a friend who had had a growth spurt.[13] Newly motherless Livvy, uprooted by a grieving father in *Dreams on Ice*, discovers after achieving some spiritual peace that the quiet gentleman watching her skate at the mall is not any random or creepy old guy but a retired coach who will train her for the love of it.[14] In

A Surprise Finish, Kristen has just come to embrace her parents' plan to relocate the family for missionary work, thus seriously interrupting her training, when she learns that they will stay put to support her grandmother through back surgery.[15]

Of course, this raises the discomforting possibility that God assisted Kristen by taking out her grandmother. But that unfortunate implication pales next to the one in *A Perfect Match*. In it, Heather decides to skate solo, dropping pairs skating with her brother even though, she admits, he is "'drop-dead gorgeous,'" as her giggly friend puts it, and "even better, . . . a positively awesome Christian." It seems that only jealousy about the brother's new pairs partner and his apparent crush-object can induce the soul-searching required to return Heather to where she belongs, literally in her brother's arms.[16] Here is the antithesis of *Blades of Glory*, which parodies the incest implications always lurking around sibling pairs teams, given the genre's dominance by narratives of heterosexual romance. In the movie, the evil brother–sister team performs as JFK and a pill-popping Marilyn Monroe, injecting drugs, infidelity, and presidential dirt into skating's supposedly clean image. *A Perfect Match* offers nothing funny unless one is tickled by the blinding effects of willful naïvety.

First, I'd Like to Thank . . .

I'm often skeptical when I see athletes on TV giving primary credit to God. Really, if there is a god, does this deity have time to help you make your touchdown? With a sport I participate in, the idea, in some ways, makes even less sense. Skating involves plenty more than the spirit can deliver. Moving at all on any kind of skates is a learned skill, no matter how smooth a skater looks. I had an amusing reminder of that watching a roller derby practice once when the coach assigned a drill that involved skating backward, which derby rarely requires. Players who ordinarily raced the track as if they'd been born on skates were suddenly tripping over their feet. Then, in figure skating, there's that "toe pick!" matter, to invoke the often-quoted line delivered by the aristocratically smug figure skater to the tough-jock smug hockey player in the 1990 classic *The Cutting Edge*. It's easy to trip. With more advanced skating, while correlation doesn't equal causation, it's hard to argue against overwhelming evidence that intensive training, certain body types, muscle memory, and, it seems, youth, are key factors in advancement.

Teresa and I talked about what God could help a skater accomplish. Not surprisingly, I was more the skeptic. Teresa didn't think God would hand her triples, or even an axel. Having been on the ice for a while she knew that those came to no one without hard work. But she seemed more willing than I to imagine God helping her accomplish feats that common wisdom put out of our reach. Then again, I don't fully discount the possibilities. I know how much frame of spirit matters. Skating can be what you shouldn't have done when you feel internally out of balance; that sprained wrist I mentioned is evidence. Or it can be exactly what you needed: a soothing respite from despair, or a source of super-sized joy, at the start, by the end, or all the way through a session. Spirit is all around the rink. Maybe that's where Joe the Bear and Sam the Mouse should go after the ice cream parlor; it worked for Teresa and me.

III

Hooks

Thinking can be a little like lacing up skates. With skates, you may have a method that works for you. Then suddenly it doesn't. Your skates are too tight or too loose. You have to keep retying them. Maybe a lace pops off a hook while you're skating. This could just mean an off day. Or your skates are starting to break down (which, like dull blades, can be a slow or sudden discovery) and you need a new pair. Or someone shows you a twist, variation, or extra knot that makes you realize that your method was never quite as good as you thought.

I root my approach to this section in two invitations that really stuck with me since I encountered them in the 1990s to shift what might be called the techniques of conceptual lacing. The first invitation occurred in 1991 during the question-and-answer segment of a lecture at Bates College by Eve Sedgwick. I don't remember the exact question but it concerned using identity categories like race, class, gender, and sexuality to understand people's circumstances, beliefs, and interactions. Sedgwick responded by asking the audience who among us had a sibling of the same sex. Then, of this group, how many were really different than that sibling? A bunch of us raised our hands again, laughing in shared acknowledgment of the funny, sometimes painful moments that this family situation can cause. Sedgwick pointed out that significant dissimilarities among siblings constitute clear evidence, right in front of most of us, of how much identity categories, though crucial to consider, fall short of explaining. After all, siblings often share our "race, class, and gender," usually matched even further according to demographic variables in upbringing like geographical location, economic status, religious training, ethnicity, nationality, and education. Yet that doesn't preclude the common sibling-from-another-planet phenomenon.

I found the second invitation in two essays by Juliet Ash in *The Gendered Object*, a 1996 anthology. The first essay, called "The Tie: Presence and Absence," considers cultural meanings connected to wearing, or not wearing, ties in several types of outfitting, including men's work out-fits, women's fashion, and schoolgirl uniforms. Through ties, Ash argues, gender norms that, in effect, come with the tie, may be "re-established or subverted," depending on various factors: how and with what ties are worn; complications of choice, aesthetics, and acquisition (the tie as gift); and attendant power relations. (The college custodian and the fashionable male professor have different reasons for not wearing ties on campus).[1] The second essay, "Memory and Objects," concerns presence, absence, and ties from a different perspective. Catalyzed by the death of Ash's husband, it considers how items of clothing conjure memories, events, intimacies, and interactions through the way they look, feel, smell, and inhabit space with you.[2] While her primary interest concerns clothes that we retain after their wearers have departed, I particularly appreciate the more general impetus to pull personal relations into analyses of how wearable (and other) objects work on us, with us, and through us.

In this section, I present my own conceptual lacing and relacing on the topic of skates themselves. I offer it in the spirit of Sedgwick's call to remember the insufficiencies of nonetheless illuminating categories and of Ash's project of going beyond such categories. My structure echoes *The Gendered Object* in the placement of Ash's essays, which have several essays between them. I like the rhythm of looking at something, travers-ing other (occupied) territories, and coming back to look again.

Here, historical and personal pieces on the gendering of skate color bookend the section. The first essay, which is called "White Skates Be-come You," considers the history and politics of the norm that females of all skin tones generally wear white, or occasionally tan, skates. The final essay, named "Black Skates, or the Stakes in Wanting," takes up my own conflicted relationship with that tradition. Between these two book-end essays are "Form-Fitting: The Bra in Three Stories" and "My Grand-mother's Shoes." Both consider other gendered wearables and look at cul-tural habits, individual idiosyncrasies, and the narratives through which people make sense of themselves, their objects, and their gear.

7

White Skates Become You

Maybe nothing about figure skates is more obvious than their gender coding by color. White skates are for women; black skates are for men. This convention can be seen in any sales display of stock skates—that is, skates "off the rack"—and in any televised competition or exhibition, even though advanced skaters usually wear custom-made skates that allow them to pick their boot color. Harlick, for instance, a major manufacturer of custom skates, offers in the base price white, black, or "Holiday Tan"—the color that conceptually corresponds, with leisure-luxury flair, to the "Flesh" crayon color that Crayola had to rename because of its white-supremacist implication about the proper color of skin.[3] Some female skaters pick tan or hide their white skates under "over-the-boot" tights, a patently imperfect subterfuge, with the shape of laces and metal hardware visible from far away. Virtually no one wears a color associated with the "opposite sex." Few choose other custom options, like the red, green, yellow, "neon pink," or "camo" offered by Riedell; the last option is a weird version of camouflage with several decidedly New Englandesque autumn leaves floating atop more standard dark blotches that gesture to the jungle. Pseudo-military whimsy.[4]

Color Coding

Like the pink and blue gender divide that is often treated as a natural law or ancient tradition, the gendering of skate color has a relatively recent history. It took off in the 1930s, after Sonja Henie, the famous figure skating personality, introduced white skating boots for women. As Ellyn Kestnbaum explains in *Culture on Ice*, white skates emphasized the line of the leg, newly visible after the also recent advent of the skating dress, instead of drawing as much attention to the boot as heavy equipment. The effect also suited Henie's aristocratic look, often accessorized with fur accents. White skates then became so normative for women that Henie moved on to beige in order to distinguish herself.[5]

How fast white spread as the dominant color for females is indicated in the 1938 *Primer of Figure Skating* by Maribel Vinson Owen, the champion skater, sportswriter, and coach. Owen writes, "White buck or calf boots are steadily replacing the old black boots among women figure skaters because they look best with a wide range of colored costumes, which may be white or pastel one day or a vivid splash of color the next."[6] That may sound like a pronouncement about the upper echelons of skating. But Owen thought that beginners could use a "costume," too, making the sage suggestion that while female novices often tried to shrink from view by dressing modestly in a "long, narrowish" skirt, they could better avoid unwanted attention by dressing in "the accepted mode" for more expert skaters: a dress or skirt with "a full circular, gored, or pleated skirt which flares at the hip line, and . . . is *never* below the knee," along with appropriate tights and bloomers. Despite insisting on the prevailing fashion in skating clothes, however, Owen did not repudiate black skates for women. On black skates and black clothes, she wrote, "Black . . . is still good and by its comparative rarity on the rinks nowadays often seems positively distinguished."[7]

Yet one person's "distinguished" can be another person's stigma. A friend told me of her mother's great disappointment in the mid-1930s, growing up in a small town in Massachusetts, when she couldn't have white skates. Decades later, she still talked bitterly about it, partly because of why she had to wear black ones. Her size-nine feet were too big to fit any available women's skates. Black skates thus doubly signaled being freakishly outside gender norms. Even worse, in a situation that could have inspired the invention of "adding insult to injury" if it hadn't long existed, her pretty younger sister had feet sufficiently petite to fit the white skates she coveted.

White/Sex, White/Race

Today, white figure skates have become so standard for female skaters that they function in a number of ways like the bodily features commonly termed secondary sex characteristics. First, like breasts or the absence of facial hair, they are considered likely evidence of the wearer's female sex. Second, and consequently, rejecting them may be interpreted as a rejection of femininity. Butch or otherwise masculine-identified women may refuse to wear white skates, just as they may dress to avoid the appearance of feminine curves. With skates, the gendering of white as female may even contribute to whether the casual or beginning skater buys figure skates at all. Because ice skating itself has gender trends, with hockey considered more masculine than figure skating, the typical sports supply store, more easily accessible to most than a skate shop, may carry few if any men's figure skates, at least in the United States.[8] As a result, someone may wind up in hockey skates just to avoid being labeled female or feminine. Conversely, the lack of white skates may deter someone from skating, too. Erika Lind, a trans woman who trained in figure skating as a child, told me, "Upon my transition I became very obsessive about white skates, just wanting to look at them as if the image of a thin blond figure skater was some kind of ideal that I could only hope to attain. For a long time I would not skate because I had not yet gotten white skates to replace my original black ones." She added that she later saw waiting as "very silly considering how many skaters prefer tan or black skates." Given how clearly skate color is gendered, it doesn't seem silly to me that she initially saw white skates as a key mark of femaleness and saw switching from black to white as integral to gender transition.[9]

Third, as Lind's vision of white skates completing the thin, blond skater look suggests, the gold standard involving this female attribute is profoundly raced. If white boots are supposed to elongate line, itself an aesthetic that owes much to the balletics of courtly, white European origin, they serve that goal only for people with light skin. White skates on dark legs, like black skates on light legs, make for shorter- and chunkier-looking legs. Transracializing leg gear—white skates, light tights—may reduce the apparent chunkiness but only at the expense of the vague relation to the natural upon which the overall look also depends, as evidenced by the market in skating tights. Most brands offer two light-skin analogs, either bearing ("Suntan") or hiding ("Classic Light Toast") the skin reference, along with one dark-skin analog, usually termed "Black."[10]

The goal to match tights to skin color may be clearest when it fails. The dissonance can be subtly jarring ("Suntan" on pale skin), or more dramatic, as happened during "A Gift from Africa," the 2007 tenth annual ice show of Figure Skating in Harlem (FIH). In the words of Tamara Tunie, the emcee and FIH bigwig famous for roles on *As the World Turns* and *Law and Order SVU*, FIH grew over the years from "15 girls" to "100 young ladies," a characterization that betokens norms of respectability associated both with FIH goals and with figure skating in general, which uses "ladies" to describe all competitors who have aged or advanced beyond "girls." In the show, the skaters performed in group and solo numbers to music from or themed to Africa in outfits made from fabrics designed to evoke traditional African attire. Their light-colored tights, however, which contrasted with the skin of many of the skaters, suggested a half-thought-out donation more than a ladylike matching of accessories to either skin or outfit.[11]

The overall effect of raced gender conventions is that to get the sleeker visual line—setting aside, for now, the question of whether one would want it—females with dark skin must choose either transracializing or transgendering attire: light legs or dark skates. Both have attendant costs and politics, besides the basic inequity of *having* to opt for trans performance. Other solutions have costs, too. For example, the African American skater Debi Thomas wore a black unitard in her short program for the 1988 Olympics. The unitard's long pant came below the ankle, extending the leg line, while the stirrups formed interesting shapes with what remained visible of the white boot. Black and white became a design issue, not a racial one. I don't know if Thomas, or anyone who helped to costume her, intended or appreciated this effect. In any case, the International Skating Union (ISU) clearly disapproved of her costume. New rules passed in 1989 explicitly forbade unitards for female competitors, along with any type of pants, bare midriffs, or excessive theatricality; men's costumes had to have sleeves and cover the chest.[12] The ruling against pants and unitards stood until 2004.

Sex for Money

In several examples above lies one more reason that white skates function like a secondary sex characteristic. They confirm femaleness through cultural norms that bare themselves especially when it requires money to address deviance: like getting electrolysis if one has hair in unwomanly places, or implants to bring one's breasts to "normal" size. Maribel Vinson Owen, I think, may have avoided stigmatizing black skates for women out of sensitivity to this issue. Despite her push for proper skating outfits, she was keen to make skating affordable for people like my friend's mother, who was hardly in the market for custom skates.[13] In general, deviation from gender coding in skates occurs primarily at the lowest level of personal economic engagement with figure skates: hand-me-downs, donations, and rentals.

Cost can also limit deviation, especially at the high end. Recommended skates even at my level can cost $1,000. Advanced skaters may spend $1,500 a pair and replace them twice a year. The price is one reason that skaters do not buy skates like shoes, with different pairs for various occasions, although some skaters may have different skates for different pursuits, like freestyle and ice dance. Skates must also be adapted through use. There is no figure skating equivalent to buying or borrowing a gorgeous pair of heels to wear with a special outfit. Heels might be considered to work even if they don't fit well, feel good, or get worn more than once. Skates don't work until they go through a breaking-in process. Damage to skates or feet result otherwise, and even small problems can affect the ability to perform hard tricks and moves. That's why television commentators sometimes attribute missed jumps to reported boot problems or the almost insurmountable situation of skates disappearing on the way to an event—an occurrence that became more common after 9/11, when skates got classified as potential weapons that could not be carried onto airplanes. That rule recently eased up.

Whiteness Isn't Everything

Skate color is clearly gendered. Yet skate color doesn't gender people in simple ways. This is partly because no one is either gendered in a simple way or gendered in isolation of other matters. Bringing out the cleavage might seem classy or trashy, depending on accessories and context—a leopard print, skin color, an expensive haircut, flashing it or not at the PTA, the shape of one's breasts as transformed by particular bras or other devices.[14] Then, experience, interpretations, and idiosyncrasies pile on. Alison Bechdel, the author of the comic strip *Dykes to Watch Out For* and the graphic memoir *Fun Home: A Family Tragicomic*, described her own white skates to me as a kind of magical, odd relic that she persisted in wearing despite the way they ill-suited her gender expression and were literally marked by miscry:

> Strangely, I wear my cheap white plastic figure skates from high school with one toe melted from a bonfire at a party at which I was so mis-

erable and socially uncomfortable that I had to skate off into the dark and prostrate myself on the ice.

I say strangely because (a) I never wear girl-specific clothing if I can help it and (b) my feet have grown at least five sizes since I was fifteen. Yet I fit into these skates. It's some kind of miracle.[15]

My own relation to white skates, for a while, was largely about my relation to white sneakers, which was largely about losing an urban environment and, more, about losing a friend. I return to that topic a few essays along, after a detour through gendered gear and attachments that live outside the ice rink.

8

Form-Fitting: The Bra in Three Stories

A few years ago, I cofacilitated part of a training for future advisors of Outright/Lewiston-Auburn, the local organization for queer, trans, questioning, and allied young people. Over lunch, the subject of bras somehow came up. I recounted my belated exposure to a standard trick for putting on bras that attach in the back. Until my thirties, I did what (I think) I saw women in my family do. I put my arms through the straps, put the straps on my shoulders, then reached back, twisted my wrists upside down, grabbed the loop and the hook ends in opposite hands, pulled them toward each other, felt for the connections, pulled a little more, and hooked. Then one day, I saw a friend do something much easier. She held the bra loosely at waist level, one end in each hand, with the cups behind her. With the hooks and loops thus visible, she fastened them almost effortlessly, turned the bra around, and put her arms through the straps last. Wow. No fumbling or convolutions. Once I saw it, it seemed so obvious. Why hadn't I figured it out myself? When I finished my story, everyone laughed. Then one of the lesbians said, "Yeah, but I bet you learned much earlier how to do the trick where you take off another woman's bra using just one hand." Everyone laughed again.

Except for me. Actually, I have no clue how to do that trick. That deficit, I explained, probably came from rarely dating people who understood their chests as erotic in a way that would be enhanced by having a lover deftly unhook a bra, or by wearing a bra like that in the first place. A sports bra, maybe, but not cleavage-bearing numbers with sexy-to-finger straps. As a result, my whole relationship to that move involves knowing how to facilitate making someone look suave using it on me. My lunch mates seemed bemused: Really? How interesting. I had the same response to them. I expected at least a few nods of familiarity, if not experience, with a gendered division of erotic labor, garb, and chest perception. Instead, they seemed to see me as an interesting oddity. That night, however, during intermission at a drag king show, I asked another femme-identified dyke if she could unhook someone's bra with one hand. "Hell no," she said. "Why would I know how to do that? I don't do that to other people. They do that to me!"

As I kept asking around over time, my casual survey confirmed two divides I had noted that day. One, corresponding to a split between practitioners and beneficiaries of the bra trick, divided more masculine- and more feminine-identified people. This was a divide grounded, I think, in several interconnected gendered and erotic traditions. These include the association of certain bras with femininity and the bra trick's status as a mark of masculine sexual prowess, experience, and, perhaps, sophistication. Consider, on this topic, the novelty book *Man Tricks: Everything Men Need (or Just Want) to Know*. It includes the bra trick along with chapters on how to buy a woman the right flowers, rip a phone book in half, jump-start a car, and throw a ball "Properly . . . and Not at All Like a Girl."[16] Chivalry, mechanical facility, muscle coordination, and a talent for fronting—masculinity apparently requires all of these and the bra trick can demonstrate each.

The other divide separated people who considered gender identity to be key to the bra trick and those who didn't. A trans man, who had earlier identified as a lesbian, told me that he knew as a teen (then going by "she") that being a practicing lesbian required knowing the trick. One dyke told me that she knew how to do it because she used to seduce younger women. Another said, "I don't know the trick [because] typically (a) I'm more interested in skin than clothes and (b) I'd fumble. Part of my style." People who answered without reference to gender, however, did not necessarily consider gender irrelevant to their erotic life or persona. Some had investments in gender that simply didn't involve the bra trick. Or gender did figure in but in a sideways relation to heterosexual stereotypes. It was like in order to have a female lover or be the sexual aggressor, two roles often associated with males, one needed to know the required bra-trick mastery.

Number Two: Sports Bra Gone Bad

A few weeks later, Ra Criscitiello, a butch dyke I'd interviewed about her extensive sports experience, showed me a catalogue from Title Nine, which sells athletic clothes for woman. Its name comes from the 1972 federal education amendment that, despite never mentioning athletics, is now primarily recognized for initiating a boom in female athletic participation by mandating equal opportunity in schools regardless of sex.[17] Title Nine was one of several companies Ra found extremely annoying for marketing a feminine image of women and girls in sports. The cover, which displayed five scenes of women before, during, or after physical activity, made the point easily. One model looked like a perky Water Bearer in a form-fitting, over-the-swimsuit, slip-on dress. All the others went floral, at least a little, for yoga, stretching, backpacking, or skiing.[18]

But dresses and floral were old news to Ra. What burned her about this catalogue was a Patagonia sports bra displayed inside that she had loved until a recent redesign. Now it looked more like a conventional bra, with thinner, adjustable straps and hooks fastening them to the bra's back. It had become useless—worse than useless, really, since she'd obviously never wear anything like that. Of course not, I replied, and I then told her about a skating friend's totally different reaction to that very same bra: "Hey, Patagonia has these great new sports bras. The straps are adjustable, just like a regular bra!" She called it the best sports bra she'd ever worn, although as we talked about it on the ice, I was standing behind her, reaching up under her shirt to fix it because the hook on one of those straps had managed to unattach itself.

Number Three: Jock Bra

In the catalogue for the photography exhibit *Game Face: What Does a Female Athlete Look Like?* Hinda Miller recounts coinventing the sports bra in 1977. A costume designer and runner—at a time, she said, when the market offered no shoes, shorts, or bras for women runners—Miller hooked up with another runner, Lisa Lindahl, to try to design a running bra. After cutting up and altering "regular bras—the 'man'-made kind that pushed the breast up and out"—they got an idea when Lindahl's husband held a jockstrap up to his chest, saying, "'Hey look, jock bra!'" His joke made them realize that the jockstrap concept, "pull[ing] everything close to the body just like the guys have been doing all this time," was the way to go. They designed a prototype formed by stitching two jock straps together, put in $1,000 (split between them and one more person) to make test models, and they refined the design as they, and other women, tried running in them. Then they borrowed $5,000 from Miller's father to manufacture about five hundred, and they set out to get it into stores, presenting it to sports suppliers as "equipment" rather than "lingerie." The inventors also changed the original name, "Jock Bra," when a woman in South Carolina, who co-owned a store with her husband, told them that women runners in her area didn't like to think of themselves as jocks. Being northerners, Miller wrote, she and Lindahl didn't see "jock" as a problem. But they changed the name to Jog Bra anyway, a name that worked extremely well. It was catchy, largely self-explanatory, and easy to translate into other languages. They founded Jog Bra, Inc., the same year; the Metropolitan Museum of Art and the Smithsonian Museum now own early prototypes.[19]

As Miller's story indicates, inventing and selling the jog bra involved switch-ups in gender attitudes on a lot of fronts. Everyone involved—inventors, marketers, and consumers—had to envision in women a market of athletes who could legitimately prioritize, at least for one garment, structural advantages for athletic activity over an interest in shaping breasts according to prevailing models of sexual attractiveness: "up and out." Sales reps had to be conversant, ideally without being smarmy, in "the anatomical components of the breast." Storeowners had to see themselves, and want to be seen, as caring about women's sports needs.[20] They also had to be willing to associate themselves with women's products, which, as Julia Serano points out, can seem to have enormous powers to feminize people upon contact. Ask a man to hold your purse, Serano suggests in her "Barrette Manifesto." You'll see: "'girl stuff' is made with the gender equivalent of Kryptonite!"[21]

The jog bra's success also depended on understanding gender identity as varied, for example by geographical region, and on other matters that involved gender, including historical timing and access to capital. It came five years after Title IX, which was too late to help the women of their generation play sports in school but helped to support a climate of female sports participation. It was also a time when, despite gains for women, financial resources remained, as now, largely under men's control. It is significant that Miller's story involves no women flush with capital, except, perhaps, the woman who co-owned a store with her husband. Miller also notes, however, that the time was ripe for small entrepreneurs: "Back then it was sort of like the Wild West. People were looking for products. They would see you if you called them."[22] This climate probably mitigated some distrust of female inventors, products, and business ventures, although I assume that getting in the door depended also on apparent race and class. It maybe also depended on gender normativity, which could forestall fears of contributing to an army of muscled, unfeminine, utilitarianly clad dykes.

Mix and Match

I assembled these bra stories because together they nicely illustrate the factors by which gender informs the history, manufacture, reputation, and use of wearable gear. Bras, worn on a body part associated with females, might seem to be inherently gendered as female. But how they function in relation to sex and gender, femaleness and maleness, femininity and masculinity, can vary greatly. Sometimes these relations are bound up in tricks and traditions passed along in many possible ways. They may be transmitted by relatives, friends, lovers, or strangers. They may be offered or interpreted as erotic advice, as sports tips, as cross-generational hand-downs or hand-ups, as girl talk, or as more than one of those at once. They may pass from person to person through ritual, happenstance, observation, word of mouth, deliberate training, or on-the-spot practice, pursued frankly or clandestinely as learning in progress.[23] They depend, too, on idiosyncrasies in interpretation, identity, and personal history. Thus, a sports bra with traditional bra straps can be viewed indifferently, dismissed without a tryout, or judged the best ever invented even if the straps require mid-workout intervention.

Through these various interactions and transmissions, bras keep contributing to gendering, and regendering, people, activities, and each other. For example, Miller recounts that before the sports bra, some women addressed the problem of painfully bouncing breasts by binding them,[24] a practice commonly associated with people keen to present themselves as male or masculine by camouflaging evidence of female-characterized body parts. Once invented, the sports bra, although rooted not at all, it seems, in any transgendering intentions, could now be used in the service of them. More generally, it offers an alternative to bras that might be labeled "girly," which, in turn, might read differently against a sports bra alternative. Maybe bras used to be read as feminine when they were lacy versus plain; now they may read as feminine partly by having hooks, straps, and cups, since one might choose a sports bra instead. Conversely, the sports bra contributed to developing feminine looks in contexts apart from traditional bras. The "uniboob" feature of sports bras migrated to built-in "shelf" tanks, including the skinny-strap camisoles that, literally reshaping the look of femininity, have become standard feminine fare. As sports bra technology continues to change, so, too, will gender signals and also markers of athleticism. A 2008 *Today* show feature on new innovations in the sports bra, for instance, showed some bras reincorporating hook-and-loop technology; others, like one with an iPod pocket, have little pretension to support vigorous activity.[25]

One More Twist, Please

Reconceptualizing the bra as a device to pull bodily protrusions inward like men did was a huge breakthrough—although it is one that seems as obvious in retrospect as how to avoid the visually unassisted arm-twist maneuver. That each could appear as a light-bulb moment, and that generations have struggled to learn the one-handed bra trick, testifies to the strength and endurance of beliefs and traditions concerning gender, breasts, sex, and sport.

I'd like an additional paradigm shift for people like me who pursue vigorous sporting activity in feminine costumes. One year, needing both structural support and invisible straps for a skating outfit, I wound up with a padded push-up number from Victoria's Secret. Even though I don't sweat much, I was drenched after a few minutes of skating. Where's the moisture-wicking fabric that is now a staple of athletic wear? Really, if people truly thought of feminine-coded sports—or that night on the town with dancing—as athletic, the enormous marketing potential would be obvious.

9

My Grandmother's Shoes

My grandmother was extremely proud of her small feet. She repeatedly bragged about wearing size four-and-a-half shoes, and she used to admonish me when I was very young that small feet were the sign of a true lady. It was as if foot size constituted biological evidence of a gentility that people might not expect to find either where she grew up, in New York tenements, or where she ended up, in the modest, comfortable circumstances of a public-school secretary with a steadily if not prestigiously employed husband. I remember her disappointment, and my half-skeptical sense of doom, when my own feet passed far beyond four (and my weight passed the ninety-six pounds she trumpeted weighing at her wedding). I was also awed at how many shoes she owned. Her closet displayed seemingly a hundred pairs of strappy sandals with one- to two-inch heels, in solid red, white, blue, pink, gold, silver, beige, green, or yellow, and in various color combinations. She sometimes attributed her shoe bounty to deals that rewarded the few people dainty enough to wear the "sample size." I recognized when I got older, however, that some of the shoes were simply cheap, as firmly rooted in a lower-middle-class economy and sensibility as her habit of splurging on a few expensive suits and then dressing them up with rickrack (although that last was a bit idiosyncratic).

Decades later, when her Alzheimer's had advanced far enough to require nursing-home care, a nurse pulled me aside on a visit in the hope that I could assist with a problem. It seemed that my grandmother frequently forgot that she couldn't really walk well anymore, but she vividly remembered that she wore only heels. The combination made her very susceptible to bad falls. Could I do anything? I went to K-Mart and bought black sneakers in size five, since they didn't have half sizes, along with fancy rainbow-colored laces, hoping to disguise the nature of the shoes through their color and bit of flashiness. Sure enough, the shoes appealed.

But after initial delight, my grandmother began to quiz me. "I hope these are small enough," she said, even though she already had them on and they fit perfectly. "I have very small feet, you know, size three and a half. And those aren't sneakers, are they? You know I would never wear sneakers." By that point she recognized family members only intermittently, and I'd had plenty of opportunities to rethink my assumptions that it was always dubious and condescending to shield people with illness from painful information. I'd seen her fresh anguish at every soon-forgotten answer to questions about the whereabouts of her husband, who had died twenty years earlier. What end would honesty serve? "Yes," I lied, "size three and a half, and of course they're not sneakers." She smiled again, happy to have new shoes that met her specifications.

Class Act

What makes for an investment in femininity so deep that it outlasts re-membering intimates? I harbor no suspicion, harsh or morose, that she loved us less than her heels or her claims to being a lady through and through. It may be tempting to view what remains in memory as more important than what doesn't stay. But even features of memory loss that seem to scream of the particular person may turn out to belong to broader patterns. When I recounted my surprise, for instance, that my grandmother could still summon the word "egregious," I heard other stories about people who hung onto adjectives long after the names and nouns that one might imagine being easier or more ingrained had faded away.

Besides, my grandmother was hardly the only person of her genera-tion, or outside of it, to idealize small feet or to use shoes in the project of gender maintenance and class uplift. In "Life in the Passing Lane: Exposing the Class Closet," Victoria Brownworth writes about how her mother's also impressively large shoe collection contributed to perpetu-ating the illusion that the genteel poverty in which they lived was really genteel affluence. Brownworth recounts, "[She] owned at least (to my memory) thirty pairs of high-heeled shoes to go with her dresses and suits," clothes rarely worn but associated with a "mythic class status" that then, in the sixties, still forbade pants for women. Like me, Brownworth saw the shoes differently over time. "I was in high school," she writes, "be-fore I understood that there were shoes and clothes that weren't like my mother's: shoes that didn't have a big black crayon mark (25 c) scrawled on the instep; dresses and suits that smelled of sizing, not mothballs or stale sweat."[26]

Maybe that's part of why shoes can be so memorable. They are good candidates for a bit of dissembling, yet they resist dissembling at the same time. They're down at your feet; maybe they don't get seen too closely. If they really match your outfit, they can seem like evidence of disposable cash, accessories made of necessities. But as Brownworth notes, "physicality" frequently interrupts passing for richer: "There is, for example, no difference between dirt-poor food and genteel poverty food. It all revolves around powdered milk, white bread, canned mushroom soup, peas and Jell-O. It revolves around how four people can be fed on scant money for one."[27] Shoes bare their origins in ways visible and visceral. Shoes from Payless simply don't look like Jimmy Choos. Used shoes may smell enough to generate a bodily reaction or to conjure what is familiar, or not. Oh, yes, these are my mother's, which first belonged to someone else. They may have creases and bad fits, so tight that you can hardly avoid grimacing or so loose that you need to curl your toes to keep the shoes from flopping around. (Expensive shoes unwisely purchased — they're so cute, maybe they'll stretch — may have related effects but that's a different story.)

Brownworth's essay underscores one more point for me: that the stories we tell about what bears intense meaning for other people reveal what bears meaning for us. I do not mean that my narrative or Brownworth's is fictional or primarily about us instead. Clearly, my grandmother valued her femininity enough to remember, and exaggerate, what she took to constitute biological and material claims on it. When I tell that story to people who knew her, they smile and nod, "Oh, yes, that's Sophie." I have no reason to doubt Brownworth's understanding of her mother either. At the same time, our stories reflect what impressed us early in our lives, illustrate what came to matter later, and serve larger points in essays that exist as they do on the page because we picked and repicked words, deciding what to add, edit, move, and delete.

For example, I wavered over including another story of my grandmother's occasional flashes of deep herself-ness in dementia, this one political. She told me, during the 2000 presidential campaign, that she didn't recognize the candidates but knew that while the Democrats and Republicans were both bad, the latter were usually worse. Compare that to the 1980s when her postretirement activities included teaching a current events course in the senior program at the YMHA — "maybe if I have a heart attack on the spot they'll understand how bad American intervention in Nicaragua really is." Or to November 1998, shortly before confusion made living alone impossible, when she got the program's bus driver to stop at her polling place so that she could vote against Al D'Amato. The story doesn't relate directly to shoes or to classed femininity. But wouldn't it misrepresent my grandmother, and, consequently, the issues in question, to imply by omission that maybe nothing mattered to her as much as her tiny, well-shod feet? She was "all about" her shoes, to use outdated slang that also postdated her, but hardly only about them.

In the end, that's why I decided to include the story. In tandem with Brownworth's account, it nicely suggests how much being all about one's shoes can and can't reveal, as well as the diverse ways in which similar economic circumstances may be lived, understood, and handled, including through physical objects interpreted or proffered as tokens of gendered class status. Brownworth describes her mother as a brilliant, also politically leftist woman, a linguist who came from a family of esteemed intellectuals and attended a Seven Sisters college after family misfortune made passing as well-off a requirement for appearing to fit in there.[28] My grandmother's economic trajectory was slightly up rather than dramatically down. She had to pursue postsecondary education in bits and pieces throughout museum courses, university audit programs, Elderhostels, public lectures, and independent research partly because she had been forced to take the secretarial track in high school. Interestingly, her story is quite like that of my New England stepgrandmother, Iola. Both involved poverty, a prettier younger sister, the same educational destiny, and the same underlying rationale: that a girl with a plain face can't count on marrying her way to financial support. But, oh, those legs, the asset Sophie emphasized whenever possible in posed photographs, with one leg slightly bent, crossing slightly in front of the other. It was a semi-decorous pin-up pose that we all, less than consciously, learned to emulate. You can make that pose happen barefoot, but a nicely tapering shoe with a bit of heel really makes for the whole effect.

10

Black Skates, or the Stakes in Wanting

I figure skate partly for certain feminine enticements, or, more precisely, for enticements that I experience as satisfying my pleasures in the feminine. I love the glitter, the emphasis on grace, and the occasional opportunity to wear a great miniskirt with an apparent purpose other than the pathetic denial of middle age. To at least as great an extent, I dislike donning the trappings of masculinity. While I enjoy, often immensely, watching others do so, it's not for me, even for alleged fun. ("Let's all cross-dress for the drag show!" No, thanks.)

Nonetheless, and despite the rigid gender coding that prescribes white skates for women, for the first five years I skated as an adult I really wanted black skates. It had nothing to do with gender bending, but with the kind of female I saw myself to be. Female skaters may officially be "Ladies" but I'm not much of a lady on or off the ice, at least in terms of demure manners, classy refinement, and that ethereal ballerina demeanor that skaters often inhabit. Black skates, I thought, could serve a more satisfying and accurate self-representation. I saw them as part of an urban-girl look, urban with certain inflections—to the left, to the more punk side of bodily proportions. I wanted black skates just like I prefer black athletic shoes, which came to epitomize urban for me after I moved from Chicago to Maine in 1990 for a job. Two decades later, black high-tops still reside in my imagination with bottles of green chili salsa as the objects whose apparent scarcity then emblematized the grief and panic of culture shock involved in moving away from the city. I thought I wouldn't be caught dead in largely white athletic shoes. Apparently I would be caught alive in them, at least until I discovered that surplus and salvage stores, a better source where I live for oddities than less-plentiful boutiques, may bring goods to a cultural market deemed ill-suited to appreciate them at full price. That discovery rescued my feet, but the initial loss connected to sneakers added meaning and intensity to the desire with which I eyed men's skates.

Desires change. As it happened, during my first venture into writing about black skates, my skates wore out. At first, I expected to buy white skates again because I considered the options for getting black skates to have unacceptable risks or costs. I could buy men's skates, but the fit would be off. I could get custom skates. But, aside from paying for them, what bothered me was how obvious my purchase of custom skates would be. Knowing that women's stock skates are white is not like knowing whether a "flex notch" is a custom or stock feature. (It's an upscale stock feature.) Maybe I'd appear arrogant or idiotic for buying far more boot than I need. Did I think my single jumps would soon be triples? The options for faking black skates seemed equally dubious. If I tried to paint white skates or have them painted, I'd risk living for several years with a botched job on footwear too expensive to replace for cosmetic reasons alone. Boot covers didn't appeal either. I just don't like them. Besides, as the website for the queer organization SkateOut warned beginning figure skaters, "Boot covers, fancy outfits and sequined warm-ups might make you feel special, but they will do little to improve your skating and instead you'll stand out as [a] beginner that's trying too hard to be the next Olympic Champion."[29]

I had every reason to think I'd correctly assessed both my options and my desires, a view reinforced by several other women who shared thwarted dreams of black. Then, a few days before my appointment to get new skates, I discovered on the web another option for black skates: Riedell, which makes the stock boots I ordinarily buy, now offered custom-stock hybrids, including a stock boot in a different color. The company's website did not indicate the price, but it surely cost much less than a fully custom skate. What now?

I could have inquired immediately. Instead, I reasoned my way out of it. If I got my skates right away, I'd have two months to break them in before the spring ice show. A special order would set me back a month at least, and it would require an extra trip to the skate shop, one hundred miles away, for a fitting. I did find a few clues about cost on the web, like pink Riedells on one site that could be compared in cost to the white version offered on another. More important, however, was that as I dawdled in those searches I knew exactly where to find swift answers. The guy I bought my skates from would probably know off-hand, and

I'd recently received quick responses from Riedell's contact e-mail address. Sure enough, when I did e-mail Riedell, after 9 P.M. on the very evening I came home with my new skates, too late to act on information that I nonetheless wanted to write about, I heard back at 8:07 the next morning: three to four weeks, $52 more. As I suspected, black skates had moved to the realm of reasonable splurge from what I took to be the performance of posturing profligacy.

The Stakes in Wanting

Why I didn't jump at the chance to get the black skates of my dreams I attribute to several factors. Some involved my interactions with other skaters. I wasn't sure that I wanted to enter every skating encounter as that woman with the black skates. Did I want to set myself apart from the get-go when, for fun or research, I might want the chance to fit in or at least to look like I might? This is not to say that adult skaters require conformity. To the contrary, I have found my local skating community to be very welcoming. Where else could I develop friendships with both a Republican nurse and a Pentecostal minister who have come to take it in stride, or at least relatively in stride, if I show up with a girlfriend or a trans boyfriend or a skating outfit passed down from a porn star? Yet nurturing friendships and research ties takes time, negotiation, displays of interest and respect, and decisions about what to reveal when. If nothing else, black skates would immediately announce that I was trying to announce something, whether about style, sexuality, gender, freakiness, or something else. I wasn't sure that I wanted that hurdle even though I could not predict exactly what that hurdle would do or when black skates would sometimes offer a benefit instead.

Second, the issue was not only utility. Figure skating, I've found, brings out an impulse for gender conformity in me that little else has done. In 2002, I shaved my legs and underarms before my first ice show. I hadn't done so in twenty-three years. No one told me to do it. I simply knew that I wanted to, just like I knew I would rather get with the program than make a fuss at the first rehearsal when I learned that in the adult group number, called Artists and Models, the men would play the artists and the women would play the models. As a feminist historian of visual culture, I've worked to challenge that gendered vision of the art world; surely, women can be artists, too. Yet I soon realized one possible result of pushing that criticism. I'd be assigned to play an artist, wear male drag, and forego the women's costume: a sexy little black minidress with skinny, sparkly vertical red stripes. I really wanted to wear it. Besides, something really appealed to me about being a girl like everyone else, which offered pleasures that followed me out of the rink. Once I started shaving again, for instance, I loved it and never stopped.

Finally, as I realized only in retrospect, I had a stake in wanting black skates that outlived actually wanting them. Looking back, I found it telling both that I related my desire for black skates to a sometimes still wrenching geographic move and that I could see plenty of signs, once I stopped beating them down, that I was not the same girl that I had been back then, at least in the fashion details. People still ask me what happened to the kick-ass boots I used to wear, by which they mean the (skate-height) black boots with metal rings that rarely leave my closet now; for kick-ass boots these days, I tend to favor a hint of perversity in lacing. More important, when I picture the look to which I connect black skates, I imagine not myself, but my friend Nadine, who died in 2004, as she looked in the 1980s and early 1990s when we spent a lot of time together. In a way, loss simultaneously amplified my desire and masked its disappearance. It is as if my actual desire for black skates quietly evacuated a story that I needed to keep telling myself in order to keep ties that I can't bear to break.

Ties That Break, Ties That Bind

A lot more than color contributes to how skates affect skaters, even setting aside their function on the ice. One factor for me was the bit of long-buried muscle memory they awakened. Muscle memory has numerous functions in figure skating. Mastering new tricks depends on it. So does refining a routine so that you "skate the program, not the elements," which is figure skating language for no longer needing to move methodically through a brain-memorized sequence of moves. It can also make one's relation to skating gear resonate with familiarity. Long before I could do much *on* my skates (muscle memory helped a bit there, too), I could do once-known things *to* my skates, which, in turn, heightened my faith in and desire for a skating future. Lacing skates up, which requires certain gripping, twisting, and pulling motions; using the one-handed back-and-forth trick for speedy unlacing at the hooks; standing on one foot to remove or reattach the blade guards; wiping the blades dry after use; slipping on the soakers, those protective, soft covers for storage; returning skates to a skate bag that somehow inevitably, inexplicably gets crowded with seemingly nothing over time—all these can make you feel like a skater, or a skater again, before you can do much that looks like figure skating. So can attendant sounds and feelings, like the little whoosh when the laces get pulled against the holes, which diminishes as the laces age, or the way that lacing skates can callus or cut one's fingers.

My relation to skates, like my relation to skating, is hardly universal. Skaters rarely seem to share my reticence about discussing skate expense; it's just genetic luck anyway that my feet fit right into a stock boot. Few people, I imagine, consider skate color so central to their skating thoughts and pleasures.

Yet I am also struck by commonalities that reveal how rooted personal investments may be in the interconnected histories of gender, technology, politics, and sport. Yes, that's specifically me who linked mourning to footwear; it was my friend who used the bra trick to seduce younger women; and it was classic Grandma Sophie to have Alzheimer's actually enhance her pride in ladylike small feet. At the same time, grief keeps infusing all sorts of owned and imagined possessions, people keep situating themselves in relation to the bra trick, foot size keeps being measured against prettier younger sisters, and footwear keeps abetting gender aspirations if only one can cover the cost. And that can all be before the gear gets put to use.

IV

Ladies

INTRODUCTION *Athletic, Artistic, or Just Plain Perverse*

Before I started figure skating as an adult, my primary take on standards of femininity in figure skating revolved around a pair of terms that commentators throw around for female skaters: *athletic* and *artistic*. As many people have noticed, the terms frequently function as codes akin to *butch* and *femme*. "Athletic" female skaters, especially opposed to "artistic" skaters, may be identified as such for stunts beyond what most female skaters can do—Tonya Harding and Midori Ito, two top "athletic" skaters, could land triple axels. "Athletic" also implies that a skater's prowess is achieved at the expense of femininity. Athletic skaters, it seems, hurl themselves up and around in undisguised displays of brawn, without refinements directing attention from muscled labor to the feminine grace that "artistic" skaters exhibit.[1]

This contrast between athletic and artistic is dubious on many levels. Why should extreme athletic accomplishments, or willing displays of strength, be gendered masculine? Using them as an exit marker for femininity is also related to using them as an exit marker for femaleness and one extremely troubling, unjust consequence: sex verification testing of elite athletes in women's sports. (I return to the topic in part 6.) Besides, the judgment "athletic" as opposed to "artistic" has been applied especially to female skaters of color (Ito and also the dark-skinned Surya Bonaly) and/or with visible lower-class roots (Harding), suggesting raced and classed feminine ideals that not all skaters can come to embody.

Regardless, why should either artistry or athleticism performed by women require a particular display of femininity for maximum support, scoring, or even participation?[2] Such notions hurt athletes not only in figure skating, famous for subtle or direct pressure to conform to gender ideals, but also in numerous other sports. Female bodybuilders have faced judging standards that reward them for quitting short of their best muscle-developing effort.[3] Throwers competing in women's track and field may feel pressure to counter the masculinity associated with the massive shoulder and arm muscles required to compete at elite levels, even visibly wearing feminine makeup when they throw. This is not to say that throwers only wear makeup as a ruse. Jayne Caudwell cautions us to remember that some athletes presenting as feminine in masculine-coded sports do so because they prefer feminine expression in general, not to deflect prejudice labeling them masculine or labeling them queer because masculine; some feminine-expressed jocks happily identify as queer, too.[4] But for throwers who identify as butch, or otherwise un-feminine, both conformity and refusal to do so have costs. Besides, as one elite thrower, Keelin Godsey, pointed out to me, throwers of all genders ought to be getting credit for grace the way figure skaters should be getting credit for strength. The two sports, we realized in conversation, have a lot in common. In both, people twirl around, balance, and utilize strength. Yet figure skaters are viewed as pretenders to the title of athlete while throwers are characterized as hurling lumberers, like the football players, such as Emmitt Smith or Jerry Rice, who surprise viewers when they shine on *Dancing with the Stars*.

Not Me?

In short, the sources and effects linked to athletic versus artistic reek. I know that. But that knowledge is mixed up for me with my own plea-sures in gender. At figure skating, hockey, public skating, and skating class, skaters engage with movements associated with masculinity or femininity: reveling in them; ignoring or straining against them; aspir-ing, struggling, or refusing to learn them—all more or less consciously in relation to gender. I can't stand watching gender coercion of any kind: people pushed to butch up, femme out, or skate against their inclina-tions, gendered or otherwise, to twirl, check, speed, pump their fists, ex-tend their arms, whatever. But I'm entranced by the rest, partly because, simply put, I find both gender contrast and intense interest in gender quite hot. Put differently, I love spectating consensual gender, just as I love participating in it. Skating suits my strong identity as femme, and while I don't want figure skating to require femininity, I experience it, as I've said, as an expression of mine.

That's why, despite my clarity about the foul tinge of the divide be-tween athletic and artistic and my fondness for calling myself an athlete especially when it challenges expectations—yep, a femme jock; yep, the girl who failed gym class; yep, get over your ideas about skating not being a sport—I was stung, during a group lesson, when the coach, illustrating that skaters have diverse styles and strengths, called me the athletic one and someone else the artistic one. I felt hurt and misunderstood, even though I knew that she intended to compliment characteristics I strive to achieve, and that "athletic" directed to someone my age bears meanings independent of gender about unexpected strength and push. I might, then, have at least been gracious. Instead I protested, anxious to fight off the unwanted label and, more important, the recognition of something that I could not keep denying. In the context of figure skating I frequently fail to register as feminine to people whom I encounter, so much so as to render invisible even the most standard feminine accoutrements. Six years into skating regularly on the same ice, another skater said to me, "Hey, you're wearing nail polish—I've never seen you do that before." Actually, no one has seen me without nail polish since 1995, when I turned my nails into twenty bright spots of mandatory color to flash at the emotional-wreck-making of the tenure process.

What made my femininity invisible? Was it my skating? I like to think I'm graceful. Was it my clothes? My favored practice garb has what I consider clear feminine markers, like spaghetti straps or scoop necks, and the near constant quality of being form-fitting; I avoid hiding my standard feminine contours of breasts, hips, and waist. What canceled all that out? In queer contexts, especially where butches and femmes are a familiar presence, I can take for granted that my visible feminine curves will be read as a deliberate choice to display femininity in contrast to people who signal a masculine expression by hiding hips and breasts. Maybe the old notion that femmes need butches to make us visible as queer, for people who don't know how to look, held true in a sports environment where butches were scarce. Or was it more simply my disinclination to practice or perform, at least in solos, in typical skating dresses? Either explanation might figure into how people perceived me in my costume for "Piece of My Heart," which might not read as feminine if my status as the only female performing a solo in pants outweighed the top's skinny straps and cut (figure 5). In general, those dropped-waist, flared-skirt numbers are not for me, although I could happily skate daily in more tube-like skirts—the kind that suit derby practice and, outside of rinks or tracks, call for seriously good boots.

5. Illegible gender? Me, with Janis Joplin–ed exhibition hair,
skating to "Piece of my Heart" in the Portland Ice Arena's show,
I ♥ Skating. Photograph by dvmsports.com, 2007.

Perverse Normalcy

The following pieces look at the mechanisms, contradictions, exclusions,
and effects involved in maintaining gender norms for those skaters who,
if they competed, would compete, officially, as "ladies." "Skaters who
would compete as 'ladies'" may seem like a laborious way to say "female
skaters." But I want to work against taking for granted the use of "lady,"
which does not always refer to people of classy refinement who demurely
cross their legs. I have noticed, for instance, that if I'm at a restaurant
with someone who presents as male, genderqueer, butch, or otherwise
masculine and who might also be perceived as female-bodied, the server
often pointedly addresses us as "ladies." It requires interpreting other

clues to discern the server's intention. It could be a bigoted refusal to ac-
knowledge my meal companion's intentional departure from femininity;
an affirmation of female masculinities as legitimately female; a nod to
our possible status as a nonheterosexual couple; a queer wink of some
kind, in the genre of calling gay men "ladies" or "girls"; or a conventional
gesture of politeness by someone ignorant or unconcerned that "lady"
might not please someone deliberately departing from femininity.

In sports, similarly, "lady" operates in diverse ways. Semiofficial team
nicknames using "lady"—like "Lady Rams" or "Lady Yachstmen," to
name two jarring results of the convention where I live—bear at least
the residue of the notion that women should or do play more delicate,
less taxing, versions of sports played by men.[5] Granted, "lady" is far less
insulting than the "whole subgenre" of "homophobic and just plain mo-
ronic" YouTube videos discussed by Jennifer Doyle that viciously trash
women's basketball as hardly being a game.[6] Still, Glenn Jordan, a sportswriter for the *Portland Press Herald*, generally refuses to use "lady" nicknames, calling them "dated and sexist with a hint of condescension."[7]
(He also refuses to use official team names with Native American references; in his writing, the Chicago Cubs would thus beat "Cleveland" in
the World Series.)

Yet "lady" can work differently, too. Jordan himself makes an exception for the University of Tennessee "Lady Vols," for "Volunteers," because their legendary coach Pat Summitt embraced it to distinguish her
championship team from the less successful men. "Lady" also remained
firmly within the category of kick-ass at a Maine Roller Derby players'
meeting I sat in on. A player praised her teammates as "true ladies" for
declining to match an opposing team's dirty tactics at a recent bout.
Ladies, by this definition, may flatten someone with legal maneuvers but
they don't brawl or start fights. Then there are the e-mails starting with
"Hey Ladies" that I routinely receive on a list for women hockey players.
Since "ladylike" hardly describes players' on-ice goals, or, uniformly, their
off-ice demeanors, I take it as a slightly ironic but polite salutation.

Figure skating has the distinction of using "ladies" both more officially—thus Jordan makes an exception here, too—and more prescrip-
tively than in most other sports, although its bottom-line use to signify
"female" is no more prescriptive than any sport dividing athletes into two
sexes with the tacit implication that two suffice. Such divisions exclude
intersex people as well as trans people at stages of transition labeled offi-

cially in-between by governing bodies controlling their participation in the sport.[8] To the extent that "lady" also signals prevailing desired characteristics of elegant femininity, it also points to barriers, sometimes fundamentally unbreachable, for numerous skaters. These include skaters identifying as females who find "lady" intolerably dissonant and those who aspire to "lady" but lack the resources to acquire or hone the characteristics that, to borrow a classroom term, count for credit. Even people who consider themselves well, or well enough, to be accommodated by the "lady" classification do not simply step into a category that reflects their identities, but may be challenged, defined, and altered by it.

While skating is commonly understood to enforce rigid, often bizarre and archaic, gender rules, the dimensions of the perversity of these rules are not always so obvious. And perverse they often are, in various senses associated with the word. As the pieces in this section suggest, they can be weird, wrong, and hurtful to be slapped with, or crazily pleasing to observe, adopt, or to mess with. The essay titled "Skank or Ballerina? Codes of the Crotch Shot," takes on one of the most convoluted hypocrisies that affect, if variously, female skaters of all ages: how moves and outfits that involve panty flashing may be considered evidence alternately of skanky classlessness or of athleticism, flexibility, and grace. The following two essays focus specifically on adult skating. They consider first what can be freeing and then what can be confining in feminine norms. In "Cracking the Normative," I work to decipher how dominant feminine norms in adult skating, which both follow and contradict norms outside the sport, may, for some people and in varied ways, contribute to making adult skating so deeply compelling and enjoyable. In "Oh, Right, Policing Femininity: Nine Inch Nails at Adult Nationals," I recount my surprisingly painful, and surprisingly surprising, experiences of finding my own femininity possibly censured in figure skating competition. The final essay, "Booty Block: Raced Femininity," begins with a look at *The Women Who Raised Me*, a memoir by the actor Victoria Rowell that wonderfully illustrates how racial matters factor into all facets of our lives, which nonetheless can never be fully explained by or reduced to them. Using her account of training in ballet to set up key issues, I consider how raced feminine ideals affect skating's look, standards of excellence, and cast of characters.

11

Skank or Ballerina?

CODES OF THE CROTCH SHOT

A defining feature of skankiness is lack of subtlety. People are called skanks for allegedly embodying a sleazy sexuality that is crudely unrefined, baldly displayed, predatory, and easy-access. Yet codes of skank can be mysterious, especially from the outside. I had a hilarious conversation once with a seasoned derby skater about sexiness in derby-girl attire. The tough, sexy derby-girl look comes in many varieties. Players often have a lot of leeway about how they participate, although some teams invite a specific erotic fantasy. The Holy Rollers, for instance, a Texas Lonestar Rollergirls team, goes for delinquent jailbait, with pleated plaid skirts and the slogan "the baddest bullies in the Sacred Heart Schoolyard."[9] But many accoutrements of derby sexiness are optional, unless you count those that also constitute protective gear. Fishnets, the iconic derby garment, wear them or skip them; knee pads, wear them no matter what.

In any case, the skater talking with me mentioned being horrified by a red pleather hot-pants jumpsuit that another derby girl wore at a recent bout. She called it shockingly skanky. I was confused. Derby girls frequently wear miniskirts, very short shorts, and tight, low-cut tops. Did pleather set this outfit apart? I thought that the limits essentially concerned function, which could disqualify pleather as bout wear. It's the antithesis of breathable fabric (not that this always stops figure skaters). But the girl in pleather wasn't bouting. She was "fresh meat," the derby term for players in training who don't yet bout but participate actively at events: working the doors, selling "merch"[andise], getting the crowd going. Besides, did red pleather hot pants really differ conceptually from, say, the red laced, ruffled hot pants (Hot Topic, circa 2007–8) that I'd seen on other players?

I asked, laughing, what made something skanky. She laughed, too. An outsider, she admitted, might not even discern that her team maintained a line between sexy and skanky. She was adamant, however, that the line existed. Other team members drew the same one; fresh meat would learn.

Gilty as Charged

In dance and dance-related physical activities, the ability to draw an approved line between sexiness and skank often marks the difference between insider and outsider. This is a recurring theme of TV talent contests, especially during cattle-call episodes where judges pick the finalists to constitute the season's cast. Season 2 of *Dallas Cowboy Cheerleaders: Making the Team* (2007) includes an admonishment about the difference between sexy dancing and pole dancing. Judges on *So You Think You Can Dance* (SYTYCD) often evince shocked dismay at female dancers who perform inappropriate crotch displays, often by sitting with spread legs facing forward. In one featured example from 2009's Season 5, an auditioner performed a splits-heavy routine wearing a tiny shirt that covered only the very top of her breasts, baring a bra-shaped top that matched small velour shorts. The bra's push-up construction and gold lamé detailing accentuated her breast size and cleavage even more. The judges chastised her for too much sex and too little technique, although the latter complaint came off as really about sex, too—a deliberate escape, in the face of gilded cleavage, from sexual excess too glaring to look at.[10]

The show's editors clearly slotted the dancer into a stock talent-show role: the clueless performer who solicits audience judgment and ridicule. But I want to draw attention to how little distanced her presentation is from what counts as appropriate, even classy, in such contexts. What sets her apart, I think, is the pushed-into-even-more-roundness Pamela Anderson cleavage, as opposed to the sleeker look that dancers often cultivate. But cleavage itself, a bare midriff, booty shorts, body-hugging clothes, accentuated sexiness—dancers commonly display all of those. Even the auditioner's mysteriously short shirt has a bit of a counterpart in an enduring item of ballet practice garb: the short ballet sweater that ties in the front. Albeit with a hem that falls *under* the breasts, it often also looks weirdly truncated.

The difference depends not, or not only, on the details, but on how they signal, which depends on other features—including body shape, skin color, movement, age, adornment, and overall demeanor—that support raced, classed, and gendered stereotypes. Thus, I suspect, dark skin contributed to making this dancer's outfit and splits look skanky to people who would also see "ghetto," akin to the skanky "white trash" judgments faced by Tonya Harding, the figure skater famous for gender-defying triple axels, a hard-life upbringing, her link to the "whack heard round the world" that injured her competitor Nancy Kerrigan in 1994, and her outfits sometimes deemed inappropriate.

Queried much later about being downgraded for a costume at the 1994 Nationals, Harding scoffed. There was "nothing showing," she said, adding, "Too risqué? Come on. Look at what the girls [female figure skaters] are wearing."[11] Well, yes and no. Harding's dress exposed no more quantitatively than the clothing of many other skaters did—or implied that it was exposing, given the liberal use of "illusion fabric." Nor was it garish by figure skating sparkle standards. It stood out nonetheless for its low and wide gold-trimmed v—think a step more modest than Jennifer Lopez's green Versace dress for the 2000 Grammy Awards ceremony—that highlighted a push-up look and implied barely covered nipples. Those features might especially be considered excessive and dé-classé with the constant buzz over her lower-class origins. Even a "sympathetic" journalist, Stephanie Foote notes, commented that Harding's costumes "'reek of polyester.'"[12]

As Foote also writes, however, the common use of *polyester* to signal *cheap* plays a bit differently in the context of figure skating. *Polyester* often connotes *lower-class* by its implied contrast to natural materials that more affluent people are understood to embrace. But "most skaters use artificial fabric in their costumes to wick away perspiration and to ensure that the costume conforms to their bodies. It need hardly be said," Foote adds, "that rayon, elastic, and sequins do not grow on brightly colored, organic farms." Nonetheless, polyester on Harding stands for "White Trash."[13] Meanwhile, 11,500 rhinestones apparently do no such thing on the $13,000 dress that the designer Vera Wang made Kerrigan, also of modest roots.[14] Instead, they upscale her.

Spread Head

Maybe what most fuzzes the borders of alleged skank in dance and figure skating concerns codes of crotch display. Sometimes spreading one's legs and exposing a covered crotch area is judged one flimsy bit of fabric away from a beaver shot, designating crude, unthinkably inappropriate, intentional, or congenital lewdness. At other times, it is treated as the unmentioned yet acceptable by-product of moves described to bespeak grace, extension, flexibility, and elegant line. Panty flashing is so embedded in figure skating, a sport widely associated with old-fashioned, balletic gender presentation, that virtually all skirted costumes—that is, most costumes for girls and women—include a matching panty sewn in to accommodate routine exposures that might read in other contexts as "I see London, I see France" embarrassing accidents.

The extent to which panty display in skating has been coded as sufficiently modest can be seen on the covers of the Christian skating novels for children that I mentioned earlier (see figure 4 in essay 6). On three of them, short billowy skirts fly up to signal twirling, landing a jump, or doing a fast, ice-spraying hockey stop.[15] A fourth, for *Dreams on Ice*, illustrates a girl doing a spiral. Although it shows the girl from the front and slightly to the side, so that her loose (extremely short) skirt hangs down to shield her panty area from the viewer, the image suggests that she could well be flashing the audience sketched in behind her as she raises her leg to a horizontal position.

At least as notable is the use of a 1998 photograph showing Nicole Bobek from a similar angle in news articles about her 2009 arrest for alleged participation in a meth ring.[16] Frequently presented alongside a mug shot in which she has stringy dark hair, a bad complexion, and a grim expression, the smiling, spiraling, blond skater is clearly intended to represent the angel before the fall. Yet the nearly full-splits extension must have flashed her original audience, while the sight for the photograph's viewers includes white panties discernible under a diaphanous, barely butt-covering, white skirt. The dress's neckline seems as close to nipple reveal as the one on Harding's downgraded 1994 dress. Perhaps the Snow White, Heidi-esque, puffed-sleeve, milkmaid cut made the neckline more acceptable.

The spiral in that photograph, at the time, was Bobek's signature move. It wouldn't be today. As the new judging system codified and recodified which spirals and spiral sequences can garner the maximum point value, extreme extension became mandatory. Now common variations, used in spins as well, include the catch-foot and the Spiral 135°, which entails creating an angle at least that wide by holding the leg up to the front or side.[17]

For a time, as clarified by the 2009 *ISU Communication* no. 1557 (the thousand-plus number itself indicating the confusion/clarification morass engendered by the new judging system), a skater seeking credit for a maximum Level Four spiral sequence virtually had to go for the crotch-barers, which look even more intentionally crotch-baring when the skater needs to hold the free leg in position.[18] *Communication* nos. 1611 and 1619, issued in 2010, removed leveling from spirals, presenting "full extension," "good flexibility," and "creativity and originality" as desired but seemingly less prescriptive criteria.[19] The spread remains, however, in both spirals and spins.

The Stretcher and the Gynecologist

People blame the extreme extensions in skating for many ills, ranging from monotony to physical injury. Debi Thomas, an Olympic medalist turned orthopedic surgeon, attributes "impingement, labral tears, subluxation, and subsequent early degenerative arthritis" to excessive range of motion imposed on the hip joint. "That is why people like Mary Lou Retton and Rudy Galindo have hip replacements at a young age," she posted to the Facebook group she started, "Fans for Downgrading Grabbing Your Skate" (figure 6). It's for people "fed up with the beauty of figure skating being completely ruined by painful displays of contortion as skaters desperately try to earn every point possible by grabbing their skates every three seconds."[20] A later post by JoAnn Schneider Farris about a variation called the "donut" expands on the extremes and absurdity. She describes learning at a USFS national seminar for technical specialists that "if you grab your skate and pull it to your head, but the skate only touches [your] bun," you will get "a Level 1 or Level 2 on a move that could have got a Level 4."[21]

But I do love one effect of the new rules: It's increasingly hard to maintain all this Emperor's New Clothes hypocrisy about crotch display. The decorated skater and renowned coach Ron Ludington memorably commented in an interview for Allison Manley's *Manleywoman* podcast: "The spiral sequence, what you need now is a person to stretch you and a gynecologist to work on [pause] you know, you know, you know."[22] Ignore or don't the somewhat gruesome image of gynecological prying. His comment makes clear that these spirals scream "Look here" and maybe "Come here."

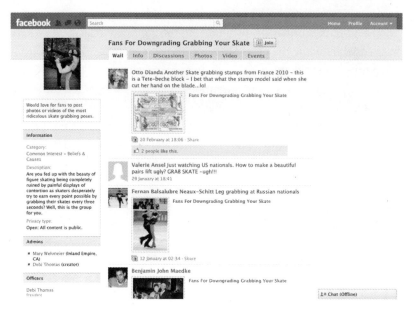

6. Facebook group, "Fans for Downgrading Grabbing Your Skate." Photograph, http://www.facebook.com, April 2011.

Those Invisible Panties Cost a Gajillion

If it's hard to imagine why it requires a full-on view to expose the crotch-shot nature of spirals in general, I suggest two reasons. First, it's easy to become acculturated to notions that figure skating comes with a free pass for crotch display. I have. More than once I've mystified nonskating friends when I asked whether a prospective costume showed too much. I'd have in mind specific issues. Did a fitted skirt ride up during a sit spin? Did a more flared skirt get stuck in the up position after flying up? But, to them, the question made no sense. If you spread your legs in a skirt, things show. Why could you possibly be asking?

Second, codes of the crotch shot depend on and support enduring, interconnected elements of privilege and prejudice. Ludington's reference to stretchers points to the expensive cross training and bodywork that help prepare skaters to glide on the ice in a vertical split and to display the look of elegance that invites viewers to see spiral extensions, among other moves, as classy. It's what Johnny Manzon-Santos, an adult skater who has worked to secure resources for promising, unmonied

7. Mixed signals. Sasha Cohen skates during the championship
free skate at the U.S. Figure Skating Championships in Spokane,
January 23, 2010. AP Photo/Elaine Thompson.

skaters, calls "polished-toepoint-that-cost-a-gajillion-dollars-thru-ballet"
skating.[23]

A photograph of Sasha Cohen performing her long program at the
2010 U.S. Nationals perfectly displays both that polish and the contradictions (figure 7). Skating to the familiar melody (although I had to look it
up) of Beethoven's somber and lyrical Moonlight Sonata, in a dress that
the writer of a story in which this photograph appeared called a "stunning
silver, gray, and black outfit," Cohen holds her leg up in a final spin.[24]
Her tensed face, muscled arm, and determined grip on the skate show
the hard work of maintaining the position that has as an effect directing the eye crotchward. Perhaps the panty's very plain fabric is intended
to message "nothing to see" against the jeweled neck, diaphanous skirt,
and satiny material across her chest, themselves typical ingredients of

skating-costume mixed signals. But its starkness, at the meeting point of her pale legs, makes it nonetheless a visual target.

The hold on elegance can be tenuous when skank lurks close by. Maybe that's why people have a bigger stake in hanging on. But that tenacity also supports the stereotypes about who is likely to display skanky excess. If flashing panties, artificial fabrics, and short shorts don't really separate skanks from ballerinas, must it then be something intrinsic to color and class?

That's only one problem with *skank* as a category, which is based on a fundamentally dubious judgment regardless. What's wrong with being sexually frank or brazen? On what principles and according to whose scales do certain kinds of abundance become excess and certain types of excess become obscene? Something is very wrong with the model by which the "gajillion-dollar" outlay for training and finery to dress up a crotch shot is considered less obscenely excessive than the crotch shot itself.

12

Cracking the Normative

Normal 90210

Tori Spelling might not seem like the obvious go-to source for insights about normality and normativity. She's been routinely linked to weird foolishness: foolishly extravagant parents, with a bowling alley in their mansion; foolish roles, like the virgin-through-college Donna Martin on *Beverly Hills, 90210*; foolish decisions, like allegedly having ribs removed to look even thinner; foolish TV movies, like *Mother, May I Sleep with Danger*? Yet as her 2008 autobiography *STORI Telling* makes clear, her freakish history and embrace of families "we choose and create"—along with, perhaps, her less-publicized work in smart family weirdness like 1997's *The House of Yes*—gave her ways to rethink the norms she had previously envied. "My whole life," she writes, "I wanted to be normal." She discovered, however, that "there is no black-and-white definition of normal. . . . There's only a messy, inconsistent, silly, hopeful version of how we feel most at home in our own lives."[25]

I find in Spelling's formulation a key to understanding what skating's tweaked feminine norms may offer some of us: a chance to be at home in our lives by accommodating inconsistencies both within ourselves and in relation to dominant social norms. My point here relates to something Juliet McMains argues about DanceSport in *Glamour Addiction: Inside the American Ballroom Dance Industry*. DanceSport, like adult skating, involves prescribed gender performance that is at once traditional, weird, regimented, freeing, and often intensely compelling, part of what draws people from a toe-dipping venture into a substantial investment of time, money, and identity. McMains, who shaved her legs for DanceSport as I did for figure skating, proposes that it can offer women "an access point through which to validate their own relationship to the feminine," sometimes partly because it involves some masculine-coded characteristics like physical strength and athleticism.[26] For women ordinarily required to display studlier postures, McMains suggests, the combination may be especially appealing.

Although I might articulate the combination of enticements a bit differently, McMains highlights well, I think, two big potential appeals in both DanceSport and figure skating. First, they can provide occasions to display gender expressions considered inappropriate in other facets of one's life—even more, I would add, as one ages. Cleavage, bared shoulders, form-fitting clothes, visible thighs, dramatic makeup, or patent enjoyment of sexuality frequently get read on older women as ridiculous, delusional, predatory, excessive, inappropriate, and disgusting. Cultural practices that demand "showing a little leg" can offer a break from that prejudice.[27] Second, they refuse to pit femaleness and femininity against being an athlete, an opposition that permeates sport on diverse levels.[28] For example, as Debra Shogan explains in *The Making of the High-Performance Athletes: Discipline, Diversity, and Ethics*, the insult in "you throw like a girl" involves more than sexist presumptions about what females can do. It also refers to a particular type of throw, using just the arm, that is at once untrained, in terms of deliberate sports instruction on how to put one's whole body into the throw, and highly trained: consistent with formal or informal training in feminine comportment, with its mandate to occupy minimal space.[29] (Thus, females learn to cross our legs even when wearing pants, because concealing panties is only the half of it.)

Especially for women who grew up before or early into Title IX, training as an athlete may constitute a slap at learned expectations, including one's own. I heard this point often from women in hockey and roller derby, where the component of rough contact makes the contradiction with learned femininity obvious. But rough contact isn't required. In a 1993 essay about her own adult skating that appeared first in the *New York Times* and then later in the anthology *SportsDykes*, April Martin, then in her mid-forties, wrote, "It still sends a shiver through me to describe myself as an athlete": "My coach bellows across the ice, 'You call that *speed*? My dead grandmother can move faster than that!' I bend deeper, push harder, feel the sweat start to run. There is deep pleasure in being pushed to my limits with the same gruff encouragement used for the serious competitors. I'm just another jock."[30]

The fact that skating also tapped into Martin's childhood ballerina fantasy, truncated at the time by a tight family budget, speaks to the piling up of feminine-linked pleasures that "nurtured and replenished" her despite their regressive elements. It also speaks to the common failure to perceive dancers as athletes, partly again because prejudice about femininity masks physical strength and accomplishment. As a result, "ballerina" or "figure skater" may be an acceptable fantasy when "jock" isn't. If you like the trappings, so much the better.

Muscles and a Bouffant

Martin also suggests that, for female skaters, pursuing athleticism with femininity partakes of a common "feminine mandate": "Take fiercely honed skills, raw power, and courage, and mask them with an illusion of fragility and vulnerability."[31] While the portrayed surface may by now have strayed a bit from fragility, Martin astutely places skating within a large genre of feminine contradiction that can generate indignation, admiration, pride, or pleasure, depending on the contexts of constriction and interpretation. Two weeks after my grandfather died, my grandmother, the one with small feet, went to a hardware store, bought caulk, and repaired a decades-old leak around the rim of the bathtub, that, in her understanding (which doesn't make so much sense in retrospect), caused wayward shower water to drip into the bathroom downstairs. I can't say for sure why she lived with a no-showers rule rather than call the super or fix it herself earlier. Who knows what's really up in someone else's relationships, or sometimes even in one's own? But I'd seen plenty of evidence that she could maneuver around my grandfather's more conservative values and little if any investment on his part in being a fix-it guy. So I leaned toward seeing it as more fascinating than sinister. Maybe it was her way to snare the luxury of a daily bath.

Or consider Olivia, whom I met during a public-skating session at a mall. Three decades after skating had brought her and her husband together, their sweet interactions included a care-giving strategy that one of my other two grandmothers had used frequently. Get your husband to rest by offering something else: a chance to watch (or sleep through) a favorite TV show; a semitrumped-up reason to get off the ice yourself. But "sweet" characterized Olivia no more than did her small frame and minimal flesh, which might suggest a frail, tentative soul to someone who didn't know her history. Hip and knee problems, along with her mother's disapproval of dance lessons, had thwarted her childhood dreams of being a Rockette, which required not only dancing but dancing in high heels. As a teen, she needed braces and physical therapy just to walk. After she fought her way back to mobility, she found skating easier on her joints than dancing. It also offered some similar thrills, like moving to music, and some extra ones, like "being able to move faster than my two feet will carry me."

Interestingly, this last figures prominently in the description of what makes skating deeply satisfying in George Plimpton's *Open Net*. It recounts his own participant-observation venture on ice, which culminated in several terrifying minutes as a professional hockey goalie. But Plimpton admitted that he was only watching the thrill of "great speed" and the "maneuverability of a dragonfly" that remained "foreign" to him as a novice skater.[32] Olivia, in contrast, had lived it. She'd fought her way back from some serious skating injuries, too, as well as a recent bone break she had incurred in some daredevil skiing incident. She declined to elaborate on it except to admit that it was "foolhardy." Her femininity on the ice included all of the above plus an amazing bouffant hairdo, both airy and massive, as well as the "fancy outfits" that she loved. She wore them even to public skating, with her husband sometimes in matching attire.

It's My Party

"I am stronger than you know," as Stevie Nicks says in the lyrics to the duet "Leather and Lace." I love the private satisfactions, open secrets (why gallantry can be so hot), and satisfying reveals evoked in that line. Like the garters I used as my tiny lifeline in hockey, they function, sometimes with an erotic tinge, as a kind of feminine-strength muscle memory, resonating with histories of strong women making their way. Along with the other cohabiting contradictions that I discussed here, they contribute mightily to making figure skating a passion that, to recall Spelling, helps me feel at home in my own life. They embolden me to recognize myself as an athlete even in sports environments where figure skaters don't appear to fit the profile—a situation hilariously dramatized, in terms of surface appearance anyway, when I showed up for the Gay Games opening ceremony on a 90-plus-degree day as seemingly one of about ten women athletes wearing a skirt or dress among thousands in shorts. They help me dismiss idiocies that might otherwise really grate. I suggested to an adult hockey player once that she could generate more power in her skating by pushing out to the side with her whole blade rather than rolling over her toe. She responded dismissively, "Thanks, but I'm not trying to look pretty." Whatever, I thought, after futilely trying to clarify the science of it. Hang onto a habit that's worse than useless while I decide whether to bother blowing by you next time we're both at public skating. Try out your quads on a sit spin while you're at it.

But the satisfactions that involve maneuvering around ideological poisons, like prejudice against the feminine, often require other people's participation as co-conspirators, appreciative spectators, or at least willing nonobstructionists. These positions may be precarious when stereotypes and conflicted stakes pull toward different ones. Patrick Califia illustrated this point with a great example, from the realm of butch and femme relationships, that has stuck with me ever since the 1990s, when I found it in an article he wrote for *On Our Backs*. He was warning butches not to let their own displays of chivalry and masculine prowess fool them into having a misogynist sense of superiority over femmes. When you're out in the rain dealing with a dead battery, Califia wrote, there's a good chance that those femmes waiting in the warm coffee shop know as much about jumper cables as you do. You can choose to view them as helpless, or you can appreciate their participation in the gendering that animates butch/femme erotics and prize the way they honor your masculinity with a respect too scarce for butches in a society with rigid sex and gender norms.[33]

People's interpretations of others can have varied effects on them. I felt a little betrayed by that hockey player I just mentioned, a friendly acquaintance. I'd thought we shared a mutual admiration for our respective athletic endeavors. Even so, I could laugh at her foolishness, skate away, and get quite a kick from telling the tale—and then from the aftermath of querying one of her coaches. Without using the player's name, I asked the coach about her assertion that coaching opinion varied regarding my theory. Although he handed me the same line about looking pretty, I gleefully spied him the next week subjecting his scrimmage-hungry players to thirty minutes of skating drills. But judgments can certainly hurt and harm in numerous ways. As Califia's example suggests, they can infiltrate intimate interactions, violate tacit or presumed bargains, shake your sense of self, and affect how people treat you.

In skating, permission and censure, flexibility and rigidness, freedom and regulation butt up against each other constantly. But how? Even what fits into which category can be hard to determine. A skating dress may be modest up top to conceal a chemo port or ample below to accommodate protection against indelicate leakages associated with age. Or the same features may serve perceived standards of age-appropriate propriety, like the use of illusion fabric to fake unwrinkled arms. But whose standards are being accommodated? How do you weigh the complicated interplay of skater preference, personal aesthetic, social norms, and anticipated judgments? How do we even discern what those judgments are? As I discuss next, it's not easy to figure out.

13

Oh, Right, Policing Femininity

NINE INCH NAILS AT ADULT NATIONALS

I made a little splash at the 2009 Adult Nationals. It wasn't for skilled skating. Besides competing in the lowest freestyle level at AN, I botched most of my spins and jumps. Instead, I stood out for violating the unwritten rules of music, dress, and gender presentation for women. My music, harder edged than most, came from the Pink Floyd song "Shine On You Crazy Diamond" as well as an instrumental version of Nine Inch Nails's "Closer," which is better known by its primary lyric "I want to fuck you like an animal," although people familiar with the song might not have placed my excerpt. Unlike my competitors' costumes, which involved skating dresses and skin-colored tights, my costume featured black leggings under a short, pleated black skirt from Hot Topic (figure 8) that had silver-colored studs and chains. Besides accenting the music with a bit of mainstreamed bondage fashion, the metallic elements provided the requisite skating-costume sparkle ordinarily met by jewel-like stones. My hair, instead of the common bun or ponytail in natural, or natural looking, hair color, had red chunks dyed into a relatively short bluish black.

I hadn't considered the costume or music to be so outrageous; neither had my coach. So I was surprised when people sought me out later to praise my refreshing deviation from the norm. "We don't think the judges liked it," someone tracked me down in the parking lot to say, "but we did." A skating friend, Sara Shley, put it another way as we considered that possibility: "Well, who's your demographic for that number? Not judges who are looking for ethereal pink ballet dresses."

Had the judges really downgraded me for look and music? Clearly, I hadn't been lavishly rewarded for creativity. Yet I hadn't skated well enough to attribute my bad placement, eighth out of nine, to disapproval. I decided to investigate further by keeping the program for another year,

8. Sparkling tastefully: code violation. Skirt from my 2009
and 2010 Nine Inch Nails/Pink Floyd costume. Photograph by
Paul Heroux, 2011.

a relatively common practice, changed merely to incorporate a year's
worth of improvement. If I skated the same program better but still got
low marks, maybe I'd know more about why.

The experiment failed in almost every aspect of execution. Any pretension to vaguely scientific controls—same program, same costume,
same event—was compromised from the start because between AN 2009
and AN 2010, I aged from Ladies Bronze III (the forty-one to fifty age
group) into IV (fifty-one to sixty), with possible advantages accruing to
being the youngest rather than the oldest. Plus, my coach, Ann, wound
up rechoreographing the program. Ann, to the great benefit of my skating, will have nothing to do with programs that primarily alternate tricks
with crossovers. More difficult, generally longer, jump and spin elements
couldn't simply be plugged into existing spots. Finally, while my skating improved noticeably over the year, I did not master the jumps that
many people competing at my level can do, and, in competition, I did
not successfully accomplish all the elements in my program. As a result, I had no credible evidence to attribute placing fifteenth of seventeen to violating norms, although two nonskating friends in the stands,
new to the whole scene and hardly objective, thought that they could:
"Your skating seemed stronger, less tentative than some of the others,
and you were doing some choreography the whole time. But we noticed

your arms didn't flutter. Do judges really like those fluttering arms?" There, perhaps, were the gender codes that make my own sense of femininity largely illegible as such in many skating contexts. But my friends also simply didn't understand the importance in scoring of jumps and spins.

Standard Deviations

If the experiment failed to help me parse my score, it did confirm that standing out in 2009 had not been a fluke. Happily, I did not acquire another creepy semistalker like the skater at AN 2009 who seemed to be everywhere I turned, calling me "wild child" and asking for my professional opinion about why women can orgasm "four times a night," which he considered "nature's way" of helping us want to reproduce. Yet my costume and program differed in the same way within this new set of competitors. People continued to flag me as unconventional and, consequently, as a risk taker, given the common understanding that judges rarely reward what one skater, who had thought of using Pink Floyd herself, called "the edgier" choices. "There's something to be said," she noted, "for picking music the judges recognize," although she had actually set aside Pink Floyd because a competitor had recently skated to it. Codes of skating etiquette against poaching from other skaters in one's training and competition vicinities complicate wisdom about the strategy that dictates using music that is already familiar within skating culture.

Her comment also reflects the way that Pink Floyd, whose music plays daily on rock and oldies radio, actually functions, like Doc Martens shoes, as a rather standard signifier of the "unconventional."[34] Many bold skating choices are old-school in other contexts. Herbie Hancock's 1983 "Rockit" was over two decades old when Stephanie Rosenthal gained tremendous buzz for using it at the regular Nationals in 2006. Simply skating (quite well) to hip-hop sent the video of her performance viral among skaters.

My 2009 costume, too, had standard "unconventional" on offer, at least for a white woman. As Gayle Wald emphasizes, white women have more history, and permission, in putting forth this particular type of rough, aggressive edge that does not necessarily have "portability" across race.[35] The predominantly white populations of roller-derby players as well as Riot Grrrls, the topic of Ward's study, support this point, and I can't help thinking here of *Bring it On 3: All or Nothing*, in which Hayden Panettiere plays a shallow, booty-disparaging white girl who transfers to a high school in the 'hood after her dad gets laid off from a fancy job. After learning the street-tough, show-your-rage dance style of crumping from the male cheerleaders there, she winds up being the one to teach the squad how to incorporate it into legitimate, rule-following, competition-winning routines — and to trade in their penalty-garnering sexual excess for a controlled display of the booty that she newly appreciates. But room for ass-kicking females is different than room for ass-kicking females as serious athletes. Derby players always have to push the point that their sport is not a free-for-all with brawling babes but a sport with specific rules of contact requiring fitness, training, and strategy. As Killer Quick, also known as Maureen Wissman, nicely explains, derby skaters pursue athleticism with an antisexist ethos that works against pitting sexiness and athleticism against each other. "[Derby] promotes an image of strong women who don't need or want to give into the societal pressures of how women should look, think, or behave. Roller derby skaters are proud of their sport, their athleticism, and their strong bodies of any shape and size, and their sexiness comes from that strength and athleticism."[36] Figure skaters, in contrast, are often taught to hide our athleticism as not ass-kicking at all.

Save It for Halloween

At AN 2010, I also understood more clearly that my violation came from doing that program in a "technical" as opposed to "interpretive" event, the other type of solo competition offered at AN. Technical programs are regulated by the Well-Balanced Program charts that form the basis for serious competition on all levels. "Interps" are more like exhibition or show programs, designed to entertain and, in theory, judged less by the spins and jumps.[37] Skaters can use props (if they don't touch the ice). Music can have lyrics — now allowed, but still rarely used — in technical programs at lower levels as of the 2009–10 season. Costume rules for technical programs don't apply. You did not have to observe the overall directive that costumes be "modest, dignified, and appropriate for athletic competition — not garish or theatrical in design" (USFS *Rules of Sport* no. 4031) or more specific rules like requiring men to wear "trousers" (4033) instead of tights.[38]

As a result, interps provide a relatively approved occasion for transgressing norms of sexual decorum and gender presentation—often, like at Halloween, in highly predictable ways. There are hot mamas and women in feline or dominatrix catsuits. There are exotic personae signaled to hail from places distant geographically, racially, or both, like the harem girl I saw in 2008 who prompted a guy in the stands to snarl, "Yeah, like we haven't seen that before." People sometimes also cross-dress to be humorous (Richard Simmons) or expressive in other ways (Roy Orbison). As my friend Debbie and I concluded, however, in a conversation after an amazing "Singin' in the Rain" interp that Debbie performed while costumed as Gene Kelly, skaters more often dress like animals. She noted later that primarily women cross-dress, although Jay Kobayashi gained fame among adult skaters about ten years ago for his performance as Michelle Kwan. Overall, however, the adult skating environment contrasted with queerer environments we hung out in, where a lot more gender variation might seem unremarkable.

Gender conformity off the ice may affect what people do or don't do on the ice, which, in turn, can affect off-ice presentation. For example, no one planning to compete with standard-competition hair could have worn her hair like I do ordinarily—in minimal variation from my costume hair. (My hair also, however, is styled to accommodate skating, with front sections long enough to tie back for practice yet short enough to immobilize with gel and hairspray for costumes.)

Once More with Feelings

Had my Nine Inch Nails and Pink Floyd program been an interp, it might have been read as an impersonation of someone transgressing boundaries. In a technical event, I simply was that someone—a someone affected by inhabiting that position in ways I didn't always predict or understand. In fact, my biggest insight about judging that came from keeping the same program another season occurred when I competed at the 2010 Colonial Adult Winter Challenge a month before AN. Three-quarters of the way through my program, as I arched and dropped forward into my catch-foot spiral, appropriately choreographed to aim the crotch view away from the three judges, I found myself looking directly at them for a second. To my surprise, while two had the expression I had come to imagine—at best, impassive; at worst, disdainful—I saw the middle judge smile broadly. She looked delighted, and, it seems, she was. I placed fourth out of six overall, but she'd ranked me second.

I make no claim that her score constitutes meaningful evidence about censure. But I do know this: When I saw her smile, my own body and spirit lightened. I suddenly felt energized, joyful, able to remember, maybe even execute, some of those instructions that my coach keeps hammering on: "bend your knees," "push don't just step," "head up." It felt like that moment every spring in the sunny warmth of daylight when I sense a haze of blues physically exit my body, alerting me that a bit of seasonal affect that had weighed me down for months was gone.

In affecting my emotions and performance so strongly, the experience also, like my foray into hockey, offered me a bit of access into the layers of injury caused by bad gender fits—injuries I usually engage most consciously as a gender-conforming ally of people who reject their assigned sex or prescribed gender norms. It was eye-opening to realize both that I was among the injured and that I was surprised to be. Figure skating is famously policed, and, intellectually, I knew better than to think that feminine-coded, nomatively bodied women live in any simple relation to norms. I have written and taught for years against some hierarchy privileging butch or trans as the glorious heights of complicated gender, or, as Julia Serano so eloquently critiques, genderqueer as the glorious heights of trans genders.[39] Yet friends in those categories often saw more clearly than I that I did not always securely inhabit the position of the unscathed. "You know, the whole thing actually felt like crap," I told one such friend several months after AN 2009, recounting an episode in my lingering notoriety when a skater volunteering at the rink entrance waved me through as I fumbled for my competitor badge: "That's OK, I know who *you* are." My friend's response: No kidding, the whole thing sounds awful.

Freak Factor

What was up with my disconnect and why did I let AN get to me so much? Partly, it was the overall heteronormativity, which, on occasion, even takes over competition logos (figure 9). Partly, I'm sure, it was simply the duration. Inevitably I descended over the week from interested surveyor to an "annual weepy freak moment," as I texted to a friend while I hid in the back seat of my rental car in 2010. It also involved being among

9. Competition swag. Logos often bear hetero couplings, visible here on these souvenir towels. Photograph by Paul Heroux, 2011.

relative strangers. I said in the last piece that figure skating helped me feel "at home in my own life" partly because some features of its feminine norms resonated with me. But that comfort depended on encouragement to feel at home where I skated. I might have been the only one slipping Tuscadero's "Latex Dominatrix" onto skating CD mixes, or the White Stripes' version of Dolly Parton's "Jolene," with male vocals imploring "Please don't take my man." I might be most expected to reuse the Naughty Nurse costume, a bizarre, oddly Swiss bit of ruffle-accented polyester, from our 2010 adult-skater spoof of *General Hospital*. But by then, people in my local skating community had stuck with me, as I wrote in my bio for the show program, "through everything from a health scare to some ups and downs in a sort of unconventional personal life." Over time, they demonstrated some interesting vagaries themselves. It takes a while to find out which gentle traditionalist in modest ballet skirts used to be a tomboy or who gets off on flashing truckers. At AN, I was still in the early stages of making friends and getting to know the scene.

Most important, perhaps, were the fact of being literally judged combined with the kind of crazy-making peek-a-boo standards that can cause misery in many contexts, including daily life. In figure skating, gender policing is legendary, obvious, and palpable. Stories abound of U.S.

Figure Skating (USFS) judges and other higher-ups working to impose the look of high-class femininity. By their own accounts, Debi Thomas had a nose job courtesy of a benefactor who was also a skating judge, and Tonya Harding was pressured by USFS officials to stay in an abusive marriage because being married looked better than being divorced.[40] By other accounts, the skating powers that be also tried to up-class the working-class (and athletic versus artistic) future national champion, Elaine Zayak, even by lending her mother a fur coat to wear during the 1980 Nationals. Various skaters I interviewed who had skated as children remembered increasing pressure to act and be correctly feminine the higher up they got.

Regardless of the truth value in each particular story, evidence of pressure and reward appears at every competition in the uniformities of dress, music, movement, bodies, and overall style. But it's hard to prove for sure exactly whether and how judges have acted on disapproval, especially given other inconsistencies and subjective elements that may happen in scoring. Little versions and variations happen all the time such as with the Johnny Weir controversy at the 2010 Winter Olympics, where some people believed that judges robbed him of a medal because his extraordinary artistry flouted preferred displays of heteromasculinity, while others said that his technical elements fell short.

Adult skating may lack the same stakes, and it certainly lacks any USFS investment in particular adult skaters. Yet it's easy to see that adult skaters are affected by, and contribute to, unarticulated standards. Every adult woman who talked to me about competing in pants or an otherwise nontraditional costume wondered about its effect on her scoring. Perhaps just as telling is a conversation I had in the stands at AN 2010. I entered the conversation as one woman credibly and angrily itemized evidence that judges at a previous competition had applied an unfortunately common form of censure that skaters call the "fat deduction" or "fat girl deduction." A little while later, however, she opined that the skater on the ice in a unitard could look so much better in a slimming dress. Telling, too, is that, back home two weeks later, another adult skater in our ice show asked me if, as she'd been advised, she really needed the deeper shade of lipstick that made her feel clownish and untrue to herself. I'd resisted stage makeup myself at first for similar reasons but I told her yes anyway. Even those who are critical of policing can contribute to the practice.

Yet to end on a snarky note would mischaracterize AN. In general, figure skating rewards conformity to arcane gender norms and can reek of the bleak hierarchy that Taylor Swift economically referenced in "You Belong with Me," where mean girls wearing just the right outfits sideline losers to perpetual misery. ("She wears high heels, I wear sneakers / She's cheer captain, and I'm in the bleachers.")[41] I remember visiting one rink where two teenage girls, wearing just the right warm-up clothes, club jacket, and groomed bun, looked at me disdainfully and then, within earshot, muttered something about adult skaters to their coach, who smirked in collusion with their haughty ridicule. I'll admit relishing my knowledge that as skaters in their later teens competing in the Novice category with only single axels in their programs, they were doomed to rule at most their very tiny corner of the kingdom.

Adult skating has the reputation for being the nonsnarky branch of figure skating, where people cheer on their competitors instead of worrying that someone will tamper with their skates. Adult Nationals, in my experience, largely bears this out. In the stands in 2010, two AN mainstays, Maureen Linhardt and Kristin Godfrey, aimed Harry Potter wands and a loud "Shazaam!" to confer magical powers on each skater coming out to begin a program at every event they attended. Their gesture was an extravagantly showy version of widely visible mutual support. Long before feeling the least bit at home at AN, I knew that needing a book project to embolden me — I can talk to those people, it's fieldwork — was largely about my own shyness. Many skaters, I observed, happily engage new people, and not just the ones writing books. They are open to making new friends, are generous with tips, and are willing to take your skating as seriously as you do regardless of your level.

Plus, despite being surrounded by visual models of femininity I would never try to approximate, ballet buns hardly appeared on everyone, and many skaters, bunned or otherwise, exemplified how often gender stereotypes fail to describe anyone. More typical in complication, perhaps, is Wendy Bauer. An astronomy professor at Wellesley, she makes much beloved "tossies," the gifts tossed to skaters after they finish, by knitting little sweaters for stuffed animals, with "AN" and the year knitted right into the sweater (figure 10).

Besides, I'm happy to see skaters perform in almost any hairdo, espe-

10. A Wendy-bear tossie joins the swag and program from AN 2010. "Tossies" are the gifts thrown onto the ice after a skater finishes. My haul in 2011 included skating gloves, party-favor body glitter, M&M's imprinted with the AN logo, a medal with an inspirational saying, and "champagne" (actually soap) bubbles. Photograph by Paul Heroux, 2011.

cially skaters who aren't young. Messages that it's time to get off every stage come earlier and in more contexts than I had imagined before I started receiving them. They can sting as derision or even when meant as deference. An audience member put it well at a 2009 event about radical queer activism: "Thanks for the respect, but we don't all want to sit on the couch, delivering some fucking wisdom of the elders." At AN we have a present, not just a past, and in 2010 I think I found a role model for my next decade or two: Joan Chanel, in her late sixties, doing a technical, not interpretive, program to a Rolling Stones medley, wearing fishnets and a black hot-pants number with a giant version of the band's tongue-and-lips logo on the front.[42] "I think I have a future," I excitedly texted friends from the stands. They often texted back, "We already knew that." Sometimes I needed a reminder.

Yet despite being low on snarkiness, AN conforms closely to the content of Swift's song in one crucial way. The video for the song portrays a scene dominated by a sea of white people in which white models of femininity rule the day in ways largely unspoken as white. (So, too, with the rush to protect Swift and to squash Kanye West after he interrupted her acceptance speech for Best Female Video at the 2009 MTV Video Music Awards.) At AN, my red-chunked hair made me an outlier. My light skin didn't. In the next piece I look more at why.

14

Booty Block

RACED FEMININITY

In *The Women Who Raised Me*, Victoria Rowell details the childhood training to pursue a career in ballet that also figured in her first big television
role. As Rowell explains, William Bell, the cocreator of *The Young and the
Restless*, "customized" Drucilla for her, although her own story differed
greatly. Drucilla appeared in 1990 as a streetwise, thieving, illiterate African American teenage runaway. Ballet, introduced far from home and
from above her station, helped to transform Drucilla into a glamorous,
sophisticated model. Rowell, of more complicated racial origin, was the
child of a white mother and black father. Born in Maine in 1959, she
first encountered ballet at home through her unmoneyed second foster
mother, Agatha Armstead, a loving, fierce advocate for Rowell despite a
happenstance entry into foster parenting that recalls the legend of Lana
Turner being discovered at a drugstore counter, except with explicit racial
criteria. Armstead and her husband, visiting a Portland hospital where
they hoped to find work for him, were spotted in the lobby by social
workers desperate, in a region largely populated by white people, to find
"Negros" deemed suitable to foster-parent black children.

When Rowell was six, Armstead discovered that Rowell's Keds were
wearing out so fast because she had been imitating dancers on TV. Herself an accomplished pianist trained at the New England Conservatory of
Music, Armstead determined that Rowell should learn ballet and taught
her the basic positions from a text she'd scrounged up. Rowell's dance
training from then on proceeded with the support of family, advocates,
friends, and mentors. Armstead kin chipped in funds or housing. The
white woman running the Cambridge School of Ballet saw the potential
in Rowell's book-trained moves and refused the prejudice that, for many
people, made dark skin a disqualifier itself. Rowell's caseworker in Maine
fought to have the state pay for toe shoes and out-of-state residence for

training. The white, Jewish mother of Rowell's ballet friend Robyn invited Rowell to live with them. She then sent both girls to the American Ballet Theater's prestigious, expensive summer program, a chance to be seen by ABT's gatekeepers that was ordinarily available only to affluent white kids.[43]

Rowell's training regimens, like her access to training, were marked at every turn by race, which informed expectations about appearance, carriage, and movement. This point emerges beautifully in two passages when Rowell talks about ballet's preference for what might be called, although Rowell doesn't, the flat look of "white-girl butt." At nine, Rowell learned that while "ballet training had [her] tucking her tailbone under," other girls living in Roxbury, the largely black-populated section of Boston, were "flipping theirs out." Her friend Lauren, for instance, who could mesmerize any boy, had mastered a different set of skills in feminine performance: "Lauren demonstrated a slightly separated fourth position as I followed along. 'Good, now put your hand on your hip, and rock back.' She was the prima ballerina of our neighborhood."

Proper training, then, could minimize or emphasize one's rear assets. It might never, however, minimize the rear enough for ballet. "The one thing about our anatomies that we could not manipulate were our robust derrieres," she writes about herself and Robyn as they starved themselves through the ABT summer program. "All the tucking under in the world could not disguise what clearly was our ancestral inheritance."[44]

Out of Alignment

Rowell raises issues, connections, and questions that I think about with figure skating, too. How does racial bias inform who populates genres of physical movement and how they develop? A quarter century after Rowell's ABT summer, the company still had never had a black principal dancer, and white students still dominated the summer ballet programs.[45] Debi Thomas, who medaled in the 1988 Winter Olympics, remains one of the few famous, or one of the only, black figure skaters past or present. Besides the disproportionate location of disposable cash in the hands of white people, what else is involved?

The tailbone-tucking issue that Rowell mentions can illustrate the complex interplay of factors. "Tuck your tailbone under" is a common directive. I've received it in skating, ballet, and yoga and I understood a smaller-looking butt to signal that I might be doing it right. Then I learned from Maggie Cee—well versed in gendered movements and pleasures as a ballet dancer, dance teacher, and artistic director of the Femme Show—that the directive's intended anatomical aim is vertical alignment. This reduces apparent butt size most dramatically in a dancer with a swayback, which tightens the hip flexors and inhibits correct use of the stomach muscles in ballet, including for ballet's signature turn-out. But unless a teacher works actively, Cee said, to convey that "skeletal and muscular" matters are at issue, students might well conclude that tail-bone tucking aims to alter "body shape or size."[46]

Diverse factors encourage that conclusion, starting with how frequently costumes camouflage the serious butt and thigh muscles that dance and figure skating require. Dancers and skaters usually don't have "white-girl butt." Those who once did don't anymore. One way to tell that off-the-rack clothes are usually sized for white-girl butt is that losing white-girl butt to muscle development makes it harder to find clothes that fit.

Big butts are also freighted with negative views of fat in general. As Cindy Lop-Her emphasized when she started the "Campaign for Real Booty" on her blog *Big Derby Girls Don't Cry*, this prejudice affects even a sport trumpeting appreciation for diversely sized women that uses rather than hides heft. I named this essay "Booty Block" after a derby move in which blockers use their rears to shove other players out of the way. Ample size can help, as Punchy O'Guts, a Maine Roller Derby pivot and blocker and one of Lop-Her's featured players, explains: "I like my ass because it makes me feel like a real woman. . . . [It] helps me in derby because ain't nobody gettin' by, the sheer weight of the thing makes it hard for a girl to take me down."[47] The "stability and strength" of larger skaters, notes DayGlo Divine, a referee for the DC Roller Girls, can also "make them really effective jammers."[48] Yet, Lop-Her writes, "Open the newspaper to a derby article, and it's likely going to be the slim jammer who's gracing the page."[49]

Big butts also bear a stigma fueled by racism. They are associated with being other than white, or being white of certain (lower) class and ethnic statuses that compromise light-skinned people's identity or privileges as white. Big butts may be Italian, Russian, Latina, peasant, white trash, or Jewish, as Rowell indicates by attributing similar "ancestral heritage" issues to her friend Robyn. They may signify racial inferiority, exoticism, lack of self-discipline, unwelcome deviation from a desired norm, perverse sexuality, carnal insatiability. Fleshy, zaftig, voluptuous: the Hottentot Venus, Jennifer Lopez.

Similarly, "tailbone tucking" may serve vertical alignment, but it also has associations with whiteness and a history involving the erasure of black-linked roots. McMains explains in *Glamour Addiction* that "Latin social dance forms" like salsa, tango, samba, and rumba bear witness to their first practitioners, "African slaves or their descendents living in Latin America," in utilizing a "flexible and dynamic spine" and "privileging . . . polyrhythms over body lines." These dances were up-classed and whitened for ballroom partly by straightening the spine. Despite retaining some poses that "showcase" the butt, the dancers also followed "Western dance traditions that require tucking the butt under the body in order to enable more balanced and aerodynamic movement through space."[50] Swing dance, originated by African Americans, was similarly transformed. Arthur Murray and Kathryn Murray warned dancers in the 1950s not to dance in the old-fashioned way with their hips pushed back; McMains notes that their "illustration of what *not* to do bears a striking resemblance to the posture of the black lindy hoppers."[51] Straight spines and tucked butts enable certain movements but they also signal a racialized version of classy.

The Meat and the Motion

What would figure skating be like if different or diverse body shapes and skin tones were valued, even sought? Although some standards of excellence are patently contrived, like point-getting body convolutions in spins and spirals, others seem natural in existence and evolution. Top skaters used to do double jumps; now they do triples, maybe even quads. But all standards develop to the benefit of particular practitioners. Triples require the aerodynamic verticality that McMains discusses, leading to a field dominated by females who can stay simultaneously skinny, toned, and strong, with less protruding protrusions, and without, ideally, extreme height, which makes it harder to rotate without tipping. Because they depend on extreme precision, and may be derailed by "growth spurts," puberty, and weight changes, triples also require intensive, continued private coaching and hours of practice time first to learn and then to maintain.

None of those conditions favoring success fully or solely concern race. "Ancestral inheritance," as Rowell put it, does not endow all or only people of color with rear or chesty amplitude. Race doesn't fully determine the cultural forms one grows up with. Armstead, not Rowell's white birth mother, had classical music training. Nor does it determine what one prefers. I met an African American adult figure skater once, a music teacher, who thought it would be great if figure skating (newly) integrated African and Asian traditions. But her fantasy of breaking norms in her own skating involved skating to music by the "progressive metal" band Tool, which she traveled a lot to see in concert. Race does not fully predict disposable income, although Agatha Armstead's financial struggles well illustrate how, as the authors of *Black Wealth/White Wealth* detail, deliberate racial barriers have historically prevented African Americans from translating educational and cultural capital into the financial cushion those might offer whites.[52]

Nor would I accuse USFS of pursuing standards with the deliberate purpose of favoring white people, although people trained in the not-too-distant past remember individual USFS skating clubs that, for instance, didn't admit racial undesirables, including Jews. The African American skater Mabel Fairbanks, who started skating in the 1930s, was never able to compete, despite passing the highest tests with the help of Maribel Vinson Owen, who coached her in secret during off-hours at rinks that wouldn't let her skate with white people. No club, in the days before one could compete as an "Individual Member" of USFS, would have her; not one club within the United States admitted a black skater until the 1960s.[53] Those days of blatant prejudice are past, and many current, injury-courting standards democratically disrespect the bodies of all skaters. Yet white supremacy, white privilege, and racial bias result not only from willful, premeditated racism. They also come from complacent disregard for even obvious inequities and failure to pursue antiracist education and transformation. The predominance of white people is rarely an innocent accident.

But Accidents Will Happen

What is an accident, I would argue, at least in relation to figure skating's governing bodies, is the one notable, relatively recent departure from figure skating's sea of whiteness, which is that there are now more top skaters of Asian descent.[54] There's simply no reason to attribute this change to deliberate activism regarding race. The only factor within skating that anyone cites, the increased primacy of jumps to the benefit of all smaller people, is itself generally attributed to the demise of competition in compulsory figures. Those are the tracings—like the simplest one, the "figure 8" of colloquial renown—central to *figure* skating's genesis that, besides making for terrible sports television, sucked up training time now devoted to freestyle. Eleven-year-old Karen Berig, for instance, who agreed to have a year of her training at Skating Club of Boston chronicled for the 1979 book for children called *I Skate!*, spent three hours a day training in figures and only one on freestyle.[55] Now, freestyle dominates training. Moves in the Field, which succeeded figures, may be hard to learn, but skaters don't have to compete in them, and they rarely take the bulk of training time except before tests.[56]

Besides, counterevidence outweighs evidence of antiracist consciousness in figure skating. I interpreted the guy bemoaning the harem girl at Adult Nationals to have been wearied by white women impersonating sexual enticers from some vague Eastern land of exciting permissions and imprisonments. But he might have been wearied by the many harem-type roles among the technical programs at the regular Nationals, performed especially by female skaters of color. In fact, Michelle Kwan's breakthrough performance in the 1990s, widely hailed as her transition from "jumping-bean" girlishness to mature artistry (at fifteen), involved a Dance-of-the-Seven-Veils number as the biblical enticer Salome.

With that performance, a Chinese American girl of one often exoticized ethnicity, performs a different ethnicity, in this case Semitic, as a girl sent by her mother to seduce King Herod into killing John the Baptist. This kind of Orientalist mishmash occurs repeatedly and internationally, as do other characters that share a history of being created or viewed through sexualized racist stereotypes. Kwan also skated as Pocahontas that year, and in 2001–2, she was Scheherazade from the *1,001* (or *Arabian*) *Nights*, which the skater Kim Yu-Na, of South Korea, used in 2008–9. That was a year after Kim skated to music from *Miss Saigon*, which has generated protest about racism and sexual exploitation in the context of United States military imperialism.[57] The year 2007–8 also saw the Salome character recur at the U.S. Nationals, skated by Carolyn-Ann Alba, one of skating's few Latina skaters; her competitor, Kristine Musademba, of Filipino and Zimbabwean descent, performed to Duke

Ellington's "Caravane," a year before she played the Queen of Sheba. (This kind of ethnic typecasting will be familiar to fans of the 2011 series *Dance Moms* in which Abby, the dance director, has the one African American child perform solos first as "LaQueefa, wearing a gold lame animal print costume and Afro wig, and then in a Bollywood number.)[58]

I do not intend the above as a litany of manipulated victims, even though I assume that many of those skaters didn't choose their music. In fact, as Kwan skated her Salome program at the 1996 U.S. Nationals, Dick Button, one of the commentators, informed television viewers that Kwan did not know the story of Salome when she began working on the program.[59] But I would not presume to imagine why she skated as Scheherazade as an adult, how she thought or felt about performing either role, or why Kim switched gears in 2010, moving from *Miss Saigon* to James Bond and Gershwin. I've been writing throughout this part of the book about skaters, including me, who approach white-dominated feminine norms in skating with more or less complicated portions of pleasure, pain, and strategy. We may play or refuse the game, variously construed. We may delight, chafe, or both at obedience to rules. I presume the same about the roles I've just been talking about.

The differences I want to highlight are between roles that carry the usually tacit criteria "white"—and, perhaps, pure, ethereal, balletic, classy—and roles that carry, often explicitly, some version of "dark," which may include sexually and delightfully servile, or lethally and voraciously seductive. Like all raced, including white, stereotypes of gendered sexualities, they are shaped by histories of injustice that also shape possibilities for maneuvering. In *Dangerous Curves: Latina Bodies in the Media*, Isabel Molina-Guzmán shows how this works with Jennifer Lopez. In one way, Lopez epitomizes the ability to take charge of "ethnic" stereotypes, working her hair and legendary "booty" to designate herself as an authentic Puerto Rican, as a legitimate hip-hop performer, or as an exotic, ethnically white romantic lead.[60] But her "racial flexibility" and "ethnic ambiguity" only went so far. As she moved closer to whiteness, she was trashed in the tabloids according to stereotypes of Puerto Rican women as promiscuous, uneducated, low-class, and immoral. Meanwhile, famous white women like Julia Roberts and Angelina Jolie, in the press at the time for similar transgressions, were often "recuperated" as "sympathetic and exemplary performers of white femininity."[61]

In *The Hypersexuality of Race: Performing Asian/American Women on Screen and Scene*, Celine Parreñas Shimizu suggests that moralist condemnation is not the best overarching approach to problematic sexual representations. This is partly because of what she calls the "bind of representation": the mixture of pain, pleasure, and political potential that may be involved in "the experience of viewing, performing, and critiquing" the "hypersexualized" racial stereotypes that inform people's own histories and experiences.[62] Richard Fung gives a hypothetical example concerning *Miss Saigon*. Despite his own profoundly negative response to "watching scantily clad bar girls bump and grind for the lecherous American soldiers," he knew that people would experience the musical in various ways. He could "even imagine," he writes, that "rebellious Asian youths for whom the bar girl spectacle could be liberating in its celebration of the forbidden, having something of the allure of Madonna."[63] In addition, as Shimizu puts it, so much about race, sexuality, representations, and our relations to all of them are "unstable," "unknowable," and full of contradictions.[64] Cementing oneself in outrage—which can seem to make the most feminist, antiracist sense—can impede understanding what's up with subjugating images. It can also impede "utilizing how sexuality may open other possible subject positions besides subjugation."[65]

I agree. I want a lot of people to stop doing a lot of things, but my overarching point is not "you're bad," but "pay attention." I want white women to think twice about doing interps involving stereotypes that primarily affect other people's lives, at least without some highly readable critical edge. There's a parallel here to the interp or technical divide I noted earlier: between roles that one may be seen to impersonate and roles that one is seen, at least somewhat, to inhabit. White women can impersonate and walk away from harem-girl eroticism. Not everyone can. Besides, it's not as if, by forgoing such roles, white women lose the chance to inhabit, play around with, and critique oppressive femininities. Troubling white-dominated femininities occupy figure skating's very center.

V

Masculine Wiles

In 2007, I was talking to a guy who had brought one of his figure skating daughters to a public-skating session for a private lesson on basic hockey skills. Ray and his family, who are white, had just moved from another state where, he said, he'd figured out from watching "little seven-year-old Asian girls landing doubles" that his daughters had no competitive future. Maybe this one, unlike the younger twirl-girl "princess," would like hockey. Ray played hockey himself, but he knew he'd never find guys to play with. Why, I asked, with so many options in the area? He explained. A former professional hockey player, drafted by an NHL team in the mid-1980s, he preferred to play without a face protector, like he'd been taught. But he'd get on the ice with these young guys, twenty-two or so, who'd been raised with full facemasks and got their stick right up in your face. He'd tell them, hey, cool it, this is a nonchecking league, we're adults, with jobs, out here to break a sweat, that's the point. Obviously, recreational hockey called for judicious restraint. That's why he chose not to score as often as he could; everyone should get a chance. But the young guys wouldn't listen even when he warned them, "Really, you don't know who you're messing with." Inevitably, a kid would get his stick in Ray's face again. Then Ray would have to go after him, although Ray eventually paid a price for it: "About when they are picking up their teeth from the ice, they're writing me a letter, saying 'please don't come back.'"

Face It

Fans and analysts of masculinity have a lot to see in skating, where various forms of masculinity are constantly being developed and transformed, articulated and transmitted, displayed and dramatized, policed and permitted, enforced and reinforced, challenged and contested—sometimes all at once, as in Ray's story. It begins with figure skating's version of the myth that Asians are taking over the country, garnering honors and opportunities that white people once could count on for themselves. Surely, Ray saw little white girls outjumping his kid in the still heavily white-dominated USFS. In his view, however, changing demographics—undoubtedly viewed through some stereotypes about Asian bodies, minds, parenting, whatever—had disrupted the traditional rink gender order as he understood it and as his family, until then, practiced it. Now, to be a successful athlete on ice, the daughter would have to step into a masculine sport. In their new state, Maine, as elsewhere, changing times had already brought teams for her to play on and some shifting gender associations about which females play hockey, although structures and populations for girls' hockey in area schools were still clearly in development.[1]

A new breed of competitors had also compromised Ray's ability to feel at home in his own sport, although generation, not race, told the story for him this time. He painted himself as a tough guy from the older days of the NHL, although, in fact, he had backdated and semifudged his pedigree. He didn't quite hail from an era before facial protection. Instead, he graduated from college almost a decade after the NCAA mandated full facemasks in 1980, which the state he lived in and the Amateur Hockey Association of the United States (AHAUS) by then already required. He would have worn one at the very latest by high school whether he played in an intramural or area league.[2] Nor had he actually played NHL hockey, as I discovered by checking out his stats online after something about the way he said "drafted by" instead of "played for" made me suspicious. Despite being deemed promising enough to be drafted right after high school for a postcollege position, he played only for the American Hockey League (AHL) and Eastern Conference Hockey League (ECHL) development teams. That itself is an impressive accomplishment, but he never was called up to the NHL even for one game.[3]

Something else in Ray's story took me some rooting around to decode, not because he was circumventing, but because I was new to hockey history, fandom, and debates: the complicated perceived relationships of wearing facial protection to being a tough guy. Some people believe that refusing to wear a face protector separates tough guys, who scoff at the extra risks, from pretenders to the title, an idea underscored by disparate rules about who may forego what. Children, teens, and college players must wear full facemasks, thus associating those facemasks with youthful, less mature play. The AHAUS rules covering players under twenty superseded a rule that restricted face protectors to players who already had facial injuries, showing the facemask's inherited association, beyond weakness, with debility.[4] Women, too, must always wear full facemasks, even in the Olympics where their male counterparts (born after 1974) need to wear only visors, thus linking full face protection and "pussy," in its interconnected meanings. Don't worry your pretty little head about your pretty little face. The AHL and ECHL mandated visors starting in the 2006–7 season, leaving the NHL, which did not even require helmets until 1979, with the sole status of housing the guys who can handle going without. Marty McSorley, a famous NHL "enforcer," the term for skaters who occupy an unofficial position of designated fighter, viewed the ability to progress beyond the facemask as a measure of suitability for NHL play: "For [the college guys] to come in without that face mask on, that changes everything big time. I saw so many young guys come into training camp over the years pretending that they were tough and gritty, but most of those guys really didn't have a clue. Those guys got weeded out pretty early."[5] As Jarrett Freedman explained to me, some of the "young hotshots," like Alex Ovechkin and Nicklas Bäckström of the Washington Capitals, still take advantage of the rule that you can forgo head protection during warmups.[6]

Face protectors, then, may be seen to separate the wimps from the tough guys and the boys (and girls and women) from the men. But they may also be seen to separate dishonorable, tough-guy upstarts from honorable, tough-guy gentlemen. Some people locate mandatory face protectors among changes like the instigator rule, which penalizes starting (some) fights, that, they argue, has turned hockey from a game of skill and controlled violence, self-policed by players with honor, into a game filled with less skilled players and cheap-tricking thugs. Without fear of getting a stick or puck in the face, players are more likely simply to block the puck with their bodies,[7] and to perform illegal, unsportsmanlike maneuvers that they won't lose an eye for in retribution. These maneuvers include the high-sticking that Ray mentioned, which refers to hitting another player above the shoulders and is, in theory, penalized when done intentionally or irresponsibly.[8]

That's why, for Ray, wearing a full facemask could signal, paradoxically, both a departure from rougher, tougher days gone by and a refusal to adopt standards of risk appropriate to recreational adult hockey, where players have adult responsibilities—we all have to work the next day, as people frequently express it—and lower stakes, or, more precisely, supposedly lower stakes. An employee at another local rink told me about fist-fighting lawyers and doctors there, including surgeons obviously in need of highly functioning hands, and another player who was ejected for anti-Semitic rants at a ref. They are the disturbing among many bits of evidence that recreational hockey has high stakes, too. In any case, when someone disrespects the play or the deference that Ray is trying to engineer, he channels his (image of the) bad old days by fighting the guy and winning. He's like the aging guy in a Toby Keith song who describes backing up his old high school buddy in a bar fight in the verse after he mans up for hot twin sisters: "I ain't as good as I once was / but I'm as good once as I ever was."[9] But it's the bad old days filtered through new practices. Ray has to wait for the kid to remove his facemask. Like removing one's own to fight, it's a newer sign of toughness and honor.

Wile You Are Watching

The pieces in this section engage incidents involving masculine performance in skate sports that foreground issues and expectations about masculinity. I named the section "masculine wiles" partly to signal how beguiling masculine-coded moves and looks can be. They can certainly beguile me. While I hardly swooned over Ray's posturing, I'd almost start smoking again to have a hot butch light my cigarette—maybe the one who used to drawl "Wanna come watch me check some fluids?" when she was heading out to work on her car. I did.

But I also want to pull at the ordinary association of wiles with femininity that makes my title an obvious switch-up on a cliché. Feminine wiles are often understood as enchantments that female or feminine people deploy, seductively and sometimes sneakily, to achieve their own aims in situations that they do not have the power to control outright. Madame de Pompadour allegedly gets to rule France, and fluff up the décor, by becoming Louis XV's official mistress. Yet wiles may be diversely gendered and deployed by people in power, sometimes to uphold a dubious status quo. Both the delightful and the dubious, separately and together, concern me here.

The essay named "'I Stand Beside Him with an Axe!': Hockey Guys Together" looks at several occasions for reflection about masculine norms in hockey, considering barriers challenged and maintained in the process. The next essay, "Quads Make the Man, or What's Too Gay for Men's Figure Skating," looks at attempts to craft recognizable criteria for sufficient masculinity, and therefore heterosexuality, in a sport reputedly devoid of studly straight guys. Finally, "The Girl Who Fooled My Butchdar" returns to a topic I talked about in part IV: the sometimes disjuncture between a person's skating and nonskating genders—this time across sex-gender categories that I engaged, not as a participant, but as a beguiled spectator.

15

"I Stand Beside Him with an Axe!"

HOCKEY GUYS TOGETHER

I name this essay after a statement made by Brian Burke, the Toronto Maple Leafs general manager, that first appeared in a November 2009 article by John Buccigross for ESPN.com called "Imagine This Story of Acceptance between Brian and Brendan Burke." It concerns a topic rarely discussed in media attention to hockey that the article calls "homophobia," although I never liked the term much. "Phobia" can excuse, soften, or mischaracterize hostility and violence (physical, verbal, mental, emotional) as fear—and as an illogical, psychological problem of individuals. As the story of Brian's son, Brendan, illustrates, antigay, antiqueer prejudice is also systemically perpetuated and institutionally entrenched. Despite making the varsity team in his competitive high school program, Brendan quit hockey when the locker-room culture grew intolerable. "Homophobic slurs [became] as commonplace as rolls of hockey tape," along with the pressure to "hook up with girls."[10] It took several years for Brendan to come out to his family. Two years later, in 2009, he came out more publicly, first to players and staff on the powerhouse hockey team he student-managed, the Miami University of Ohio RedHawks, and then through the Buccigross piece. His father's support was central to the coverage: "I wish this burden would fall on someone else's shoulders," began an often-reposted quote. "But since he wishes to blaze this trail, I stand beside him with an axe! I simply could not be more proud of Brendan than I am, and I love him as much as I admire him."[11] Tragedy brought the story into a larger circulation three months later when Brendan died in a car crash on an icy winter road.

Bathed in Emotion

I stand beside him with an axe. It's a statement as poetic as it is moving, invoking images and meanings specific to its particular context and beyond. The axe may call up diverse weapons and vectors of force (hockey sticks included) and diverse arenas—sporting, domestic, and political—where the imperative to defend summons the power to hurt. "Standing beside" someone makes for disconcertingly common conditions of comfort, protection, intimacy, heat, vulnerability, and danger, sometimes shifting abruptly from one to the other. A team trade can make an on-ice foe out of a previously defended teammate. A disclosure turns a father's pride into rage, or, in this case, a united front. Intensity in relation, physically felt—it resonates through accounts of Brian Burke's support and grief. Michael Farber wrote for *Sports Illustrated* that

> . . . Brian—a hockey carnivore who embraces physical play and fighting; a 6′2″, 240-pound fishing, hunting, Harley-riding, truck-driving, tobacco-chewing father of six who says he is "a poster boy for straight people if you look at all the macho measuring sticks"—[had] embraced Brendan, a gay-rights advocate, for all the world to see. . . .
>
> Now Brian placed his hand on his dead son's chest and kept it there for the two-hour flight in the air ambulance that took Brendan's body from Ohio to Massachusetts.[12]

Brendan Burke's death really got to me, in several ways. Most simply, it moved me immensely; I cried over it more than once. Yet I was also haunted by something that I raise here without any intent to diminish the tragedy of his death: how much the story, as felt and told, can smooth over or obscure. Most glaring are the antigay policies of the Catholic Church. Farber called the ten priests presiding over the funeral Mass "another reminder that for Brian Burke, nothing is small in life, or death."[13] But it also suggests a Church on board with what Brendan stood up for and came to stand for, although formulators and agents of its doctrine keep pronouncing homosexuality to be a sin.

Subtler, as is often the case, are ways that whiteness factors into the story, including its prominence. Harm attending white, often affluent people receives disproportionate media attention; name any nonwhite equivalent for JonBenét Ramsay or Natalie Holloway. It's telling that the 2009 Matthew Shepard and James Byrd, Jr. Hate Crimes Prevention Act is generally known as the Matthew Shepard Act. The short name erases the African American man whose identity-based murder received less attention than that of the white, gay Shepard, which inspired a play, *The Laramie Project*, that is still performed in schools and community theaters all around the country. Byrd's (lack of) place in popular culture also recalls that of Phillip DeVine, an African American man murdered alongside the white trans man Brandon Teena but absent from the Hollywood movie that memorialized Teena, *Boys Don't Cry*.[14]

Significant, too, is the virtual certainty that tragedy befalling a high-level figure in hockey will concern white people, a sport largely white from the bottom up. So are the upper echelons of most organized sports, and the Burke story dramatizes one reason why. Father and son both seem to have seamlessly exited playing hockey for (less physically demanding) brainwork. Brian Burke left pro hockey for Harvard Law; Brendan had law school in mind, too. As the athletic stars turned scholars in the book *Out of Bounds* emphasize, whiteness and wealth affect the likelihood that athletes will be nurtured to view their bodies as more than instruments of success and advancement.[15] As Stanley Thangaraj points out in writing about masculinities in a South Asian American basketball league, whiteness can also enhance expectations of a judicious combination of brain and brawn. In contrast, "model-minority" South Asian Americans are seen as too brainy for physical prowess, like other model-minority Asian Americans as well as Jews; African American athletes, by racial prejudice, are all brawn.[16] (Thus, too, the response of Michelle Obama's brother, Craig Robinson, to a semijoking question from Bryant Gumbel about whether, in basketball, Barack Obama played white or played black. Robinson replied that Obama used to play black but "after thirty-five, we all play white.")[17]

The predominance of white men in hockey also underpins, I believe, a common theme in hockey representations that filters into descriptions of Brian Burke, the weapon-toting antihomophobe: the idea that the toughest guys in hockey are sweet deep down. Ross Bernstein writes in *The Code* that "the amazing thing about hockey fighters is the fact that they are without question the nicest, friendliest guys off the ice."[18] That notion got a bigger audience in 2009 on the popular Canadian TV show *Battle of the Blades*, which partnered eight retired hockey players with female former figure skaters to compete in figure skating. In season 1, the players included three hockey players notorious for fighting: Tie Domi and Bob Probert, two enforcers, and Claude Lemieux, known as an agitator but also for scoring. Sometimes the commentators emphasized the guys' softness as nonetheless heteromanly: Lemieux has the "courage" and fierceness to show a different side of himself as a "satin-shirted, romantic lady-killer," skating to "A Moment Like This."[19] Sometimes softness is the underlying truth. "[Fighting] was my job and I would fight for my teammates," Bob Probert commented, "but I think I am a big teddy bear," a point echoed in obituaries when he died suddenly less than a year later.[20]

Not everyone believes that the meanest players leave violence on the ice. Sportswriter Joe Lapointe calls it "one of the Big Myths in sports spread by the media."[21] Others swear by it, offering personal testimony and reasons for the apparent on-ice/off-ice contradictions. Enforcers aren't the stars, the possibly ego-inflated scorers, but are the guys who help out their teammates, as one fan who occasionally got to hang out with players told me. I'm inclined myself to think that it varies by case because I believe that in sports, as in sex, people may inhabit or enjoy roles that do not correspond with what they do or like in other contexts. What interests me most here is the intense cultural work to separate the essential character of these men from the unrelenting violence they are famous for. It's primarily white people, individually and as a race, who get rehabilitated that way.

Gender Is Relative

Public mourning for gay white men, like public respect for them, often also depends on normative masculine gender. "Marriage equality" campaigns don't want queeny advocates any more than that kid in *The Birdcage* does.[22] Brendan Burke, by all the public representations I've seen, fits the bill as gender normative. (I'm not questioning whether he was so, just noting the public image.) A picture in the ESPN.com father–son piece shows him looking like any fresh-faced college kid in a polo shirt. Nor does the piece tell one of those common stories about gay or trans kids whose gender expressions, sensibilities, or identities clash with the sports behaviors expected of them, even if they can perform as required. Giselle, a trans woman I met in ballet class, had hidden her identity as female, from herself and others, behind the position of enforcer in boys' hockey. Brendan, in contrast, apparently found himself suited to hockey; it was brutal prejudice, not rough play, that got to him.

Yet the article's focus on his father's hypermasculinity makes the lesser masculinity of gay men seem almost required for a coherent coming-out story. Brian Burke, Buccigross says, admits to getting as far as the AHL by compensating for an inadequate skill set with his "rough and tough qualities": "You know, like pugnacity, testosterone, truculence and belligerence. He's a man, baby." The article casts Brian as over-the-top from every perspective: looking in the mirror, through a child's eyes, from within hockey, from outside. Father and son frequently traveled forth in the media, however, as part of a simple hierarchy of manliness where gay men rank below quintessential hockey guys, even when the gay men are hockey guys themselves. *Sports Illustrated* quoted Trevor MacNeil, a player in a gay hockey league who was interviewed, several days after Brendan's death, at the Olympic Village's LGBT Pride House in Vancouver: "For Brian Burke to say, Yes, I drive a truck and I hunt, but Brendan's my son and I love him no matter what—well, for me that was shocking and great."[23] Brian Burke here is a little like the fictional Billy Elliot's gruff father, who comes, along with his embattled, striking fellow miners, to support Billy's desire to be a ballet dancer. There's a different concoction of sexuality, masculinity, and class than in the Burkes' case. The miners learn that male dancers need not be gay, as hockey players need not be straight, and they struggle with a hit to their own masculinities as the miner's strike of 1984–85 threatens their ability to support themselves. But both are moving in related ways that hardly affect only me. I was in good company crying my way through the movie and then the musical, even though many of us, I'm sure, had a rational side chafing at the bonus points straight guys can get for shedding bigotries they shouldn't have had in the first place.[24]

Since I started working on this project, various representations of "macho measuring sticks" for straight guys have popped up around sports. They can seem either Neanderthal-esque or self-consciously, amusingly excessive, depending on how you look at them and how you expect others to see them. In a famous Snickers ad that played during the 2007 Super Bowl, two mechanics accidentally kiss as they gobble to the middle of the same Snickers bar from opposite ends. "Quick, do something manly!" one says, prompting each to rip out a chunk of his own chest hair, screaming in agony from the pain.[25]

Snickers pulled the ad, which lives on through YouTube, after the Human Rights Campaign and the Gay and Lesbian Alliance Against Defamation complained that it promoted prejudice. I'd seen it, instead, as a hilarious slam against the idiotic homophobia of insecure men, although I can see the other side. As Michael Messner points out in his classic article, "When Bodies Are Weapons: Masculinity and Violence in Sport," the ability to take and administer physical pain is cultivated, rewarded, and demanded among players and fans of contact sports.[26] From this angle, ripping out chest hair could look like rising to the occasion. But I still like to think that a substantial number of viewers would read the ad like I did.

Then there are the ads for hockey sticks with hit-over-the-head metaphors of the hockey stick as a phallic weapon. In 2007, an ad for Mission brand hockey sticks in *USA Hockey Magazine*, the publication of the organization that I had to join to play hockey, announced in large letters, "TITANIUM in your SHAFT . . . now we're talking PERFORMANCE." In 2010, a web ad for the Bauer Vaporx:60, with "TeXtreme®," displayed the stick on fire as the sound of crashing thunder sent electricity pulsing through it, releasing lightning-bolt zigzags that broke up the surface below. The slogan above it, "So responsive that it finishes your thoughts," jokily toggled sensitive-guy relationship lingo and a dick at the ready when needed.[27] In one extremely clever promotional video from that year, published on the retail website hockeymonkey.com, "Mike Cammalleri discovers the unbelievable control he has with the new Easton Synergy EQ50 hockey stick." It shows Cammalleri, from the Montreal Canadiens, wielding his stick as a kind of magic-wand remote-control device to redirect the Zamboni, hoist the Canadian flag higher than the

U.S. flag, switch a rink's scheduled session to "stick time," and stop two players from other teams at the "Player's Entrance." He then uses the stick to open the door for them, turning them into unsettled recipients of his manly chivalry.[28]

I enjoy this turn to the parodic but I'm wary of it, too, because of what jokes, charm, sorrow, sympathy, self-awareness, and a will to challenge homophobia can glaze over. Charm can be fleeting or deceiving.[29] Even if it's not, a rink full of endearing guys is still a rink full of guys. It took me longer than I'd like to admit to notice that you'd never learn by reading about Brendan Burke that girls and women in hockey also face antiqueer sentiments, similarly grounded in a chain of bad reasoning about the inherent masculinity of the sport. As the logic goes, hockey players are masculine, and queer gender accompanies queer sexuality; thus female players must be queer and male players must be straight. Nor would you see evidence that women and girls even play hockey. What's visible instead is the gathering of hockey men across roles, time, and generations that often leaves women and girls fighting for ice time, given a pecking order based on status and squatters' rights. In Toronto (the home of Brian Burke's Maple Leafs), advocates for girls' and women's hockey eventually turned to the city government for help in pressuring rink operators to find them some time, with insufficient results. There, as elsewhere, the dearth of ice affects opportunities to train and play, the use of volunteer time spent on scrounging up ice, and the cost of playing, because long travel in order to use the odd available hour at more expensive rinks may be one result.[30] These resource issues only get more acute as the interest in playing hockey grows among girls and women; those issues, along with the location of rinks, also affect players living in predominantly non-white areas.

And Nonetheless

This is the essay with too many "and yets," but I have one more. Despite what the coverage of his life and death can obscure, I do not minimize Brendan Burke taking on homophobia in men's hockey. As people frequently comment, the mere handful of openly gay athletes testifies to the bleak situation. So do two hockey novels for kids that set out to challenge traditional views and ways. J. E. MacLeod's *Waiting to Score* (2009) tackles sexist hockey cultures, sexual assault, alcoholism, parental pres-

sure, problematic investments in the father and son hockey lineage, beliefs that dirty play stays on the ice, and preconceptions about good girls,
popular girls, and poetic Goth girls. The 2001 book *Cool as Ice*, published
under the name of Matt Christopher, a prolific writer of children's sports
novels, offers another set of hockey-life lessons as a small-sized, boy
figure skater named Chris comes to shine in ice hockey but also to realize that figure skating can still rock for him, too. His friends include a
girl who wins the interest of her hockey-boy crush when she stops acting all sweet and solicitous around him so he can see how well she plays
hockey. That boy helps to convince the coach that because she's "tough as
nails on D[efense]," she should join the hitherto all-male travel team for
the championships; the team has an opening after dirty-fighting, racist
bullies on an opposing team break the leg of the league's only African
American player.[31]

Both books also designate the bad guys by having them call people
sissies or faggots. Yet they don't comment about the issue or go further.
MacLeod, to the contrary, even goes to the trouble of raising and putting
to rest the rumor that the protagonist's single mother and aunt are lesbians. The book's happy ending pairs up the protagonist's mom with the
hockey scout as the aunt wistfully giggles "like a schoolgirl."[32] The Matt
Christopher franchise, according to a polite e-mail response from his
son, had never addressed the issue in more than one hundred books, at
least as of 2007:

> Dear Erica,
>   Thanks for visiting our site and reading one of my Dad's books.
> To answer your question, the issue of gay rights is not in any of Dad's
> books. Thank you for the very interesting topic.[33]

So it matters that people use the example of Brendan Burke, made
more poignant by his death, to visibly stand against homophobia in
hockey and to blog on hockey websites about antigay prejudice in the pro
leagues, among amateurs, in schools, and in the stands.[34] It matters that
Brian Burke marches in Pride parades and that the Chicago Blackhawks
sent player Brent Sopel, marching in Brendan's name, to Chicago Pride
in 2010 with the Stanley Cup they'd just won—after reminders during
the championship showed how routine are both antigay slurs as sports
insults and the sexism that backs them up. These included a photograph
of the Blackhawks' locker room, which had a poster calling one of their

opponents on the Philadelphia Flyers "gay," and the *Chicago Tribune's* dubious gesture of "Commit to the Cup" spirit: a full-page color poster in its June 8th edition showing Flyer Chris Pronger skating as "Chrissy Pronger." He's wearing a hockey jersey over a figure skating dress with the headline "Looks Like Tarzan, Skates Like Jane." Protests induced the *Tribune's* sports editor, Mike Kellams, to apologize to people offended by the way the paper tried to "connect" to fans "in a fun way." He also reassured one of the biggest name protesters, Angela Ruggiero, a four-time Olympic medalist in women's hockey, that he respected her sport: "I grew up in Indiana and came to hockey as an adult. Ruggiero vs. me on the rink would be no contest. I know that from what she and her team did at the Vancouver Olympics."[35]

No kidding. As an adult athlete, I know the ceilings Kellams refers to. But otherwise he might rival her? That's as insulting as the reason some people thought Ruggiero should lighten up: Hey, the poster's not implying that Pronger plays like a female hockey player; it's saying he skates like a female figure skater.

16

Quads Make the Man,
or What's Too Gay for Men's Figure Skating

Does twirling around in the air become manly once you can turn four revolutions instead of three? Such a claim seems absurd from various positions. If you think rotating on an axis is hopelessly, unalterably frilly—the two words in "twirl girl" being firmly attached and equally a slam—one more revolution couldn't possibly matter. If you know the strength, power, and risk taking required to master two- or three-revolution jumps, then you know that the stud credibility associated with those characteristics does not need a fourth revolution. If you question why those characteristics are labeled masculine in the first place, the notion is insulting and misguided as well as preposterous.

Yet as followers of figure skating know, Evgeny Plushenko committed this prequel to the *Chicago Tribune*'s Chrissy Pronger poster right before the 2010 Olympics: "Without a quad," he said, "it's women's skating."[36] After Evan Lysacek beat him with a quadless program, Plushenko protested, supported by two notable backers: his prime minister, Vladimir Putin, and Elvis Stojko, an Olympic silver medalist in 1994 and 1998. Neither stated explicitly that Lysacek's skating wasn't men's skating. I assume they'd learned a bit of diplomatic discretion, Putin quite literally, although his statement that Plushenko had "performed the most accomplished program on the Vancouver ice" hardly suited the Olympics' often-stated ideal of promoting international harmony through sport. Neither did the dramatic title of Stojko's essay for Yahoo Sports, "The Night They Killed Figure Skating." But despite using examples only from the men's event, Stojko contended that the whole sport had been killed by a judging system that rewarded skaters for shirking the big risks. He was "going to watch hockey, where athletes are allowed to push the envelope. A real sport."[37]

Stojko didn't gender the victim, I think, for the same reason he offered a shout-out to Johnny Weir as another undermarked skater. He'd been schooled the year before during the public relations debacle that came to be nicknamed Skate Canada's "Tough" campaign. According to a disclaimer posted by William Thompson, the CEO of Skate Canada, Canada's equivalent to USFS, Skate Canada had no official "Tough" Campaign. Instead, it intended to "message the difficulty of the sport."[38] In the service of that aim, the organization apparently asked all skaters to tone down the sequins, while its marketing director, Debbie Wilkes, encouraged skaters to talk up their rigorous training and gruesome injuries, like the eighty stitches a pairs skater needed in 2007 when her partner's wayward camel spin sliced her in the face. Wilkes also partnered up Skate Canada with Harley-Davidson to show female skaters as tough girls on bikes.[39]

Regardless of Skate Canada's aim, however, and the contributing concern that "the athleticism of the women was being overlooked," many people interpreted the organization to be "messaging" the toughness of male skaters specifically. They saw "tough" as an intended contrast to "effeminate" or "gay," rather than as a synonym for "difficult," and perceived the push to court audiences for sports like hockey as a rejection of figure skating's sizeable number of gay fans.[40]

Stojko fueled that interpretation. Although he didn't speak for Skate Canada, as Thompson reminded his readers, he might well appear to, having won seven Canadian national titles between 1994 and 2002 as well as many medals representing Canada in international competition. He was also an obvious person to interview. He was famous for athletic firsts involving quad jumps and for being visibly downgraded artistically for using nonballetic movement traditions like martial arts. Proud of giving men's skating, to quote his website, "a more masculine look and aggressive presence,"[41] he was glad to comment on Skate Canada catching up to him, sometimes in highly dubious language. "It's not that the male skating has to totally obliterate the gay guys that are skating and the gay public that's watching it," he told an ABC interviewer.[42]

Should men's skating, then, merely semiobliterate the gays? It can be hard to extend the benefit of the doubt—unfortunate word choice, sensationalist editing—when "obliterate" calls up deliberate genocidal pronouncements and actions. But Stojko denied any antigay sentiments and tried to clarify his position a month later:

> It has nothing to do with your sexual preference. . . . It's all about what men's skating is—power and strength. Whether he's gay or straight, it doesn't matter. It's what you're showcasing on the ice. If you're very lyrical and you're really feminine and soft, well, that's not men's skating. THAT IS NOT MEN'S SKATING, OKAY? Men's skating is power, strength, masculinity, focus, clarity of movement, interpretation of music.[43]

While some observers remained skeptical about Stojko's position on sexuality,[44] I care more about what he considered specific to men's skating. I'd question everything on the list from power (get over it) to interpretation of music (no clue), and even masculinity. Females should never exhibit masculinity? However masculinity is constituted, I disagree.

Credit Check

I do credit Stojko for trying to untangle gender and sexuality. A lot of people can't, or won't, recognize any difference. It's one reason that, just like with the recent attention to homophobia in hockey, the talk about homosexuality in figure skating never mentions women skaters. In hockey, gay male players were a hitherto unconsidered phenomenon because they embody masculinity; in figure skating we femmy queer girls still remain an unconsidered phenomenon because we couldn't possibly be queer. Or people play on the confusion of gender and sexuality, often cruelly for laughs. Right around when Plushenko was trumpeting his male quads, two commentators on Canadian TV joked about Weir needing a gender test—a comment echoed six months later in a Twitter post made allegedly by Evan Lysacek—who claimed that his account had been hacked after being denounced by the online impersonator he'd blamed at first. Fake Evan tweeted: "I am extremely disappointed in my actual person. . . . I, fake Evan, promise to be better than that."[45] (I wonder if fake Evan cared about his "actual person" getting in on the real-man protestations, telling reporters at the Olympics that "the tricks we're doing, they're so difficult and really dangerous. This is a very competitive and very athletic sport. I'm not trying to be balletic; I'm trying to win an Olympic medal.")[46]

I give Stojko credit, then, but no sympathy. It takes willful ignorance to miss that hostility to perceived feminine qualities in males contributes to antigay prejudice, especially growing up in a sport known for qualities deemed feminine, like artistry, and the stereotype that the males are all gay. As Adams importantly details in *Artistic Impressions*, men's skating didn't always have those connotations. Two centuries ago, some prescribed skating as a vigorous activity that could hone displays of grace appropriate to aristocratic masculinity; it was a cure for effeminacy among upper-class boys, not a sign of it.[47] But not anymore. Now the associations between feminine, soft, gay, and artistic are now too intertwined to be separated in promotional bytes or for selective repudiation. Skate Canada could not possibly have "messaged" figure skating as difficult without having the message carry a tinge of sexism, homophobia, anti-femininity, and what Tim Bergling calls "sissyphobia." It's a hostility to femininity or effeminacy in males that, Bergling emphasizes, also afflicts the legions of gay men cringing at the queens among them and flocking to the "straight-acting."[48]

Besides, declining to repudiate is not enough. Thompson said that Skate Canada "gives no direction" about a "skater's personal life" because figure skating has "always been and will continue to be a welcoming and inclusive sport."[49] Yet Brian Orser, outed in a palimony suit after he turned pro, remains the only publicly gay skater associated with Canadian skating. In fact, Orser is one of a handful of visibly gay pro athletes, who usually come out after the high-stakes part of their competitive careers ends. Asked at the 2009 Sports, Culture, and Sexuality conference why he hadn't come out publicly until he left professional basketball, another such athlete, John Amaechi, ventured that only superstar athletes could even consider surviving the revelation. Amaechi, whose memoir details diverse encounters with prejudice (including advice to enhance his NBA prospects by tanning his already dark skin for a more athletic, "blacker," look), said that gay athletes need to be so good that the organizations, sports, and geopolitical entities they represent would be grossly impoverished without them.[50] Even in figure skating, a sport widely acknowledged to have many gay male fans and athletes—one writer puts "unofficial insider estimates" at 25–50 percent—virtually none have risked it apart from Rudy Galindo.[51] According to Jon Jackson, a gay former skater turned skating judge, Galindo paid for it, being denied top assignments customary for the World Champion that Galindo surprised insiders by becoming.[52]

But Even the Snakes Are Sparkly

Locating appropriate manliness in one extra twirled revolution may easily be termed absurd, but it's hardly alone among the loopy, idiosyncratic, or fine-point gender distinctions that would be laughable if they didn't signal a large, toxic will to police gender, sometimes through, or for, policing sexuality. Bryan Safi makes this point clear in "That's Gay: Johnny Weir," a segment of his comedic "That's Gay" feature on the Current TV show *Infomania*, that went viral during the Olympics.[53] Safi has no interest in de-queering Weir or skating. He happily translates the "elegant" offered by other critics to "fruit stand," illustrated with clips from Weir's most queer-signaling routines, like his exhibition program to Lady Gaga's "Poker Face" and his much buzzed-about performance as a swan, fluttering arms included. Weir wore a costume for the latter that Jim Caple, in a sympathetic ESPN profile, said, in characteristic journalistic euphemism, would have been "over-the-top" for Elton John, with "glittery, featherlike designs across the chest, crisscrossed strapping over one arm and a single red glove he named Camille."[54]

But does any of that mean that "Johnny Weir [is] too gay for figure skating"? "Wait," Safi says, "is that even possible?"

> Figure skating is the gayest sport of all time. In fact, let's take a look at where it falls on our official sports sexuality spectrum. On the hetero extreme, there's football, then hockey, then baseball, then tennis, croquet, wrestling, ascot tying, scented candle making, competitive ass fucking, figure skating. The sport is gay, deal with it.

I love that list, which loses something on the page apart from Safi's gay-drawl delivery, because while Safi nods to the macho straight-guy stereotype by starting with football and hockey, he doesn't set up parallel gender and sexuality continuums. "Competitive ass fucking," right up next to skating, seems surely the gayest but not the least studly item on the list, which also locates croquet to the straight side of wrestling.

Yet, Safi notes, in this sport where his allegedly polar-opposite rival, the "man's man" Evan Lysacek, is "wrapped in Swarovski snakes," the sparkly decoration on a costume that Vera Wang designed for him, Weir is treated totally differently. Despite three national championship titles, commentators never refer to him as an athlete; he's outrageous, flamboyant, funny, a joke. "Well," Safi says, "the message is clear": "Ladyboys, do not enter the world of sports, not even *our* sports. Stick to what you're good at, competitive flower arranging." Weir himself commented in his memoir, *Welcome to My World*, dating the ascent of "flamboyant" to his swan-wearing days, that the "f-word" bugged him both for bringing allusions to sex into the picture, which he considered irrelevant to skating, and mostly for implying a "lack of seriousness." He was "as serious as any skater out there, just not as boring," or, as he put it less flippantly, far from the "sanitized ideal" that skaters are pushed to represent — another reason that figure skating looks at once hilarious, unmasked, and jarring up against "competitive ass fucking."[55]

It's not, Weir said, that he didn't play up the image that got him the label. But then again, as Amaechi suggests, flamboyance is hardly the province of either gay or femmy men. Amaechi calls the NBA locker room — where players primped, compared cocks, and tried on each other's clothes and jewelry, "applying cologne and hair gel by the bucketful" — "the most flamboyant place I'd been this side of a swanky club full of martini-drinking gay men."[56] But "flamboyant" usually isn't applied to (apparently) masculine guys.

Here is another reason that the term "homophobia" falls short. It often mislabels the antifemme or antifag sentiments that may drive distinctions between sparkly snakes and sparkly swans, or the continuing push on *So You Think You Can Dance* (SYTYCD) for gender-normative dancing despite patent moves to fix the show's antigay reputation. That reputation peaked in season 5 when judges trashed two men who auditioned as a ballroom pair and Nigel Lithgoe, the head judge, tweeted his distaste for "*Brokeback* ballroom."[57] By season 7, in contrast, Lithgoe was attributing to "America," not the judges, a failure to appreciate the "slightly androgynous" (code for feminine/effeminate/gay) style of Billy Bell, one of the dancers. But the show still constantly promoted gender-appropriate dancing. Male dancers expressed gratitude to icons, mentors, and choreographers for showing them that dancing could be masculine. Mia Michaels, a judge, told Lauren Froderman, a contestant, that "as an athletic female dancer, you really need to work harder to have a little bit more of a feminine quality to you." This was after Froderman performed a duet to "Let

Me Entertain You" in a slinky dress and blond bombshell persona that might have been described as oozing feminine charms.

It's athletic versus artistic all over again, with shades of skin involved here, too. For people unversed in the distinctions between masculine and feminine twirling and toe-pointing, which the judges often reference as if they are obvious, SYTYCD offers a set of black-coded "go hard or go home" styles and partners. For instance, the show butched up Alex Wong, a ballet dancer, by partnering him with the African American SYTYCD "All Star" hip-hop dancer Steven "tWitch" Boss for a crunk routine. Then, in the finale, tWitch helped butch up guest-star Ellen DeGeneres when she joined tWitch to dance a modified version of that number in honor of Wong, who had been sidelined by an injury.[58]

There's a general absence of such styles from figure skating's gender-coding arsenal, although the Japanese skater Daisuke Takahashi did a short program in 2007–8 to a hip-hop version of *Swan Lake*. Maybe that absence is partly why male skaters bearing a martial-arts style, a fourth revolution, or a sparkly snake find pressing their masculinity all the more urgent.[59]

17

The Girl Who Fooled My Butchdar

"I want that one in my Christmas stocking." Even with the grand spectacle of hotness that is Maine Roller Derby in front of us, I knew exactly who my friend meant: Jacked Rabbit, widely considered, at least among dykes I talked to, the hottest butch skating with MRD (figure 11).[60] I never heard anyone itemize what made her "hot" or "butch." Who needed to? She was obviously both. Maybe it was the display of narrow hips and broad shoulders instead of feminine curves—not that body shape determines gender identity but a person can camouflage skeletal givens. Or her highly defined muscles, built rather than discretely toned; clearly, she didn't train in the manner prescribed to avoid (allegedly) unfeminine bulking up. Or various complements of toughness like men's styled tanks, extensive tattoos, or skin darker than delicate on the "white" spectrum. None of those characteristics only or always mark "butch" but they add up. Then there was the way she skated, although it was hard to pinpoint the exact difference. She skated fast and hard, bent aerodynamically forward as derby requires of all skaters. Still, something set her skating apart.

Alas, fieldwork can be a grinch. Several weeks after the bout, I watched an MRD practice and sat in on the players' meeting that followed. As I waited for the meeting to begin, Jacked Rabbit emerged in street clothes that completely changed my impression of her. More than the low-cut jeans and slightly sparkly belt, what struck me was her top. It had a square-cut neckline, low and wide enough to reveal black straps like the chemise or bra straps that I associate with a certain feminine eroticism. Hmmm. She was still extremely hot, no question, but not butch. I confirmed my assessment several months later when we met for an interview. Her outfit matched, in gender signals, the one she'd changed into after practice and the first thing she wanted to know was who did my hair because she wanted something similar. "Well," a friend pointed out," at least that means she noticed you, too."

11. Jacked Rabbit in her uniform for Maine Roller Derby's
Port Authorities. Photograph by Matthew Robbins, 2009.

Interference

How had I initially been so mistaken? I like to think that I have great
butchdar, a term that I concoct, but hardly invent, from the more common *gaydar*. It's been fine-tuned through reading, relocation, recreation,
erotic interests, and gender-justice work. I can discern butch energy
in happily feminine-presenting women, and, conversely, an absence of
butch identity in people bearing features that confuse others, like body
hair in places associated with masculinity. After over twenty-five years of
teaching in Wisconsin and Maine, I'm also (largely) past the confusion
that commonly plagues urban transplants to more rural areas until we
learn that pick-up trucks and the proverbial flannel shirt may represent

no-nonsense functionality rather than a shout-out in what, twenty years ago, was famously called the "lesbian erotic dance."[61]

I also know how much the expression "lesbian erotic dance" fails to encompass or describe. Butches may not identify as female. Like queer femmes, queer butches might not identify as lesbian. Nor does "butch" work as an umbrella or preferred term for all people who, as Butch/femme.com puts it, claim a masculinity that is not ordinarily considered their "birthright."[62] People who are "transmasculine," or "masculine of center," to use two recent formulations, embrace a wide range of identities sometimes also marked by race, class, culture, and generation. The Brown Boi Project uses the latter term to describe "a wide range of identities such as butch, stud, aggressive/AG, macha, dom, etc."[63]

With such sophisticated butchdar, how had I so misread Jacked Rabbit?

What Nice Muscles You Have

Or had I? Unlike me, Jacked Rabbit, also known as Kathy Grinvalsky, who was surprised, happy, and gracious to learn she had a dyke fan base, didn't conclude that she'd fooled my butchdar. She thought it had detected one side of her personality, including her ability to get "down and dirty," and was glad I'd recognized an extremely different one, too. Derby suited her, she said, because, like her, it was multifaceted: "whimsical, sexual, sexy, but also about being a serious athlete and kicking ass." But some people read her as one-dimensional. They see a shallow interest in muscles when, she said, "I take care of my body more for my mind." As she elaborated a few years later, she saw mental and spiritual aspects as core to athletic training that she'd previously undertaken for the wrong reasons; she hoped to be able to impart a more holistic practice to others. People also sometimes read into her muscles an innate confidence that was actually hard won. She attributed the courage to try out for derby to having just previously learned to box. Mental barriers like "Will they like me?" might have deterred her otherwise.

Once Kathy mentioned boxing, I could see the transferable skills that had contributed to my impression of her skating: smart, quick, side-to-side movement and weight transfers; hard blocking; and the "calm focus" she said you needed if someone is going to be punching you in the head. That experience, and protective gear, contributed to her fearlessness, and thus, I imagine, to her amazingly smooth propulsion forward, which she credited also to two other factors: her love of the sport, which impelled her to better form, and a "technical mind-set," nurtured by years of working out at a gym, which helped her figure out, for instance, the best mechanics to get power from each push. At least as important were her connections with the other women, which surpassed her initial expectations. She trusted them when they said she was doing well, a comment that surprised me because her noteworthy skill seemed obvious both to me and to her most advanced teammates.

Derby transformed Kathy's life in other ways, too, including one relevant to my semi-wayward butchdar. She hadn't taken up fishnets. But she'd become newly comfortable showing her legs in shorts and short skirts, both on and off the track.

Snakes, Swans, Axes, Dust, and Fruitboots

It's common, and smart, to challenge the idea that certain gender characteristics are grounded in nature by pointing out seemingly timeless gender markers that actually belong to our time and place. Men used to wear the tights that now garner men a one-point costume deduction under IJS. Standards of masculinity that mark male figure skaters and dancers as likely gay in North America do not do so everywhere. Thus the "gay or European?" confusion sung about in *Legally Blonde the Musical*.[64]

Yet signifiers of masculinity can be so much more specific to situations, groups, activities, and individuals. As with the "skank or ballerina" situation, it can be hard to make sense of particular standards of masculinity as an outsider. Attending my first demolition derby at the Beech Ridge Motor Speedway Day of Destruction, I could confidently discern "masculinity on parade," as I wrote in my field notes. Yet I couldn't figure out why the announcer suddenly drawled, "He's doing the loser dance. We've seen *that* before" after one of many male drivers did a dust-raising, tire-screeching, figure eight of rage after losing his race.[65] Was it something about this guy's actions or merely his status as the umpteenth?

Similarly, I needed guidance about the codes of sufficient masculinity, presented as sufficient heterosexuality, in action at my local skate park. Jordan Williams took me there to survey the scene that he frequented as a practitioner of "aggressive inline skating," to use a term Williams identified as old-fashioned but functional.[66] Skateboarders, he said, may deride as "fruitbooters" the inline skaters riding the same tiny stair rails and somersaulting over the same concrete slopes that they are. As Williams later explained to me, the jibes have numerous contributing factors and effects: perceptions about equipment (is it wimpy to have the wheels attached to your feet?); perceptions about authenticity and marketability (rollerblading as a commercial, commercialized invention according to skateboarders who nonetheless command the airwaves and profit opportunities); perceptions about "extreme sports" (thus, "the relentless attempts on the part of rollerbladers to prove that what we are doing is in fact tough, crazy, hard, and different than beach cruising"); and, most simply, the function of "that's gay" as an effective insult. Pubescent boys, Williams noted, make up a huge share of the market for action sports as fans and participants. So "what better way to scare a pubescent kid out of a pair of skates and onto a board than to imply there are some sociological or cultural strings connect[ing] being gay and being a rollerblader. A thirteen-year-old will crack under the pressure of a cool dude seventeen-year-old every time, especially if the seventeen-year-old is calling him a 'fag.'"[67] But meanwhile inline skaters may throw "fag" at skaters around them who are wearing pipe-leg pants that in other contexts might have just signaled "hipster"—or some (other) variations on "poser" once remarketed as "skinny jeans."

Time and Again

Another MRD player told me once that she couldn't stand the common sweetheart-by-day and animal-by-night representation of derby players in the press as if the sport brought out secret or dormant aspects of a woman's personality. Maybe some other teams feel that way, she said, but not hers. MRD publicity, I notice, supports her claim, emphasizing differences among women rather than within women. For a long time, MRD publicized a description that I really loved because it's so comprehensively welcoming and presumption-busting:

> We've got:
> · Girlie-girls and women who wouldn't be caught dead in a skirt or stockings
> · Lifelong athletes and women who've never touched a sport in their lives
> · Tattooed beauties and landscapes of virgin skin

- Short girls, tall girls, big girls, small girls
- Moms, girlfriends, wives, and joyously single women
- Straight girls, gay girls, and anything in between
- Loud-mouthed firecrackers and quiet, reserved badasses
- The list goes on and on.[68]

What it didn't mention, however, not that I think it should have, are the varied ways that individual people relate to those categories and the potentially transformative effects of sports on gender, which I mean in two ways. First, participating in sports may transform people's general understandings of themselves on physical, social, mental, emotional, erotic, and, as Kathy and Teresa both convey very differently, spiritual levels. Second, while the sweetheart/animal trope can reek of sexist shrinkages, people may indeed understand or manifest gender within their sporting activities as different than in other contexts. More simply put, I'm not the same woman as I was before I started skating, and I'm not quite the same woman when I'm skating as when I'm not.

Neither is Jacked Rabbit, or my friend, Mary Squires, a figure skater whom I asked to rate herself on and off the ice on what dykes, perhaps more often in the past, have sometimes called the butch/femme scale, going from superfemme (1) to superbutch (10). I wondered if she agreed with my sense of a gap. She did. Off-ice, she was a 4 and on-ice an 8. Her assessment pretty much matched what I would have guessed then, and maybe now, despite the more frequent appearance of skating dresses in her costume repertoire. The difference between the two athletes for me was in the reverse-direction reveals; with Mary, I'd noticed the girl before the skating. My assessment, however, was the same. Damn, that skater is hot!

VI

Having the Wherewithal

In May 2006, annual maintenance at my home rink, the Portland Ice Arena (PIA), revealed a problem under the ice surface that required shutting down for the summer. Coordinators for prebooked hockey camps and such had to scramble for ice time at other rinks in the area, which had already, in the days before the "economic downturn," been heavily booked. As a result, public skating was largely squeezed out to accommodate displaced, more lucrative, programs.

So if I wanted to skate locally, I had to skate at the Family Ice Center in Falmouth on "club ice," the freestyle sessions sponsored by the USFS branch based there, the North Atlantic Figure Skating Club (NAFSC). That meant joining the club, which I was disinclined to do. To me, "skating club" sounded like country club, and some do function like them. The Philadelphia Skating Club and Humane Society—so-named because its original nineteenth-century members used to rescue people who fell through the ice on the Schuylkill River—requires references from three current members to join. Letters should "tell whether you believe, to the best of your knowledge, that the candidate's friends would be comfortable at the Club."[1] Eek—that rings of every exclusionary practice phrased in the patently bogus concern for the comfort of minority intruders.

Anyone with the membership fee, not minor but exponentially cheaper than some other clubs, may join NAFSC. But I still I associated the "club" concept with unsavory elitism. A bit of class-based insecurity amped up my reluctance. Probably there'd be skating corollaries of not knowing which fork to use. I belonged at PIA, the nice municipal rink down the road. I didn't belong on club ice alongside young, advanced skaters that I was fearful and embarrassed to skate with anyway.

The prospect scared me enough that for a while I avoided it by driving seventy-five miles each way to public skating in Newburyport, Massachusetts. But I didn't really have free five-hour chunks of time, the gas and tolls made the venture expensive, and the Gay Games were imminent.

Eventually I just had to deal: skate with kids zipping around me; get up the courage to hand my program music to the monitor as if I believed that my solos deserved run-through time; and try not to feel like the clumsy, delusional poser I presumed the others rightly saw me to be. On club ice, as during figure skating practice ice at PIA, a skater doing a run-through to music also had put on a pinnie, one of those sleeveless tops that gym teachers and coaches distribute during practices or scrimmages to organize a subset of the players into a visible team when everyone is wearing the same (or no) uniform. Wearing a pinnie, by itself, transported me into gym-class humiliation mode.

Keys to the Kingdom

I'm glad I did it, for two reasons. First, eventually I got over myself. I came to see, even to feel, that I had every right to skate on that ice. I also developed enough confidence, facility, and speed both to participate in sharing responsibility for crash avoidance—a collective endeavor that has baffled almost every nonskater I've brought to a practice—and to refuse to scurry away from that actually small subset of kids whose hostile glare does scream "get off my ice." I glare back. Second, frequenting freestyle ice brought a connection between talent and money before my eyes that might otherwise have taken me longer to figure out. The most advanced kids on the ice—the polished dancers, the double or triple jumpers—and the kids on their way to those accomplishments skated on that expensive ice every day, on at least two sessions, with daily private lessons, too. That wasn't the difference precisely between club skaters and PIA skaters, as I came to learn when I started frequenting PIA freestyle ice, which had some similarly invested regulars, some of whom were also members of clubs. But time and money were absolutely the difference between those kids and the kids they had started with in group lessons who might now get, at most, one short private lesson and a few hours of practice a week.

The links among training time, coaching, and results did not seem like new information. What did was the virtually inescapable correlation of amounts: the way that x skill set and y competitive potential cost roughly z time and money. In fact, as I learned over the next half decade on the ice, I was also seeing what ten hours of ice and two or three hours of coaching a week couldn't buy. Malcolm Gladwell writes in *Outliers* about the "10,000-hour rule": the amalgam of research showing that from musical prodigies to technological visionaries to chess masters to world-class athletes, no matter how much popular narratives define them through genius or talent, none get to the top of their field without 10,000 hours of practice.[2] I can easily see how that minimum, which works out to about 20 hours a week over 10 years, would apply to figure skating. The very top skaters on the ice with me generally also trained elsewhere: on routine trips to skating centers in Boston or Delaware, or at least for a few intensive weeks of summer training. Even with those extras, and extensive off-ice training, hardly any were heading to national, Senior-level competition although a handful medaled nationally several levels below that.

Nonetheless, they were clearly serious skaters—serious in the sense of dedicated as well as in the slang sense of excellent—and easily visible as such partly because the extent of their training was visible, too. One possible effect of that visibility became apparent to me only toward the end of this project when I described the book to a high-school friend, Michelle Stacey, as we reconnected on Facebook. One thing I love about figure skating at PIA, and one reason, I believe, that people praise the environment there as friendly, is that skaters are taken seriously if they want to be, regardless of what they spend or accomplish. The extensive program for adults is part of that. So is the relatively low bar, completing Freestyle I, for performing a solo in the annual show, a privilege not restricted to skaters who have private coaches to choreograph a solo program for them. Skaters who take group lessons only, with, perhaps, a very modest supplement of private lessons, are welcome to perform the program they learned in group lessons. Those skaters have resources that correspond to what I had as a child. Nonetheless, I must have internalized the criteria for "serious" that I discerned through watching advanced skaters. I was surprised when Michelle said that of course she remembered how much my skating mattered to me back then; I had misremembered my own past, including the depths of my own passions.

Have Sex in April if You Want to Grow a Pro Hockey Player

I wish Gladwell had dwelled more on who can acquire such training and how definitions of "the best" develop. Standards of excellence do not evolve independent of social forces. As I discussed earlier, for instance, the balletic posture and extension that count so heavily in figure skating and ballroom dance have a raced history. But he does identify key requirements for the 10,000-hour track, which include the virtually inevitable component of money in acquiring time. "You can't be poor," Gladwell puts it bluntly, because if you need a paying job to contribute to your own sustenance you won't have enough time left over.[3]

You also need recognition, support, maybe special programs, and occasionally some odd leg-ups. One fascinating example that Gladwell discusses concerns a phenomenon publicized in the 1980s after Paula Barnsley, looking at player stats during a boy's hockey game in Canada, noticed that most players in this advanced league for teens had been born in January, February, or March. The clear explanation was that hockey programs in Canada group kids by age using the calendar year, so kids who were deemed gifted at four years old may actually have been demonstrating developmental advantages, including size, that come from being up to 364 days older than kids born in December. Then, early attention brings advantages that continue to accrue, eventually leading to more games, more practice time, more challenging competitions, and higher-level training.[4] As Gladwell points out, relatively simple remedies could be designed for this unfair, inefficient approach of identifying talent by full-year age groupings, which occurs in various other sports and countries, as well as in nonsporting pursuits, including tracking children by apparent intellectual gifts. Remedies haven't been designed, Gladwell thinks, because we "so profoundly personalize success." We attribute it to talent or genius, not, or far more than, systems that confer advantages and the resources required to benefit from them.[5]

What's Up with the Wherewithal?

The essays in this section look at paths, and representations of paths, from talent to success. Who has talent? Who has success? How do you get from one to the other? "Buy-In: Some Notes on Cost" circles around the question "how much does it cost to figure skate?" and puts some actual figures into the contexts of various dynamics, including shifting concepts of need and entanglements of truth and hype. "So You Think You Can Train, or Why Can Joshua Dance?" turns to one of the most popular recent sources for narratives about training: television talent contests. Beginning with a manufactured scandal on *So You Think You Can Dance*,

I consider how prejudice and practices affect notions—which affect outcomes—about whom training and success legitimately belong to. Finally, "Gifts of Nature, Freaks of Culture" takes on prejudice and practices concerning the allegedly raw ingredients, looking at whispers, screams, and regulations about perceived natural and unnatural advantages.

18

Buy-In

SOME NOTES ON COST

I'm wary when people describe the intense pursuit of activities they enjoy in terms of addiction. Even though it's an easy shorthand for "can't get enough," I suspect an implicit judgment that pleasure in quantity, especially bodily pleasure, is bound to be bad for you. Or as Dear Abby counseled once, to the "Woman Search[ing] for Reason to End her Guiltless Affair," "when something feels good, it is easy to become addicted, . . . and then you'll be in for a world of pain."[6]

But now that I've been skating for a while, I see the interconnections between love, money, and time that give so many adult figure skaters the ingredients for a classic addiction narrative. It can come upon you the way that bumming a cigarette at a party can turn into a pack-a-day habit: bit by bit before your very eyes, yet before you know it and while you half-deliberately missed what was happening. It begins, perhaps, with a group lesson every week, that you attend if nothing else is up. A few years later, skating has shunted other activities to the side, involving cash, prioritizing, and sacrifices that would have seemed unimaginable at first. Maybe they seem lunatic still. But the bar for sanity, or justifiable lunacy, has surely risen. So has the bar for satisfaction. You need more to have enough. You scheme to get it. Maybe you cut your expenses by getting in on the delivery.[7] Perceived wants become perceived needs. You can't quit, or moderate, even when you know you're hurting yourself (or others). Shame and guilt—about having, spending, wanting—dampen, or fuel, the thrills.

Four Thousand Proverbial Lattes

If you want to know where your money goes, popular wisdom says, consider the $3 latte. To spend $3 is a small splurge (maybe), but if you do it twice every workday in fifty five-day workweeks it adds up to $30 a week, $1,500 a year. Skating costs can creep up like that, too. Here's how it happened to me in the fall of 2007, when I took the four skating tests I needed to compete in Bronze at Adult Nationals.

First, I paid for the tests themselves. I took the first three in one test session for $85 altogether, cheap for the region but one hundred miles away in Hooksett, New Hampshire. I took my fourth through my home club close to where I live. It was a cheaper endeavor overall, although the single test cost $43 even with a discount for club members, who pay annually to belong on top of the USFS basic membership fee ($185 versus $120 for the 2011–12 season, for example). At both test sessions I paid $10 for practice ice.

Those were the one-time, set fees. Then there were expenses for preparation that I had more control over. Nervous about the upcoming tests, I wanted to skate more. Because I was on sabbatical, or so I interpreted the situation then, I could. The increased cost of doing so involved both how many hours and which sessions. Both FIC and PIA had freestyle ice that then cost around $9–$14 for about fifty minutes, depending on whether it was municipal or club ice, whether you belonged to the club if the latter, and whether you paid in advance or "walked on." Each rink also offered eighty- to ninety-minute public sessions for $5 or a twelve-for-$50 punch card. Public skating at PIA four blocks from home was obviously the best deal. But PIA allowed jumps and spins on public sessions only in a coned-off area at the end of the rink, making it hard to practice programs or Moves in the Field, which cover the ice surface. In contrast, FIC, six miles farther away, lets skaters at lightly attended sessions have the run of the ice if we all share nicely. We can also often play our program music. (In trade for being allowed to self-police, regulars may also perform informal monitoring services. "Hi there, it's not the best idea to skate with a six-month-old on your shoulders! No, really, my friend the nurse told me. It can be really bad if they fall.")

So I frequently chose FIC public skating, even on Tuesdays and Fridays, when FIC restricts public skating to adults only and charges $9–10. I also often paid for freestyle ice on days when I couldn't make a public session, rather than just going to the gym instead like I did before, or when I wanted a lesson on days when my coach couldn't accommodate the public ice schedule. Sometimes on Sunday, to have a lesson, I paid for early morning freestyle ice, even though I had free practice time that afternoon in exchange for volunteer coaching assistance with beginning adult skaters.

Thus did skating three to four days a week turn into skating five to six days a week, often on more expensive ice and more often with a lesson. At first I saw the increase as a temporary situation. But once the tests were done, I didn't want to cut back. Skating, flying, gliding, air on skin—the pleasure portion always returns for me, bigger, more vivid by contrast, when the pressure comes off after a test, show, or competition. Besides, I had so much to work on: footwork neglected when I was practicing ten Moves and a test program; that elusive flip jump, finally right around the corner (alas, actually not) with the new back-3/mohawk entrance. Stronger now, too, I could handle longer, more frequent practices, although I'd had to face the sad truth learned by every middle-aged athlete from Dara Torres, with her midlife Olympic medals and personal stretching staff, on down: It's the slower recovery time that kills you.[8] As a result, I couldn't really handle the training I envisioned pursuing during my sabbatical, with two ballet classes, three cardio sessions, and maybe some yoga added onto skating each week.

But while I bailed on yoga (included in my Y membership anyway) and the heavy-jumping section of ballet class (although my knees eventually took me out of ballet altogether), I didn't scale back the skating. When it came to skating, I rarely subtracted after I had added. I didn't quit group lessons once I started privates. They were now a bargain by comparison. In fact, when I lucked into a group-lessons coach who really worked for me, the lessons offered cheap-ish access to the huge luxury and benefit of having a coaching team. Learning from Kristin during class to squeeze my butt for the back outside exit edge while still on the front inside entry edge helped me learn how to pull off a decent Choctaw turn. I didn't skip paid ice on Monday due to free ice on Sunday, as I'd first planned to do. On Monday, I'd think, "well, who knows how often I'll be able to skate this week. I'd better skate when I can." Yet somehow, even after sabbatical, on most days I made it happen. Now, though, there were added costs—to me and the ozone layer—associated with forgoing carpool opportunities that would have been otherwise available.

Big Bucks and Bottom Lines

It's hard to offer a bottom line on skating costs or to guesstimate how much particular individuals are spending. Key costs vary considerably by whim, market, location, and personal circumstance. Thirty dollars can buy 15 or 30 minutes of coaching time as well as 80, 180, or (much more rarely) 280 minutes of freestyle ice. Skaters might live 5 or 105 miles, at least, from rinks they skate at. They might splurge and save in ways visible and hidden. That skater at AN from 2,000 miles away has someone putting her on the ice. Did she, or she and some other skaters, fly in her own coach? Did she hire a local coach for a few hours, or did her friend act as a coach for free? Vera Wang said in 2010 that she attended Evan Lysacek's international competitions, or sent a tailor, to make sure the costumes she designed for him work perfectly.[9] Did he actually fly a designer around the world? Or was Wang, in effect, paid in publicity?

While expenses can be hard to eyeball, I can say that a pair of skates, a competition or two, and the littler costs I described above can easily add up to $10,000 a year. Kids making a serious run at being contenders require three to six times that much, even double that if they reach the top echelons. In *Inside Edge: A Revealing Look into the Secret World of Figure Skating*, Christine Brennan, a sports writer, detailed the expenses for the 1994–95 competitive season for a Senior Men's skater, Michael Weiss, who started in his sister's hand-me-down white skates painted black — and is best known, at least among my friends, for compulsively referencing the wife and kids, presumably to imply heterosexuality. (That's a better strategy, surely, than skating to music by Queen, wearing leather-type pants, and doing booty flirtations with the audience as he did during the 2011 Stars on Ice show.)[10] According to Brennan, Weiss's family used various strategies to keep costs *down* to $50,000 for the year. These included finding a sponsor for his competition costumes, which trimmed his costume cost from $3,000 to $1,000, and cramming six people into two $39-a-night hotel rooms when they traveled to competitions, which required a coach who was open to, and able to afford being on, a "low-budget joyride."[11] That $50,000 didn't include expenses that other top skaters face, like regular trips or relocation costs to train at a big skating center. Besides, that was back in 1995. There are now new expenses to pay for: like the use of Dartfish's SimulCam and StroMotion technologies, far too expensive for small rinks to own, but used, according to Dartfish, in the training regimes of 162 medal winners at the 2010 Winter Olympics.[12] Plus, costs have risen for everything. In 2007, Adam Rippon, who became the national and world Junior Champion in 2008, said that his skates cost $3,000 a year for two pairs, up from the $2,000 that Weiss spent.[13]

I'd searched articles about Rippon after the 2007 Adult Training Camp that I attended with Teresa, which took place at the rink where he then trained. Our assigned schedule included two off-ice classes with his mother, Kelly Rippon, who had a new, life-coaching "specialized transition and thinking company" called Authentic Change. In one class, she illustrated skating's investments and challenges with a situation that she faced as a skating parent on a limited income: explaining to her five other children that they could only spend $30 a year on athletic footwear because Adam's cost one hundred times that.[14] To be honest, I didn't know how she justified it. But I wasn't surprised that she assumed an audience of adult skaters would respond sympathetically. By the time we've made it to a training camp weekend, most of us have put skating in front of other activities, people, and expenses—including for the weekend itself—in ways likely to raise eyebrows among nonskaters.

We're also long past sticker shock, if not despair, about the cost of figure skates, which, expensive in their own right, can cost twice as much as comparable-level hockey or derby skates.[15] This disparity generates diverse theories about supply, demand, material, labor, and participants. The most popular theory can be summarized as "they know that princesses' parents will pay," although a skate shop owner I know disagreed. He bought that explanation for blades: "How much different can a $600 blade be from a $200 one?" (Apparently, according to another sharpener, the difference is the plating and greater specification for tricks.)[16] But with boots, he thought, it was all about quantity. Derby and hockey skates can be outsourced to China. Unions, he thought "have skate companies by the balls," given the small number of figure skates that are produced.

Hmmm. I looked around with his theory in mind, if not his distaste for unions. According to Riedell, my skates were "expertly crafted in Red Wing, MN." To me, that intends to bespeak a labor source far removed geographically and in practice from either sweatshops or union labor, although the extended description, describing "microfiber lining" and a "hand-rolled collar," emphasized not labor conditions but scientific-sounding technical advances meeting old-fashioned production.[17] Importantly, however, "expertly crafted in Red Wing, MN" offers no actual information about labor conditions, only spin.

Flat Ice, Slippery Slope

The triple jumps required of top-level athletes today can hardly be performed on flimsy rentals or arguably on skates like mine. The force of repeated landings requires more support. At the same time, truth and hype about connections between equipment and performance never simply line up, even when the hype is true. Instead, they interact in historically specific, mutually dependent ways. Some people think boots have become so built up because skaters came, through external guidance, to believe they needed boot support—short-circuiting technique development. (Christopher MacDougall details the history of a similar argument about running shoes, which includes Nike's discovery that some of its sponsored athletes were training barefoot, and the debates about correlations between the development of support-heavy running shoes and increased injuries.)[18] Skating standards change to accommodate accomplishments that depend, to some extent, on what people can, and will, pay for at a particular time. Triples couldn't be the baseline for the top, nor could back archings and leg extensions that are natural for a mere few, if the costs to cultivate those tricks had not become normalized as integral to serious training.

Meanwhile, the fact that money alone can't generate those accomplishments, while some are pulled off more cheaply than others, adds to the mystery and mystique that hype feeds on. Skates, ice, coaching, cross-training, and costumes are among numerous skating expenses that require the constant weighing of means, marketing, and evidence. Does every advanced skater need ballet (Pilates, yoga, a private trainer)? That kid who got third in Regionals has that. The specialized bodywork provided by rolfers? Michelle Kwan and Elvis Stojko used one. The twelve-sided versus the less expensive eight-sided crystals on a costume? (Not according to Ice Mom of icemom.net.[19]) To FedEx one's skates to such-and-such a master sharpener because the master sharpener down the road, or ninety miles away, simply won't do anymore? Some of those expenditures still seem crazy to me—or at least for me. But not as much as they used to.

19

So You Think You Can Train,
or Why Can Joshua Dance?

On season 4 of *So You Think You Can Dance* (SYTYCD), the judges trumped up a little scandal akin to sandbagging in skating when they accused Joshua Allen, the season's eventual winner, of demonstrating more training than he'd let on having. The scene took place during the episode that revealed the twenty dancers who had made it through the final auditions during "Vegas Week." Maybe because they were accusing a black man of being shifty, Debbie Allen, one of the judges, delivered the accusation. Debbie Allen is the African American dancer, choreographer, and actor best known from the 1980 movie and, especially, television series *Fame* (1982–87), where her now legendary call to the nitty-gritty of training appeared in the opening montage of every episode: "You've got big dreams? You want fame? Well, fame costs. And right here is where you start paying . . . in sweat." When Joshua Allen came before the judges, she informed him that they questioned his truthfulness. He had presented himself as a hip-hopper from an extremely disadvantaged childhood. "Not knowing really what you're going to eat the next day" amplified his hunger to make it, as viewers had just seen in a clip. Yet during a group number, the judges had seen him do a *brisé*, a difficult ballet move. Despite their distrust, however, they made him a finalist anyway.[20]

Now You Don't

I don't call the scandal trumped up because either the *brisé* (from the French for "broken") or its evidence of training was. They weren't. A still shot labeled "NAUGHTY BRISÉ" on the blog *Television! You Black Emperor* shows Joshua Allen doing the move, which would be hard to master on the spot.[21] Another blogger, sarcastic about insider language presented as self-explanatory, indicates why: "I knew it! . . . I totally said, 'That looks like a move wherein he swept one leg into the air to the side while jumping off the other, bringing both legs together in the air and then beating them before landing!'"[22] I call the scandal trumped up because he had already demonstrated such training during his first audition in Dallas, which two judges, more and less explicitly, had noted. Adam Shankman registered surprise to the judge next to him at Allen's port de bras (balletic arm positions) and Lithgoe praised his "elevation," not naming but drawing attention to a huge split jump that the viewer then saw in replay.

But if judges noted the results of training, they pretended not to recognize them as such. To me, Allen's split jump had two obvious sources: years of dance training, which enabled him to loft himself high into the air with perfectly straight legs and pointed toes; and a plan to show his versatility, virtuosity, and intense drive. Yet the judges treated the split as an isolated trick. Lithgoe said that it "came out of nowhere," adding "I can't wait to see if you can do anything other than that." So instead of sending Allen "directly to Vegas," despite calling him one of the "most exciting" he'd seen all day, Lithgoe sent him to the second-chance "choreography round" for auditioners whose impressive solos alone did not yet convince the judges of their broad-enough range of skill, experience, and trainability.

Really Listen, OK?

This portrayal of Allen can be attributed, I think, to layers of racist and racial presumption. Why was it a stretch to envision him as a former kid in dance class? When they sent him to the choreography round, Shankman actually said to him (unless fancy editing transferred this condescending utterance to that scene), "Focus. Really listen, okay? 'Cause we like you" as if Allen might be totally new to the whole business of choreography or had some innate disinclination to pay attention in school. Why didn't they consider his expertise in hip-hop and popping as itself a likely sign of training? They should know better than to believe in the common absurdity that black people simply have rhythm, casually picking up amazing dance skills by hanging out on ghetto street corners with a boom box.

Why did judges and editors feel free to be so careless with Allen's reputation, all the way through the season to a convoluted switch-up in the finale? Judges then insisted that he had come to *SYTYCD* untrained after even more glaring evidence to the contrary, especially during his duet with tWitch Boss, the runner-up. Appropriately for their characterization as two "street dancers"[23]—and because heterosexism ruled out SYTYCD's ordinary duet subject, romance—they performed a street-duel version of the Russian Trepak from the *Nutcracker* ballet that required moves of Allen (only) like 540-degree-turn jumps. Besides, by then Allen had long ago explained having some training, the show's bio page stated that he had training, and it had already come out in blogs that his training included stints at Debbie Allen's own dance schools![24] Nonetheless, Lithgoe told him that he had raised the standard for all future contestants, who would have to think, "Joshua didn't get training and look at how brilliant he was." Other judges fawned over his raw talent, further naturalized by comments that the duet was "testosterone driven."[25]

Dancing Outside the Race

These characterizations of Allen in the finale—untrained, driven by natural masculinity—suggest that his offense lay in violating common raced stereotypes. Hip-hop dancers, who are likely not white, are allegedly untrained; ballet dancers, who are likely white, are trained, although each type can inject the other with nature and culture, respectively. The story of the "street-dancer" Joshua Allen lifted to victory through SYTYCD is basically *Save the Last Dance* backward. In the 2001 movie, a family tragedy forces white, uptight ballerina Sara to move to a rough, urban neighborhood populated predominantly by people of color. There, Derek, her black future boyfriend and a hip-hop expert, helps her bring life into her dancing by teaching her some of his moves. The film makes clear that she's trained and he isn't. She aspires to Julliard and can perform twists and extensions that don't come naturally. He shines at the local dance club, filled with people who feel the beat in a way that apparently eludes Sara completely before an on-site lesson, despite years of moving to music.

Of course, nothing lines up by race alone. Appropriate training is set up not only against raced ideas of the natural but also against unfortunate, less classy training regimes that white people are no strangers to. At the same Dallas auditions where Joshua tried out, Lithgoe called one white, female veteran of pageants and dance-school teams a "Stepford" dancer and "pirouetting set of teeth."[26] Training also generally shines brighter when it appears to enhance a natural penchant for heteronormativity. Anthony Bryant, who had been rejected during season 1 tryouts for being too feminine, was rejected again for season 4, despite having ditched the ribbon he'd danced with the first time for a camouflage jumpsuit suggesting militarist masculinity. Lithgoe liked his technique but thought a spark was missing.[27] No kidding.

Nor do only white people have the right training. Season 3's runner-up, the African American dancer Danny Tidwell, had already worked professionally as a ballet dancer, although his dance trajectory testifies to raced barriers by featuring, like Rowell's, the key intervention of a white dancer. Denise Wall, a dance studio owner and the mother of the season 2 runner-up, Travis Wall, took an interest in the promising Tidwell, who was discovered by another dance teacher in an after-school program "funded by a grant for at-risk youths." Wall eventually adopted him.[28] On SYTYCD, judges slammed Tidwell for haughtiness, which some critics saw as implicit displeasure that he had stepped out of his place as a black man, "not smiling enough, not demonstrating enough feeling, not being humble enough, literally . . . not shucking and jiving."[29] Interestingly, one critic suggested, albeit haughtily herself, that the judges were really looking for Leroy from *Fame*, "a gritty dancer with attitude who possesses nothing but a soaring jump and the ability to spin on a dime."[30] There's Joshua Allen, or the reading of him that sees his *brisé* as new information after an audition with a Russian split.

That Was Then, Training Is Now

As Joshua Allen indicated in a 2009 interview, both representations of his training were true. He was trained and he wasn't. "Let's be real," he said. "Let's not be stupid to the fact that, yeah, I took classes when I could. I kept saying that." But "it was always stop and start. It wasn't sustained like [that of two other dancers on the show] William or Mark." It was enough, however, to teach him that he needed more than intermittent classes and annual scholarships to monthlong Summer Intensives at Debbie Allen's Dance Academy in Los Angeles. "I always wanted to be chosen for [the year-round] program to live there. I almost begged for it, but I didn't get it. I was back home crying. . . . I would ask myself, 'Am I doing this for no reason? Am I going to be 20 or 21 and still not make it and living in my mom's house?'"[31]

Times change. Money talks differently. So does training. What Allen learned as a teenager and I learned as an adult on freestyle ice with well-capitalized kids is now knowledge available free, at least in its basics, to anyone who has watched SYTYCD regularly in the seasons since Allen's *brisé* caused him trouble. As with many other televised competitions centered around vocational artistry, the notion that such shows enable raw or raw-ish talent to shine has given way to the battle of the professionally trained. *Top Chef* and *Project Runway* contestants may already have their own restaurants or clothing lines. The SYTYCD judges now flatly call the lack of a "polished-toepoint-that-cost-a-gajillion-dollars-thru-ballet" training, to recall my friend's formulation, a virtually insurmountable barrier. In 2010's season 7, it was the downfall of another "street dancer," Jose Ruiz, who actually did lack such training. Although charm, b-boy excellence, and being a quick learner elevated him into contestant material and won him popularity, his lack of proper training, mentioned repeatedly, ensured his failure at the end.

Rules Aren't Made to Be Broken

The requirement to show up already extensively trained in ways requiring opportunity, exposure, support, and cash gets in the way of another common theme on televised talent contests: representing. Audition episodes are full of would-be contestants who want to represent for people unexpected to shine in this arena: people of a particular race or ethnicity (very common); recently homeless (SYTYCD, *America's Best Dance Crew* [ABDC], *America's Got Talent* [AGT]); recently homeless *and* trans (*America's Next Top Model* [ANTM]); middle-aged (*Dancing with the Stars*); adopted (*Dallas Cowboys Cheerleaders: Making the Team*); living with Asperger's (ANTM); living post-Katrina (AGT). But realities and representation collide. Lack of resources gets in the way. So do rules and standards that belie any stated interest in opening doors.

A clear example comes from cycle 9 on ANTM. Heather Kuszmich, the contestant with Asperger's, a form of autism best known for challenges involving interpretive nuance, was eliminated after bombing the show's standard "go-see challenge" in which models race to find designers' studios in an unfamiliar city.[32] Such a charge, as I can attest, would panick and flummox many people labeled (or presumed) neurotypical, a term I learned on a great website that parodically critiques medical stigmatization of autism.[33] But it was virtually destined to trip up someone with Asperger's. Yet *ANTM* nonetheless retained the challenge, which Tyra Banks, the host and head judge, usually describes as utilizing skills required of any "top model." More important than how dubious that claim is—as if "top models" couldn't simply hire drivers who know where they are going or participate in the more common practice called "taking a cab"—is a point that this *ANTM* fixture illustrates. As I elaborate next, rules of contest work in complex ways to assign categories like normalcy, disability, giftedness, and freakishness to human variation.

20

Gifts of Nature, Freaks of Culture

How does what you can do in skating depend on the particular body you bring to it? As I worked on this project, I became keenly interested in the stakes, politics, and pitfalls of proposing answers—especially answers that may seem patently true. Consider, for example, effects on the body of aging. As an athlete, as a figure skater specifically, as a researcher, and as a middle-aged person sharing rueful smiles with others who now catch ourselves groaning involuntarily upon standing, I find it obvious that aging takes a toll. It's hardly obvious to me alone. Even Olga Kotelko, the ninety-one-year-old track star who was profiled in a *New York Times* article called "The Incredible Flying Nonagenarian," drew the interest of scientists and trainers for matching top athletes in their eighties, not younger.[34] My friend, and sometimes collaborator, Shana Agid put the situation well, in relation to his own recent venture into acrobatics and trapeze. Activities like ours, especially when pursued in the vicinity of aspiring kids, offer two inescapable and contradictory reminders: Age is less limiting than many people expect yet unquestionably limiting in ways that are impossible to transcend. Adult skaters who could land triple or double jumps as kids eventually lose them, those who began as adults very rarely get them, and we all watch kids at our rinks rush past us in their pace of learning and achieving results.

The effects of aging are so obvious, at least once they start to nail you, that one bit of data that I believe I could offer up, were I to pursue the numbers more systematically, is that no athlete over the age of thirty-two ever utters a phrase like "age, it's in your head, really." I heard that sentiment sometimes from younger derby skaters who asked why I didn't just try it. I usually responded that my knees had lived a few decades too long to handle, even with kneepads, a fraction of what they put their knees through. They rarely seemed convinced. They didn't shake my certainty either. I still think of aging's toll, the fact of it, as the opposite of rocket science.

Yet exactly how aging limits skaters is varied and hard to specify. Childhood training can help adults to perform otherwise unattainable feats, which puts adult-onset athletes at a disadvantage. As more young athletes age into newly thriving adult versions of their sport—or in, roller derby, as leagues introduce junior derby for girls still too young to hit[35]— they may push out people who started older, as has happened, for instance, in Adult synchronized skating. Advantages of starting early extend beyond muscle memory for solo moves, as an adult hockey player pointed out to me. When I watch her play, I see the facility in skating and "stick handling" that marks decades on the ice, the last few in regularized, coached hockey. What I couldn't see, she explained, was the big divide caused by the recent advent of competitive hockey for girls and young women. Even the best older players struggled to internalize plays and teamwork that players who'd been coached in college or earlier found to be second nature.

Besides, age doesn't proceed uniformly. The hot flashes that have occasionally messed with my balance since my late forties—including once right before my program music started at AN—might have messed someone else up at thirty-five or fifty-five, or not at all. (Given famously wild teen hormones, I've wondered whether upsets in Ladies championships might ever turn on the "wrong time of the month.") Maybe other people my age don't increasingly forget the correction they've just received during the few seconds when they skate away from their coach to try the trick again.

In addition, bodies never age independently of cultural, economic, and other matters that prevent universal characterizations of bodies at a certain age. Variables include everything from environmental pollution to happenstance to labor, whether "manual" by label or impactful in ways suggested in phrases like "hunched over a desk." Key, too, of course, are available resources. Once, during a program run-through a few weeks before a competition, I crashed forward out of a camel spin (a spin in an arabesque position) so hard that a bunch of those very kids I'd been afraid of rushed over to see if I was OK. Surely it affected my immediate recovery, my ongoing relation to flexibility, and the long-term health of my organs that I paid a rolfer to work on my connective tissue instead of just popping massive amounts of ibuprofen. My rolfer, Gary, told me, however, that I had initially set myself back by doing what skaters learn to do when we fall even when we can tell we're going to hurt a lot imminently or tomorrow: I scrambled up, raced to catch the music, and finished my program. Animals, he said, don't experience body trauma like humans do because when animals get hurt they lie where they are and let the shock dissipate. I should try that, he said, at least when I'm not mid-program.[36] I told him I would, but somehow I always forget.

In with the Wrong Crowd

Even if assertions about bodies primed or ill-suited to particular practices have some truth value, they can never be true in any simple way and never concern the body in isolation. Fifty isn't really the new thirty but maybe's it closer to the new thirty if you can afford organic vegetables and a gym membership. Whatever their merit, however, such assertions come tinged and are rendered rightly suspect by the terrible company they keep with sketchy ideas of a sort that have popped up in this book already. More and less mutable bodily features may be laden with dubious meanings. True ladies have small feet; thin people exercise virtue and discipline.[37] Apparently innate talent may have other or additional explanations, like the standard developmental advantage of being four-and-a-half instead of four.

So many ways of grouping people are questionable, most notoriously when it comes to race and ethnicity. For example, as Amy Bass nicely details, studies concerning the alleged superiority of "the black athlete" in certain sports bear shifting premises about who even fits into that category. As she notes, C. Montague Cobb, an African American former athlete and physical anthropologist—who was not, Bass argued, without some dubious racializing premises himself—pointed out in 1936 that athletes who were considered "Negro stars" had not a "single physical characteristic" in common that "would definitely identify them as Negros." Jesse Owens himself, whose four Olympic gold medals would soon be taken as a slap at Hitler's claims of Aryan physical superiority, lacked, Cobb argued, a preponderance of physical characteristics considered particular to or dominant in "Negroid" peoples.[38]

Alongside problematic assertions about physical commonalities come problematic notions about what they signify. In her 2010 article about why "Figure Skaters of Asian Descent Have Risen to Prominence," Jere Longman writes that "Asian skaters are often small and willowy" and she quotes a famous coach saying, "They have bodies that are quick and light;

they're able to do things very fast. . . . It's like Chinese divers. If you look at those bodies, there's nothing there. They're just like nymphs."[39] To me, these descriptions suggest a certain exoticizing eye (willowy, nymph) and counteract the article's emphasis on "cultural factors," not that any such factors are as universal or necessarily so specific to Asians as the article suggests either—as if one never sees white skating parents who are strict and driving! People aren't naturally "quick and light" or "able to do things fast." Those descriptions imply that products of labor and training are natural. It's the same language used to justify relegating people described as nimble- and small-fingered to repetitive, crippling work with needles and microchips.

Hormones and Hemoglobin

Between high-profile disciplined sportscasters and, I'd like to think, some popular education less focused on avoiding censure, people often shy away from pronouncements about the physical characteristics of groups who noticeably populate particular sports. Evidence of that wariness appears both in the relatively tentative claims of people like Longman and in some interesting silences and diversionary moves, exemplified, perhaps, in recent attention to the early predominance of Jews in men's basketball. Accounts of the phenomenon—four Jews played for the Knicks in the first NBA game ever! With two more on the roster!— appropriately slam racist explanations of the time. Often quoted is a 1937 comment by Paul Gallico in the New York Daily News: "The reason, I suspect, that basketball appeals to the Hebrew with his Oriental background is that the game places a premium on an alert, scheming mind, flashy trickiness, artful dodging and general smart-aleckness."[40] (Visible, by contrast, is Longman's relative subtlety.) Yet in explaining why virtually no Jews play pro ball in the U.S. now, these same sources seem fully willing to promote another unfounded stereotype: that Jews are all rich. Apparently the theory that Jews now play golf in affluent suburbs is preferable to entertaining out loud what seems like one reasonably likely contributing factor, without discounting shifting populations of the urban "ghetto" training ground, which is that once men's basketball becomes a game in which the shortest player on a roster may be 6'1" (although basketball's not-so-distant history includes a very few exceptions like the 5'3" Muggsy Bogues), the pool of Jews might be smaller.

In contrast, categorizing natural ability by sex functions most often in sports as if disparate abilities between two distinct categories should be taken for granted and organized around, even if those presumptions have repeatedly been contested: when girls or women play, or fight to play, in "male" sports or leagues; when male versus female becomes a spectacle (Billie Jean King playing against Bobby Riggs); when female-categorized or self-categorizing athletes do not conform to rules of femininity set for them, causing hostility, accusation, and sometimes required medical verification. Perceived incompatibilities between femininity or female-ness and significant athleticism have contributed to a history of sex veri-fication testing that has included thirty years of mandatory testing for all athletes in women's, and only women's, events at the Olympics and the continuing practice of testing people competing as female whose achievements, or appearance, are seen to place them outside the bounds of the category.[41]

The preeminence of sex segregation in sports and the policing of those boundaries around male and female testify to their durability and the stakes in maintaining them, especially because they don't accomplish the tasks of managing natural advantages that they purport to accom-plish. As the 2010 report *On the Team: Equal Opportunity for Transgender Student Athletes* emphasizes, we should not let the fuss over patrolling sex categories fool us into thinking that trans people have similar physi-cal advantages any more than do non-trans people. Nor should we forget that advantages differ across sports, or imagine that regulating bodies by sex division will account for all natural advantages. In other words, trans women aren't all tall. Height doesn't help in all sports. More than hor-mones matter. Swimmers, for example, may benefit from naturally high levels of hemoglobin, which facilitates oxygen intake. Yet no one tries to regulate advantages like that.[42]

Instead, Sarah Teetzel comments, athletes with most natural advan-tages other than those linked to sex and gender are seen to have "won the 'genetic lottery.'"[43] Thus, Jane Devlin notes, Yao Ming, a 7'6" professional basketball player, gets an NBA contract for extreme deviation from recog-nized norms of tallness, while Caster Semenya's extremely fast times as a world champion runner, along with perceptions of her body as being insufficiently feminine, resulted in highly publicized accusations and forced testing.[44]

12. Still from "Proof that Muralitharan Does Not Chuck" showing Muttiah Muralitharan being manhandled on *The Cricket Show* in 2004 by the segment's host and a doctor. Island Cricket website, uploaded on December 14, 2008, http://www.islandcricket.lk.

In fact, the label "natural gift" often functions as the ultimate stamp of an advantage's legitimacy. A great example appears in a 2004 segment from *The Cricket Show* that staged tests to disprove recurring accusations, sometimes by umpires, that Muttiah Muralitharan (nicknamed Murali), a cricket star from Sri Lanka, utilized an illegal bowling maneuver called "chucking," which involves straightening one's arm beyond the allowed limits. The host, Ravi Shastri, a former cricket player for India, explained that the alleged offense was an optical illusion due partly to Murali's unusual anatomy. His shoulder and wrist have greater than ordinary rotational flexibility, enhancing his abilities, while he cannot fully straighten his elbow, making it impossible to violate the extension rule. After Shastri and then a doctor gave a hands-on display of Murali's rotation and extension (figure 12), Murali, with his arm immobilized in a brace, demonstrated his technique by bowling to Michael Slater, an Australian former opponent, proving further that he can execute glorious moves without straightening his arm. Murali, then, has a gift of nature that is rightly unregulated and legitimate because it is natural, as Shastri loudly declares: "That is simply amazing. You can see he's BORN WITH IT. It's not something he's manufactured one night." Murali's advantages are congenital, a point emphasized through Shastri's recurring joke locating potency in the sperm donor: "If there is to be another [person with Murali's bowling arm], senior Murali needs to get on the job again."[45]

Freaks Born and Bred

The case of Murali, and its representation on *The Cricket Show*, offers a great dramatization of two key points about how the attribution of natural gifts plays out in sports (and often elsewhere). First, it often involves an implicit coding and treatment of outliers as freaks. In the video segment, Murali, strikingly, says not one word as people manipulate his body and put him through tests to demonstrate what's "simply amazing." The fact that he is also the darkest-skinned person in the video, from the least powerful country of the three represented, adds a historic echo to the scene, recalling the human specimens put on display as freaks or oddities.[46]

Second, the value accorded the natural is inconsistent, contested, and created through technologies that mold and measure both the criteria and the bodies. Sarah Rebolloso McCullough uses the great phrase "technologies of naturalization" to describe the complex of ideas, tools, and practices used to determine and police what counts as natural as opposed to unnatural — unnatural in the sense of either artificial or contrary to acceptable norms in nature.[47] In Murali's case, nature is verified by photographic media, "Dr. Mandeep Dillon, Orthopaedician," and a device made of "steel rods" in "heat-moulded plastic," as the host and superimposed text doubly reassure us. It rescues his right to play. In contrast, when athletes face issues concerning sex categories, the same sophistication is marshaled to make natural variation a disqualifying factor, although again, significantly, only for people competing in female categories.

The criteria for natural *enough* are as varied and fraught as the criteria for natural. Definitions of health itself aren't uniform or stable. Champion athletes used to promote cigarettes the way they now announce plans to visit Disney World.[48] The medical registry form for my 2009 Adult Nationals registration form included "menstruation" as one of the problems that competitors were asked to disclose, as if the very fact of menstruation might denote compromised health. The phrasing was changed to "menstrual complications" in 2010, and "disordered eating" also joined the list. Given how recently "disordered eating" supplanted "eating disorders" as a preferred phrase, I think someone with an eye on more modern interpretations of health had gotten involved, although I still don't understand why "menstrual complications" require advance disclosures like other items on the list, such as hypertension, asthma, and seizures, might.

Definitions of enhancement aren't fixed either, as Tara Magdalinski elaborates in *Sport, Technology, and the Body*. Nor are lines between repair, restoration, and enhancement.[49] Even when lines might seem easy to draw, standards aren't consistent. "We allow athletes," Teetzel writes, "to improve their vision to 20/15 or better using laser eye surgery and to use any performance-enhancing supplement not explicitly banned by the World Anti-Doping Code, and yet we prohibit them from transfusing their own blood or topping off their natural testosterone levels with exogenous sources."[50] Where does the body end anyway and what may gear legitimately transform? Skate boots affect how much I can bend my ankles (which also depends on my strength), and they help me land without twisting my ankles. Blades, although distinctly cultural and detachable products, function in some ways as extensions of the body.

Design and access can complicate issues of nature, training, and fairness. McCullough demonstrates how through the example of the Speedo LZR Racer. The LZR Racer is the advanced-technology full-body swimsuit worn famously in the 2008 Summer Olympics by Michael Phelps and later banned. Some of the suit's material mimics shark skin, and some outperforms it, thus rendering at issue the boundaries of the human and nonhuman as well as the boundaries of the organic and nonorganic. The suit reduces drag and actually "chang[es] the physical capabilities of the body—increasing blood flow, maximizing lung capacity, and compressing muscles to increase proprioception," which means, roughly, sensing where your body parts are.[51] It's expensive and requires help to put on. Its development also demonstrates that while it's generally sketchy to sort ability by race, nation, or ethnicity, it does not serve the study and practice of sport, any more than it serves any antiracist project, to maintain pretenses to color- or other such blindnesses. McCullough writes that "white bodies from [the United States, Australia, and the United Kingdom] dominated the design production and marketing materials for the suits, racializing swimming as predominantly white."

If we consider that "ancestral inheritance," as Victoria Rowell put it,[52] may involve trends in shape and size, the suit's racial ancestry matters, especially because the suits, which were designed partly by taking laser scans of four hundred elite and predominantly white athletes, do not mold themselves around the body but force the body to adapt to the suit. Speedo's advertising, McCullough adds, also centers male athletes, while the suit itself flattens and androgynizes female athletes, further rendering hips and protruding breasts anathema to the athletic body. It's like the fate of the "womanly figure" in figure skating after the ascent of tricks best served aerodynamically by compact bodies. In skating, however, outfits return the womanly, more precisely the white womanly figure, to the sport, by depicting femininity, often with a gesture toward cleavage even on the prepubescent.

Conjugating Brisé: Break, Broke, Broken

The opening lines of Avril Lavigne's 2002 hit "Sk8er Boi" invoke the apparently fixed characteristics of some of the sex categories and cultural activities that I've been considering in "Having the Wherewithal":

> He was a boy, she was a girl
> Can I make it any more obvious?
> He was a punk, she did ballet
> What more can I say?"[53]

Common understandings about sex, gender, and class make the lines easily legible, economically setting the stage for the song's sad tale, which concerns a snobby girl whose prejudice makes her reject the advances of a skateboarder who will later be "rocking up MTV." "Boy" meeting "girl" can appear to paint an "obvious" picture of who's involved and what happens: naturally, a story of fulfilled or thwarted heterosexual desires. Doing ballet is replete with apparently self-evident meaning about class, training, and movement that the downscale street style of skater-boy "punk" highlights by contrast.

Then again, regarding nature and training, the very same things may be both obvious and opaque. Girl, boy, punk, ballet, and the "boi" as spelled in the song's title—none of those terms have guaranteed occupancy. The categories "boy" and "girl" do not simply reflect truths of the natural. They can function to police notions of natural difference and deflect attention from differences that might be more relevant to the situation, within and outside sports. All five categories have potential queer attachments—to identities, relationships, and transgression—and raced content, sometimes varied in relation to different genders and sexualities. Raced exclusions, for instance, contribute to making ballet seem the purview of snooty white people. So do resources required—although labor conditions complicate the relation between movement and money because dancers who live off their dancing can inhabit at most the look of aristocracy.

So what does it mean when narratives of talent camouflage narratives of money, when a *brisé* suggests cheating, when the wrong limits and boundaries are passed off as the natural way to go? It means that nothing and everything is broken.

VII

Blade Scars/Biopsy Scars

RETHINKING RISK AND CHOICE

> My girl, wine on her lips
> Tonight's the night she wraps around my fingertips
> I know she'll look good with a scar
> 'Cause that's how we are
> —Neill C. Furio, *Black Dahlia Blues*

I sometimes have slice marks on my right shin. Like the little gashes that score my right skate, they come from messing up when I'm trying to cross a slightly lifted left leg over my straight right leg in order to achieve the standard jump or back-spin position for skaters who rotate counter-clockwise. The scars, then, are accidental, although I can't describe them as completely unwelcome. I have to admit that if the cut isn't too deep, I don't mind the sharp little sting or, perhaps, a few minutes later, the slow recognition of a damp, cool sensation caused by little blood drop-lets emerging along a scratch line. It makes me think that I understand a little about why some people view cutting as an erotic practice, even if I'm most fascinated by mechanics and visuals that I experience on another register. Why does the blade occasionally cut my leg without ripping what covers it, even jeans? Conversely, why can it rip thin tights but leave the skin intact? I'm interested in how scars overlay each other, whether they fade or don't, how I no longer get off the ice to check out the situation. What's a little blood? Who needs to get off the ice for that?

In that bit of bravado lies another appeal. Scars are signs of being seri-ous about skating, tough enough to take the rough and tumble, evidence that there *is* rough and tumble, that I have cuts and bruises to show and tell alongside derby girls displaying the physical evidence of their own fierceness, which they may sometimes feel the need to spotlight, too. It's an impulse I see in Killer Quick's "How to Spot a Derby Girl":

> Know what happens when you fall at high speed and slide along the floor? It's called track rash, baby, and o how it burns. Now imagine

someone wearing tiny criss-crossing ropes of fabric all across her legs taking a big fall and sliding along the floor on an upper thigh/hip. The results come in fascinating shapes and patterns, and sometimes take months to fade away.[1]

Fishnets as "criss-crossing ropes of fabric": the description toughens up a staple of derby attire that, to the displeasure of many derby girls who defiantly wear them anyway, compromises derby's reputation as a serious sport, at least among people for whom the combination of sexiness and rough play on the track always equals "catfight" no matter what signs of sport might be staring them in the face: athleticism, rules, refs, evidence of serious training.

But derby girls have a different image problem than figure skaters. Derby action looks tough all the time. Skaters knock each other across the floor. They scramble up after sprawling and hop right over fallen skaters; according to the rules of the Women's Flat Track Derby Association (WFTDA), fresh injuries do not stop play as long as the player can crawl off the track before her injury poses a threat to the others.[2] Figure skaters, in contrast, do a lot to make hard work look easy. We often forgo postures and movements common in other skate sports that both facilitate, and symbolize, the whole body working as one unit in an intense coordinated effort. Think of the derby girl's or speedskater's canonic forward-leaning stance, those runnerlike arm movements, or that sleek, hot combo for speeding around an oval: the inside arm held behind the back for aerodynamic advantage while the outside one pumps. Figure skaters, meanwhile, present torso positions and floating arm gestures that often camouflage the challenge of executing them and may seem to do anything but help propel the body forward.

Add in the outfits that may mask indelicate muscles and the common cultural habit of associating anything labeled feminine with weakness, and it's no wonder that only people prepared or predisposed to see what's hard in figure skating may view it a serious, grit-requiring sport. I can laugh at that misconception or occasionally even play off of it for a laugh myself; I'm the first person to describe my brief foray into hockey as a crash course in confirming that I'd rather be twirling around. But maybe my blade scars feed a desire to have a story that sounds more fierce: Do you know what can happen when you put knives on your feet and hurl yourself around backward into the air to land on the mere tip of just one of those blades? It's called perilous, baby, and it's a risk I choose every day.

Spin Out

Sure, whatever; those musings about skate marks started to feel shallow and distant after biopsy marks started to join my collection of freshly ac-quired scars. In 2008, I acquired two on my left breast. One is a small red bump from the first biopsy, an in-office procedure that involved, basically, drilling a little hole to remove suspicious tissue pinpointed by a mam-mogram. The other, an incision mark following the border of my areola about an inch around the top, came from a follow-up biopsy, done in a hospital under sedation, after the first biopsy revealed noncancerous but abnormal, rapidly multiplying cells, or "atypical ductal hyperplasia."

Given the spin I'd concocted for my skating scars, I was surprised by how much I dreaded the incision scar. I was just starting to process sen-tences about abnormality, another biopsy, surgery, the hospital, sedation, and the fact that the word "probably" still modified "not cancer," when I heard myself asking the doctor if the biopsy would leave a scar. Coming so early in the conversation, the question suggested, as the tone of the doctor's response confirmed, that I would factor her answer into my deci-sion about whether to proceed. Actually, I kind of wanted to, even though I knew I shouldn't.

What I didn't ask this time was the question I'd urgently posed to medical personnel when I sprained my wrist six months into skating: How long would I be off the ice? I didn't have to. Six years later, skating was often already a known issue in any given conversation. I remember from right around then the extremely painful discovery upon meeting a lover's close friends that they knew virtually nothing about me. "You figure skate? How interesting." Somehow that seemed a lot more telling than their lack of a clue about my job. My doctor had learned about my skating from the mammogram practitioner, who'd listened graciously when I tried to ward off nerve-racking medical news by telling her that I didn't want to get it right before our ice show. Maybe it was an extra reason that she took the initiative to corral a doctor on that late Friday afternoon, determined not to send me home for the weekend with only a passed-along diagnosis from a radiologist.

I also got unsolicited but extremely welcome advice from my skating friend Mary Squires, who had called me as soon as I e-mailed her about the impending surgery. A veteran of several such biopsies herself, she had two pieces of advice. First, if I was wondering already about whether I should really stay off the ice for the whole week that she knew my doctor would recommend, the answer was yes. That admonition made me smile. It's the tough-skater intense determination that I adore in her. A cliché in coaching and skater interviews involves "attacking" the elements of your skating. She visibly does; that's one reason I find her skating so hot to watch. I was flattered that she knew I needed a little lecture about heeding the doctor's orders. (Actually, the doctor's assistant charged with telling me what to expect gave me a different example: "no vacuuming." It was a convenient illustration of literally the least of my concerns.)

Mary's second bit of advice fit into the tough-girl genre, too. She told me to think of the biopsy scars as battle scars. That one I couldn't even pretend to do, despite so much to help me along: the tough-girl spin on scars already in my repertoire; the cultural commonplace of the cancer "battle"; and my prior assumptions about the feminist models I would emulate in related circumstances. Once the prospect became less abstract, I knew immediately that, should the diagnosis require mastectomy, I'd be no Deena Metzger, the woman defiantly posing open-armed and single breasted in Hella Hamid's iconic 1978 photograph of her, now sometimes known as *The Warrior*. Nor could I even begin to live up to the example of Audre Lorde. Widely credited and associated with the warrior metaphor, she took it far beyond the political position now most commonly linked to it, a feminist defiance of patriarchal beauty standards:

> For me, my scars are an honorable reminder that I may be a casualty in the cosmic war against radiation, animal fat, air pollution, McDonald's hamburgers and Red Dye No, 2, but the fight is still going on, and I am still part of it. I refuse to have my scars hidden or trivialized behind lambs wool or silicone gel. I refuse to be reduced in my own eyes or in the eyes of others from warrior to mere victim.[3]

I was stuck, in contrast, where Lorde puts Eudora, the troubled if knowledgeable character who bore the author's own scars in her 1982 "biomythography" *Zami: A New Spelling of My Name*. Eudora, Audre's older lover, finds her scars "hard to take . . . Not dashing or romantic." It's Audre who calls them a "mark of the Amazon," insists on making love "in the light," and finds herself, through her relationship with Eudora, growing into "a woman connecting with other women in an intricate, complex, and ever-widening network of exchanging strengths."[4] That's precisely the network I caught myself wanting to run from, or at least toward the part of it that embraced feminist cleavage.

Little Knives, Bigger Problems

Skating on little knives. Biopsy scars made me revisit what, in neologizing homage to the term "bootylicious" popularized by the musical group Destiny's Child, I've come to think of as a taste for the perilicious: a certain relish in a kind of risk taking that is delicious to survive and delectable to narrate.[5] I'd always been somewhat embarrassed about my urge to concoct a studlier narrative for figure skating. It made me feel like the idiot that marketers probably had in mind when they decided to sell to skaters little knit gloves under the name HandGards, despite their inability to protect hands from much more than the cold. I know figure skating is plenty hard; why should I care who else does? Worse, what foolish behavior might I undertake in the quest to prove it to myself or to others? The more often I deferred admitting injury, got on the ice even when my body hurt, ignored the familiar twinges signaling use turning to overuse, or skipped the weekly recovery day that athletic wisdom generally recommends—and the more I paid attention to other athletes pushing through pain—the more pride in injury seemed like a slippery slope in the direction of lunatic risk and recklessness about permanent damage. A student once introduced himself on the first day of a seminar by proudly announcing his one hundred trips to the emergency room, many caused by injuries incurred trying to recreate stunts from MTV's aptly named show *Jackass*. The fact that I had come even to fathom his delight disturbed me. Besides, posturing about figure skating's toughness inevitably panders, if indirectly, to the sexism and sexist-related homophobia that contributes mightily to figure skating's reputation as a lightweight endeavor in the first place.

Looking back and forth between the skate scars and the biopsy scars did not eliminate my appetite for the perilicious. It did, however, illuminate nicely, I think, some of the complicated ways that gender and economics figure into risk, choice, and consequences. I take them up further in the next three essays.

21

Parsing Perilicious

"Can't You Waitress with the Other Arm?"

No, you can't. Not if you have a broken collarbone, as surely any medical practitioner who is familiar with the anatomy of collarbones and, presumably, restaurant table service would know. But that's exactly what a doctor asked a Maine Roller Derby player, Patty O'Mean, also known as Crystal Vaccaro, as he was treating the injury that kept her out of work for a month and unable to scrimmage for five months. She could have started blocking and bouting earlier, she told me, if she had stayed out of work until her collarbone healed. But she couldn't, not without paid sick leave or the economic cushion that inherited wealth, moneyed connections, or a higher paying job might have offered. Neither then nor in 2008, when she broke her leg, could she easily access less physically taxing temporary employment; jobs are hard to come by.

Patty's interchange with the doctor reflects, I think, several common disconnects in the realm of physical activity, labor, and health care: between jobs that do and don't allow for accommodations regarding taxing, or newly taxing, physical components (lifting a tray, word processing all day); between people who do and don't notice the physical labor of others, even or especially labor performed on their behalf; between people who can and can't expect to take health care for granted. I use *expect to* as a qualifier to signal both disparities in access to health care—only some people can reasonably presume available services—and possible disparities between expectation and actuality. Insurance coverage runs out, copays and consumer costs add up to far beyond what's expected, new categories like "unemployed" or "preexisting condition" change one's relation to health-care resources.

I think of these disparities often when I read chronicles of skating injuries on Facebook pages like "Figure Skating Will Eventually Kill Me . . . or at least give me arthritis" or "You Might be a Figure Skater if . . ."[6] One skater completes the "if" with "you fill out a medical form for injuries and make a box at the bottom saying: all of the above CHECK!" Another suggests long-term problems she has no reason fully to worry about yet—"your toes just plain WONT [sic] lay flat anymore"—in the context of a presumption of free-flowing resources: "You think that paying $60 for a pair of soccer cleats or $200 for a pair of riding boots is nothing . . . because even that crappy first pair of 'real' skates you got cost over $500 . . . not to mention how much the custom harlicks you have now cost." A third skater answers with, "you have a brace for every body part laying around your house just in case," followed by a long list of injuries. Some answers involved chronic pain, requiring long-term physical therapy, or needed surgery. One skater's comment "I thank god my parents have good medical insurance" represents virtually the only such reference I found on a thread I consulted when it had 585 responses, suggesting how many people in this dangerous sport may take that access for granted. You get injured, you get treated.[7]

Front and Center at the Back of Your Mind

Yet the luxury to assume receiving medical treatment is hardly a precondition of failing to parse perilicious—to itemize the risks and potential consequences of dangerous choices—or of choosing to ignore, or half-ignore, the results of parsing, half-parsing, or beginning to parse. Plenty of people put obstacles in front of fully imagining themselves in worst-case scenarios or lesser permanent consequences. These may include the mix of pleasures that make the risks worth it, like a pleasure in danger, pain, crashes, pile-ups, bragging rights, and risk itself (physical, mental, emotional), as well as a healthy or unhealthy dose of denial, normalization, distancing, and selective memory. Factor in, too, more or less careful and conscious calculations of risk, which depend themselves on all kinds of matters, including skaters' abilities to assess their own talents. I see people on the ice all the time who look like a concussion waiting to happen because they are trying skills beyond them. Yet I know also from how often I've said or heard "I'm tilting how?" or "My arm is where?" that we just may not know what we're doing.

How much evidence we may push away, even when it's staring us in the face, was underscored for me when I first visited the website of Sin City Skates in February 2008. A well-known "derby owned and operated" supply business, its homepage had a prominent link to a site dedicated to fund-raising for Tequila Mockingbird, a Chicago derby player who had severely injured her spinal cord during a bout five months earlier. "Since that day," helptequila.com explained, "Tequila has been in hospitals, re-learning old skills: how to hold a pen, feed herself, and operate her wheel-chair. . . . The injury has limited most of the movement in her limbs, re-stricting her freedom, independence, and most importantly, her ability to work."[8] Reading this account, I wondered if anyone who got to the link as I did, through Sin City, would rethink purchase plans. Tequila's story certainly brought to mind my own risky activities, including one practice that mystifies even many other risk-taking athletes. Unlike other athletes who might easily crash or fall, figure skaters almost universally don't wear helmets, an idiocy that, a jock friend pointed out, I had nor-malized enough not to include in my perilicious boast about skating on little knives.

Maybe some Sin City customers paused. But few, I imagine, walked away from derby, a sport that continues to grow exponentially. Tequila's teammates didn't walk away. Two months after her accident, they earned a place at the WFTDA national championships. Had a different girl been injured, Tequila would have certainly played on, too. She was a battle-scarred veteran of dangerous sports who was planning for more. She had figure skated in childhood, recently recovered from a derby-induced back injury, and contemplated trying amateur boxing in derby's off-season.[9] She saw her accident as an "anomaly."[10] A derby girl should expect to be part of a falling skater pileup, not to have someone's skate land with force on her neck. The latter, she said, was as likely as walking across the street and getting hit by a bus.[11]

That's a common type of reference, I found, for people who partici-pate in dangerous sports. Nancy Theberge noticed its frequency when she interviewed high-level women's hockey players. For them, it served a slightly different point: Hey, life itself is dangerous. That was just one facet of the skaters' complicated attitudes toward the risk, pain, and in-jury involved in their sports. In describing their histories to her, skaters often downplayed these features, omitting, or omitting at first, some big injuries or what they considered routine wear and tear. Yet embracing the danger and consequences was central to their identities as people and players.[12] I found the same mix of responses from derby skaters. For instance, I usually asked skaters if derby was as hard on their knees as it looked. An initial "not really" often belied the ills and injuries they told me about as time went on: knees that never stopped hurting; knees that seemed to house gravel; ligaments that were healing or shot for good, including the famously vulnerable ACL as well as the less-well-known PCLS, and MCLS.

Athletic Supporters

Tequila's accident was as rare in derby as the terrible 2008 pro hockey incident in which the blade of a Florida Panthers' teammate accidentally sliced Richard Zednik's carotid artery, setting off renewed debate (which continued after he recovered and, in the next season, returned to the ice) about whether and for whom neck guards should be mandatory. If both athletes had unusual accidents, however, the situations in which they had them were far from anomalous. Zednik, unlike women competing on any skates at virtually any level, played for an organization that paid him to skate, accommodated recovery from injury as part of the job, and had trainers and a physical therapist on paid staff.[13] Presumably, the Panthers paid for his insurance. Derby players, in contrast, have meager coverage under WFTDA insurance, which is meant to supplement a skater's primary policy.[14] Tequila did not have one. According to an article two years after the accident about an upcoming benefit for her, "Not long out of law school and living under a mountain of debt," despite her lawyer job for the city of Chicago, "[she] did what millions of Americans do. She took a chance and went without." Besides leaving her in debt for emergency care, her lack of coverage, as Tequila emphasized, left recovery aids like physical therapy, "$50 for half an hour," out of reach.[15]

The risks of the perilicious are far from uniform, with divergence across unsurprising lines. Some athletes can afford more expensive protection. More than a few derby girls recounted learning the hard way that instead of scrimping with the $50 knee pads they should have spent twice as much. A high school hockey player whose parents could afford expensive gear told me that she took over as goalie after two predecessors fell to knee injuries. One had required knee and hip replacements that resulted partly from using hand-me-down pads. The women's hockey team that Theberge studied depended on volunteer medical support and went without a trainer during one of the seasons in which she followed them. The competitive cheerleading teams that Kate Torgovnick studied for her book *Cheer!* also frequently practiced without a trainer present, as most do, despite high-risk stunts like somersaulting tosses off human pyramids.[16] This was the case even at schools where trainers attended practices in the other sports, like football, in which breaks and bruises equally constitute badges of honor.[17] Meanwhile, at one school Torgovnick profiled, the team with men on it had more resources than the all-women's squad, and the difference between schools resembled the disparities shown in the film *Bring It On*.[18] In real life, however, the cheerleaders at the historically black institution were trying to get to a separate, less prestigious national championship for schools like theirs, which they eventually had to forgo when they could not find a funding angel. Their coach told Torgovnick, as his team practiced for one shot to win a paid trip to Nationals, "We gotta get that award tomorrow. Otherwise, we'll be calling Oprah."[19] His comment testifies to how taken for granted it is that some teams and competitors have no hope but charity to finance their perilicious pursuits.[20] As his team's situation demonstrated, too, Oprah generally isn't coming.

Then there are the ways that, as with early spotting of talent, support breeds more of it, as some athletic twists in health insurance highlight. For athletes on NCAA college teams, several staged policies supplement their required personal coverage if they are injured: an "excess" policy provided by the school (akin to the "excess" policy WFTDA offers); and a "catastrophic" policy, provided by the NCAA for free to participating institutions, which takes over after the school has paid $75,000. Thus, benefits attend playing a sport as a varsity athlete—or cheering for varsity athletes. Cheerleaders are covered for injuries incurred in connection with cheering at varsity intercollegiate games. But because competitive cheerleading is not a varsity sport, the NCAA doesn't cover cheerleaders for competitions, although perhaps competitors will benefit from cheerleader-safety measures initiated by insurers after discovering that cheerleader injuries accounted for 22 percent of their claims costs.[21]

Additionally, very highly ranked athletes in some sports may qualify for Elite Athlete Health Insurance (EAHI) coverage. The United States Olympic Committee (USOC), for instance, allots coverage for a designated number of athletes in each participating sport. In effect, then, top athletes are also competing to be eligible for insurance coverage. USA Swimming's policy on filling its fifty-six EAHI-eligible slots makes this point clear. It has "tie-breaker" criteria for slots left over after members of the

World Championship Team accept or decline coverage.²² As the case of a former University of Georgia football player, Decory Bryant, illustrates, some athletes have access to other forms of health-related insurance, if they can pay for it. A defensive back with a promising future in the NFL, Bryant had been deemed eligible for the "Exceptional Athlete Student Disability Insurance Program," which protects student athletes against the loss of projected professional income through a career-ending injury. Bryant had such an injury five days after he informed the athletic department that his parents would pay the $5,103 premium to enroll him but before he had a chance to sign the paperwork.²³

Sun-Kissed Heroics

A profile I read of a young Latina figure skater describes her pursuing the sport even though "day after day, the only Latina she sees is her own reflection in the ice." She draws inspiration from her immigrant grandmother, who came from Mexico, packed Sunkist oranges in Fullerton, California, by day, did other jobs at night to make ends meet, and then, before the skater was born, died of cancer at age forty-seven.²⁴ I can't help suspecting that pesticides and overwork—as integrally related to brown skin as her granddaughter's isolation on the ice—abetted her death. As environmental justice activists document, carcinogenic toxins, much more than not, saturate areas inhabited primarily by people who are of color and/or poor.²⁵

Visions meet toxins. From one angle, parsing the perilicious simply gets in the way of pleasure. You don't want to stop so you don't want to know. But that impulse to avoid surfacing risks and costs also threatens to obscure the systemic inequities that extend into and beyond sports, especially when stories of daring, exceptionalism, and triumph sometimes seem to have unmatched appeal, when holders of power benefit from the camouflage, and when their cues may be subtle. In the next piece, I turn from the blade scars to the biopsy scars, using a small incident to elaborate on more and less subtle forces bearing on risk, choice, and inequity.

22

Telling the Mrs.

One little moment of gendered misery that occurred the day of my second biopsy encapsulates for me how multifaceted can be the gendering of risk, choice, and the lack thereof. It involved the doctor tasked with a single job: to insert a needle into my breast, using mammogram films as a guide. The procedure pinpoints what the surgeon should remove when the cells of concern have not formed a palpable, visible lump. In my case, the doctor explained, his was a very tricky job because the location of the cells meant that he had to go in from the side instead of down from the top, which, I could discern, required having to squat or kneel. I can't remember exactly when it happened, but somewhere during his explanation or execution of this task, he called me "Mrs. Rand." Ick. Ordinarily, I would have corrected him. I don't like the presumption in "Mrs." that I am a heterosexual, married lady whose primary identity comes from her husband. Yet I hesitated to risk annoying a guy who, balanced precariously, would have to keep piercing my breast with a needle until he hit a microscopic target.

I have a vivid memory, emotional and visceral, of sinking into silence. Yet I must have corrected him once because the radiology intern asked me, when we were alone between phases of the procedure, if I had a "partner." In other contexts I might have bristled at that, too. I don't like the presumption of marital two-by-twoness as the desired norm, the privileges that attend marriage, or, to be honest, my own susceptibility, especially in situations like this, to the common equation between being unpartnered, which I was at the time, and being pathetically alone. It can be hard to fight the feeling, which cultural clichés stand ready to help you articulate, that the wonderful people gathered to support you are "stepping up to the plate" because you "don't have anyone." But in this context, I knew that the radiologist was using "partner" as a coded reference for "gay." The question was her way to let me know that she had heard me say "not Mrs.," discerned that I might have meant "not straight," and would continue to extend her friendly demeanor.

Old News

In some ways, my encounter with this doctor far from typified my experience. He was the only male doctor of the four that I saw from the first consult through follow-up, and he seemed decidedly old-fashioned. His kindly older-white-guy voice and outfit recalled TV doctors of yore like Marcus Welby MD. In fact, he looked exactly like the guy I had pictured about ten or fifteen years earlier when a girlfriend's sister, about forty at the time, explained to us the source of her by then perpetual haze. Her family doctor, in rural Maine, had prescribed Valium, rather than, say, counseling or divorce, after she confided in him about her loveless marriage to a quietly abusive jerk. Really?

I didn't suspect my doctor of being anything like an overmedicating abuse enabler. But certain behavior did suggest that privilege had helped him evade discovering that he was behind the times on respectful behavior. For instance, after he'd introduced himself from the back or side of my chair, I had to ask him to come around in front of me so that I could associate a human with the disembodied voice; I wanted him to see me as more than a body part, too. Plus, apparently he had never noted that "Ms.," which avoids frontloading marital status, had joined the mainstream or the growing statistical likelihood that his female patients might also have a professional title like "Dr." Only circumstances like these make me want to trumpet that, technically, I do.

Dude Deference

That last point, however, is fraught with its own issues of hierarchy. In standard protocol, Dr. trumps Mrs., Mr., Ms., and Miss. Meanwhile, other people in the very same space as the Drs. and Mrs.'s may be addressed by first names instead (such as, in my procedure room, the radiology technician and her female intern). That version of proper manners suggests a guiding principle that people are due different degrees of deference based on some problematic criteria. For example, I frequently ask my students to consider why custodians and food service workers at

Bates must display their first names on their uniforms, which effectively invite people to use them. Meanwhile, numerous cues, including building directories, course catalogues, prior training, and common practice, direct students to address faculty and some administrators by Professor, Dean, Mr., or Ms. The gesture honors our professional training. But why should we presume what training people who clean or cook have, why should only certain training confer honorifics, and why should training of any kind put some people above others anyway?

Besides, the practice of parceling out honorifics always has problematic resonances and historical echoes. Like many private institutions, Bates has a predominance of well-off, predominantly white, young people among the students, and there is a huge disparity in pay between the majority of faculty and most people on staff (raising the question of why such disparities make any sense either). As a result, the honorific or no honorific divide likens Bates to an affluent household where children learn to address their parents' friends with honorifics but domestic workers by first names. If this analogy seems farfetched, it is justified by the following ratio, observed by many besides me: Students seem comfortable using first-name familiarity with faculty, whether by invitation or presumption, in relatively direct proportion to (1) how much the professor's race and gender might likely match that of the "hired help" and (2) how much the student's own does not. My own early impulse to understand "call me Erica" as a rejection of hierarchy made this correlation hard for me to see until African American colleagues clued me into my white privilege on this matter. They made clear how far from revolutionary it is to participate in practices that encourage rich, white young people to address older black people by their first names.

From this perspective, it is impossible to evaluate a single instance of using honorifics without having others to compare it to. My doctor might well have meant "Mrs." as a gesture of respect. Still, neither the term nor the intention fully reveals his criteria for this deference. Did my apparent age, skin color, or class status have anything to do with it? That last might be harder for him to guess on-site given the equalizer of the hospital gown. But other factors imply it, including, unfortunately, my very appearance for health-care services—particularly services like interventions for small abnormalities detected early by "routine" screenings that are far from routine in the U.S. for the un- or underinsured. Even mainstream news venues like the syndicated Sunday *Parade* magazine announce this disparity these days.[26]

So Gay, So Straight

Yet deferential or not, "Mrs." also roots me into a heterosexual domestic context. When the host of season 3 of *America's Got Talent*, introducing the judges, says "Y'all make some noise for the **gorgeous . . . Mrs. . . . Sharon . . . Osbourne**" he suggests that her primary credential is being married to crazy Ozzy, not her work as a manager, author, producer, and philanthropist as listed in her bio on the website.[27] Of course, Sharon and Ozzy are no Ozzie and Harriet, and married people in a couple may be queer-identified, nonnormatively gendered, or have all kinds of queer relationships to each other. They might even throw around "Mrs." out of perverse delight in a tweaked bow to tradition: Let me do my wifely duties to help you relax, dear, after your hard, hard day at work.

But the doctor's use of "Mrs." suggested no awareness of anything like that. Nor do many references to marriage lately, even or especially when pronounced by advocates of "same-sex marriage," or "marriage equality." To the contrary, as numerous critics have pointed out, the focus on conjugal-couple units has obscured, and for some people replaced, the work of queer communities historically to create, honor, and support diverse social, family, and partnering arrangements, erotic and otherwise.[28]

There is a mighty portion of tradition in the nonetheless specific contemporary moment in which the doctor called me Mrs., a tradition that includes differential access to health care. As Mrs. Rand, I might have health insurance by virtue of my husband's job. Would having access to health care by virtue of a wife's job be any more legitimate, as opposed to criteria like "human being"—especially when a recognition of marital, family, and parental ties depends on matters like race, immigration policies, and economic status?[29]

Gendered Little Prick

One more key factor probably motivated the doctor to call me "Mrs.": my apparent gender normativity. I was highly conscious as I sat in that chair that my opportunity to accept whatever benefits of goodwill "Mrs." had to offer depended on my apparent conformity to a certain model of suitable femininity. That model, like all gender ideals, is bound up with ideals and perceptions related to race, class status, age-appropriate behavior, and sexuality, for which gender, in turn, is often seen to constitute evidence. Because people often use their assessment of gender normativity to gauge sexual orientation—the feminine woman is likely straight; the butch woman is likely not—strangers often assume that I'm straight until they discover otherwise. That discovery may then cause them to revise their impression of my gender normativity if they see "straight" as a criterion for "feminine."

Yet here is something else to consider about conveying gender and sexual normativity in the context I have been describing above. Clad in a hospital gown for "breast surgery," the ability to project one's desired relation to normativity is highly compromised because of limits relating to the very body parts of focus. The requirement to be naked from the waist up under the gown precludes the use of tops, undergarments, or other devices that people may use to shape how their chest appears in terms of matters like volume and cleavage. The term "breast" itself, used universally regarding the bodily site of medical intervention, may grate against one's sex or gender identity. This point may seem most obvious regarding people with breast cancer who were assigned the category "male" at birth and who also identify as male because they generally aren't understood to have "breasts" until they have breast cancer. Otherwise, they have a "chest," not those body parts often labeled "female secondary sex characteristics." (I avoid using "secondary sex characteristic" for the same reason that I referred above not to "men with breast cancer" but to people both assigned and identifying as male. I don't want to imply that body parts determine or fix a truth about sex and gender. To do so disrespects the identities that trans, genderqueer, or otherwise gender nonconforming people may claim; having grown protrusions doesn't disqualify someone from "male" nor necessarily root someone in "female."[30]) But people who are assigned "female" at birth, whether they do or don't identify as women, might also experience a disjunction between their own identity and the physical, medical, and cultural meanings commonly ascribed to breasts as womanly, as I discuss further next.

23

What Sticks Out

During the long mammogram appointment that initiated my biopsies, I stole a breast cancer magazine from the waiting room. I'd been reading an article about Peggy Fleming until I saw that she'd been diagnosed at my age. I panicked. She was forty-nine. I'm forty-nine. She's a skater. I'm a skater. Of course, she's an Olympic champion, and I'm the farthest thing from it. But still. I tried to figure out whether it would be bad luck to keep reading or cosmically worse to act superstitious. I have no idea why theft might have seemed more auspicious. Maybe furtive pilfering complemented the frantic quality of my magical thinking.

I didn't hoard anything else. But my desperate attempt to secure just the right position, literally, in relation to Peggy Fleming's story inaugurated a series of mental interactions with ready-made narratives that I saw just waiting to cast me in them. By the time I had lost the magazine, discovered that I had actually "stolen" a giveaway staple of breast medicine waiting rooms, taken another one, and then lost it again, never to be found or replaced, I had daily relationships with several other narrative predators, including the standard human-interest stories about heroic people pursuing sports during or after illness.

Just Because You're Paranoid . . .

I was actually right that narratives would be waiting to grab me if cancer had detectably done so. Barbara Ehrenreich details many of their components in "Welcome to Cancerland: A Mammogram Leads to a Cult of Pink Kitsch." They include a character with virtually mandatory cheerfulness, supported by "spiritual upward mobility," who follows a path to adult warrior from infantilized patient gifted with a weird profusion of breast cancer teddy bears.[31] Her "battle," which offers many opportunities to maintain or even enhance her feminine charms, is bathed in corporatized pink "awareness."[32] (That awareness now includes "Pink in the Rink" days where male pro hockey players wear pink—which, of course, they would never wear otherwise—to raise money for breast cancer research.) S. Locklain Jain, in her astute "Cancer Butch," calls the inescapable pink a part of the "redoubling of femininity that fissure through the entire biomedical complex of cancer treatments." She also cites "the pamphlets that let women know how soon after mastectomy they can return to 'washing walls,'"[33] encoding the same reigning hypothesis about breast cancer that probably underlay my own experiences of being called "Mrs." and being told when I could resume vacuuming. Breast cancer most likely, and importantly, interrupts a marital caregiver role associated with equations between breasts and nurturing.

Blues in the Pink

Dominant breast-cancer culture depends on assumptions that people who have body parts labeled "breasts" have uniform understandings even about the situation of having them, not to mention the possibility of losing them. They don't. I had been reminded of that a few years earlier when I tried to help find resources for a friend with breast cancer. She'd been frustrated by the apparent disinterest of her health-care providers in addressing, or even acknowledging the possible importance to her, of a matter she cared greatly about: the future of the immense erotic pleasure she got from breast sensation. I thought I had a great contact for her: a friend extremely well connected in the world of sex educators, workers, and artists who had also recently faced breast cancer. But this second friend responded as if (although, of course, who knows) this issue had dropped from her mind with the appearance of cancer. She totally blew me off saying, in effect, "who cares, the point is trying to survive!"

That story bares differences even among women who enjoyed having breasts that, as the coinventor of the Jog Bra put it, came "up and out,"[34] and who saw their breasts as core to their erotic life as female. Yet as Eve Sedgwick notes in the essay "White Glasses," the "formal and folk ideologies around breast cancer" operate "as if the most obvious thing in the world were the defining centrality of her breasts to any woman's sense of her gender identity and integrity."[35] This model didn't work for Sedgwick, who described herself in the essay both as someone who identified, significantly, as a gay man, and as "a woman . . . whose breast eroticism wasn't strong." Overall, her breasts were "relatively peripheral to the complex places where sexuality and gender identity really happen" for her.[36]

That model didn't work for Jain either. The issue came up especially after a first mastectomy, when Jain found herself apparently cast in yet another narrative, courtesy of the warrior images I discussed earlier. Visible scars or having one breast, she wrote, had become so coded as a "radical political statement" that "one breast seemed to force [her] into permanent warrior status."[37] Jain doesn't disavow a radical position on breast cancer: far from it. To the contrary, she offers one in the essay, which updates, extends, and offers a critical homage to Lorde's understanding of breast cancer's gendered and environmental politics. Yet, just as people might embrace a certain masculinity associated with the bra trick but not locate their own masculinity in performing it,[38] she didn't want her radical position located in a display of one-breastedness. Deciding what to do about the situation also involved other issues, among them a gender identity that, while female, having breasts did not support: "Breasts forced me to live in a sort of social drag. Rather than being a welcome harbinger of womanhood, 25 years ago breasts had stolen my tomboy youth. Not only did they require cumbersome bras and add weight and heft that had to be dragged around the soccer field, but they also came with a set of expectations about my behavior."[39] A second mastectomy gave her "an opportunity to have [her] body approximate her body image."[40]

I've heard similar sentiments from several other women who identify to some degree as butch and have had cancer-related mastectomies. Also like Jain, who explained "I did not want to be a guy nor do I experience myself in the wrong body,"[41] they frequently described themselves in contradistinction to another group of people whose uneasy fit between gender identity and breasts lately gets more attention: female-to-male trans men. Trans men may have mastectomies, in that situation commonly called "chest surgery," to help their bodies fit their gender identity. I situated my own impending biopsy in relation to trans men, too, but for different reasons. Jain writes of thinking that maybe her scars "render visible the cultural sacrifice of cancer, showing that, because [she] bore the disease, the six other women of that one in seven stat will escape." She adds, parenthetically, "can I please choose who they will be?" suggesting the convoluted cosmic bargaining that the languages of sacrifice, statistics, and unexpected blessing can produce.[42] I had my own convoluted cosmic bargaining. Hadn't some chest-altering quota been filled in my world by all the people I knew who *wanted* it? It took me a while to realize that my convolution echoed the dubious need versus want opposition used by insurance companies to deny funding for "sex reassignment" procedures. They are generally labeled "elective," a matter of choice, despite the huge evidence that substantial risks to a person's mental and physical health and safety may come from withholding such services.

Feminine Directions

As I've been discussing in *Blade Scars/Biopsy Scars*, narratives and ideologies have material, physical consequences in relation to risk and choice. A proper, heterosexual, light-skinned, well-insured, gender-normative Mrs. Rand has resources at her disposal that may help her catch cancer early; enable her to live farther from carcinogenic toxins; cushion the consequences of her taste for the perilicious; and receive the diverse benefits, not always easy to pinpoint, that accompany deference and respect.

In addition, people advantageously placed in relation to risk and choice are also advantageously placed to shore up the very characteristics that place them advantageously. Jain, Sedgwick, and Ehrenreich, each unserved by it, discuss the huge institutionalized apparatus of care designed to help women with breast cancer preserve the feminine "you" threatened by amputations and other effects of treatment.[43] Implicit in that apparatus are both an acknowledgment of how much gender expression matters and a disregard for anyone whose preferred gender expression deviates from the feminine. As implied by the "Before and After" pictures on the website for the program *Look Good . . . and Feel Better*—a postcancer makeover program that is free to the extent that "free" can describe a service underwritten by companies purveying cosmetics that contain carcinogens—both looking good and feeling better belong, 100 percent, to women heading in feminine directions.[44]

24

Losing Her Manhood

At a conference on Sport, Sexuality, and Culture in the spring of 2009, I had the sports studies version of love at first sight when I saw Katharine Kittredge present a talk called "Losing My Manhood and Losing My Mind: A Female Hockey Player's Experience with Post Concussion Syndrome." The scene had all the ingredients for an intoxicating new crush. Opposites attract, with a twist akin to butch/femme, one of my very favorite kinds of twists. She loved being one of the guys in hockey, so much so that she had generally played on men's teams (figure 13). I loved the girly features of figure skating. But, wait, look how we're exactly the same. We had each found homes in sports known for gendered reputations that, for some people, suggest or enforce stifling stereotypes. For us, instead, they offered access to gender expressions that felt both natural and learned, easy to slip into without thought yet simultaneously a topic of interest, fascination, and analysis. Not only that, we both wanted to affirm the absolute pleasure of what we were doing, even when it came abetted, surrounded, and compromised by some dubious practices and values. We also, I learned later, liked to compare how much we love skating to how much we love sex (a lot), and we shared a determination not to let the tolls of sport deter sex. Of course, we had a few different issues to work around. Hockey players don't need a charming way to say "right now, please, but don't mess up my hair!" when an opportunity arises to have nerve-calming distraction before heading to the rink for a big event. Helmets make that a nonissue.

Cruel Blow

No matter what sports-studies romance might loom, however, Kittredge was more importantly in the throes of a different relation to sports: heartache. Several years earlier she'd developed Post Concussion Syndrome

13. Katharine Kittredge playing with the Tuesday Night Pond Hockey League, Polar Cap Ice Rink, Chenango Bridge, New York, February 2002. Photograph by Alexandra R. Darion. Courtesy of Katharine Kittredge.

(PCS) as a by-product of being "clubbed on the back of the head" during a game. The symptoms, including uncontrollable crying, exhaustion, and a "brain haze," lasted ten months, but one consequence, she was sure, was permanent. She had to quit hockey. She'd thought about it previously, particularly in 2002 after an injury-filled three months, which included two of her five total concussions. She wondered then if it was "worth being supremely happy if the cost is chronic pain," or if she could live with the terrifying risk of more serious head or spinal injuries than she had already incurred.[45] Then, it was worth the risk; this time, it wasn't. Her medical practitioners had concluded that another concussion could bring "catastrophic and permanent brain damage."[46] (By 2010, too many concussions had also taken out a number of derby girls I had interviewed several years earlier who had never anticipated being permanently side-lined by injury.)

From Kittredge's eloquent description of what she found and lost in men's hockey, her decision not to quit after the first scary injuries made total sense to me. A lot was familiar, including the shift from act to iden-tity as she went from being a person who plays hockey to a hockey player: "Like many athletes," she writes, "I had come to see my sport as much more than a physical activity; ice hockey was my 'secret,' my 'true' iden-tity. Although I played many roles in my life (professor, mother, wife, and scholar), for fifteen years I had felt that I was most fully 'myself' on the ice."[47] Plus, I saw my own urge to run from hockey collisions primarily in terms of distaste. It wasn't about prudence, self-protection, or aversion to pain, except that I wanted to avoid wasting on hockey what I had come to see as a finite amount of abuse or even use that vulnerable body parts can handle over a lifetime.

Generation

I could also see more clearly, thanks to Kittredge, how our age-specific re-lations to our jock lives could contribute to making our risk-willingness seem both appealingly ordinary and appealingly distinct from ordinary bad ideology. While she is a half-decade younger than I am, we both grew up before opportunities linked to Title ix could impact our child-hoods much, although compliance requirements led to Kittredge's first encounter with hockey when her college, looking for ways to comply, re-cruited female athletes from other sports to form a women's team. The minimal resources provided to them—like way-oversized jv uniforms to borrow for games only—shows how half-assed gestures to Title ix could be. We both also grew up in families far from involved with sports: watch-ing, doing, or facilitating them. Neither of us had family sports-watching tv time; her family didn't even have a tv. My bit of childhood skating, a sport with an even more precarious hold in the 1970s on the category "sport," was an oddity, unlike my conformity to the long-standing family-and-friends tradition of struggling through gym class. Kittredge did more sports in childhood, including some figure skating, but still with noth-ing like the intense full-family investment more common now—in some families anyway—since the advent of more organized sports for girls and the ramping up of kids' sports in general.

Thus, as Kittredge points out, when we claimed or experienced sports identities that resembled those of the young people around us, we did so without precisely the same sources of origin attributed to their more noxious features. For instance, Kittredge found her identity as an athlete to be as "hopelessly hypermasculine" as that of the college football players in her first-year seminar, a course on "Experiencing College Athletics." Yet her own "attachment to a masculine athletic identity had not come about as a result of [the] years of social pressure and media indoctrination"[48] that she and her students had read about in texts like Messner's "When Bodies Are Weapons." Kittredge, far from being taught or rewarded, had been "scolded, penalized, and shunned" for the kinds of behaviors that concern critics of sports masculinities, like "aggression" and a "willingness to produce and experience pain." She writes, "My family, my coaches, my teammates, the officials and the spectators made it clear that the way that I played sports—the time when I felt most myself, and most alive—was unacceptable and wrong." Thus, playing men's hockey, where men interpreted her as "rational and effective, the kind of guy you wanted on your team" was all the sweeter.[49] It helped her live as the "bi-gendered" person she understood herself to be: happily female in many roles, happily male on the ice.

That doesn't mean, of course, that, by virtue of feeling true, right, and life-enhancing, Kittredge's gender identity, gender expression, and gendered behavior were freer of external influence. She asks without being able to answer whether her masculinity, having been fed later, was "less of a capitulation to societal norms" than that of the other players on her team. One complicating factor in figuring this out is something that, Kittredge notes, she and her students interpreted very differently than Messner had. The athletes he interviewed believed that their success came from natural talent and yet, simultaneously, from intense training. Messner considered this apparent contradiction an "aha" piece of evidence about the successful imposition of bad ideology. Kittredge and her class had a different reaction: sure, of course, so what?

The Best of Times

Maybe that's why pleasures honed through training can seem even more compelling if they are right for you and even more mystifying, deluded, or both if they are not. From the inside, training, means, and models can look like gifts or lifesavers—routes to the person you were meant to be. From the outside, they can look like blindfolds, partly, I think, because what people tweak or set aside of their training may be opaque from the outside, too.

In a way, our pursuits both of the perilicious and of gendered identities in women's skating and men's hockey function a lot like the butch/ femme erotics that I lent to my sports-studies dream date. They can all look so, so regressive: investments in toxic, old practices that should have been banished long ago. A person with a decent critique of sexism shouldn't enjoy masculinity, wear bad-for-your-body-and-mobility high heels, "do roles" that appear to mimic tired straight-person moves, crash into people for fun, risk injury, or twirl around, if not inside archaic costuming, then surrounded by it. The way that pleasures get tied up in what it looks like is one of the recurring topics I return to in the next, penultimate section.

VIII

The Politics of Pleasure

25

Pleasure on Its Face

I started the book describing the beginnings of pleasure. I begin this section near the book's end with a story about the middle of sadness when I melted down on an airplane in the spring of 2008. The occasion actually involved remembering a very funny incident from a decade earlier. One evening, I returned home from work around 10 P.M., exhausted but reluctant to go right from work to sleep without a pleasurable or relaxing interlude. Settling on a plan, I turned on my Hitachi Magic Wand, a popular model of vibrator. Suddenly, all the power in my apartment went out. Had my vibrator done that? What now? I didn't want to call Bates College Campus Security, which took maintenance calls at night for people who lived, as I did, in faculty housing. But after seeking advice from the power company (no, it wasn't their problem) and unsuccessfully trying to locate my handy then-girlfriend, I did. Two guys came over, determined that something had tripped the main switch in the electrical box in the basement, flipped it back on, and climbed the three flights back up to report. I thanked them. They took off.

I should have just gone to sleep. But I couldn't believe that my hitherto reliable vibrator, which I still wanted to use, had been the culprit. I turned it on again. Damn, same result. I decide to find the circuit box myself. But before I could, the lights came back on, and I soon heard a knock. The Campus Security guys were back. Seeing the lights go out again as they walked away, they had returned to remedy the situation and ensure that it didn't recur. One of them said, as they must routinely say to repeat offenders in dorms, "You have a faulty appliance causing these shorts. We'd like to take it away so you won't be tempted to use it again." I told them that I had determined the culprit and would dispose of it on my own. They politely insisted. I promised again. They insisted again, clearly planted at my back door with no intention to budge empty-handed. Finally, too tired to invent a story, or to weigh how widely this juicy tale might circulate, I blurted out, "Look, it's a vibrator, and

I'll throw it right out when you leave." They looked at me quite startled, mumbled OK, and left, taking only the story with them.

Magic Wands, Electrical Shorts

While I hoped they would be discreet, I told the story often myself, and in the conversation I remembered on the plane, from six months before the flight, my friend Paqui had brought it up to me. We had been discussing the recent unexpected deaths of two former colleagues at Bates, where we'd each been teaching by then for about seventeen years. We noted a discrepancy in how people's deaths were narrated on campus. While circumstances exaggerated this contrast between the two people in question now, it seemed to us that straight or partnered dead people tended to be memorialized in some fullness while official communications about people like us, queer, unpartnered, or both, often offer little if any information about erotic and intimate lives. If the person doesn't have a surviving spouse, the Bates "survived by" conventions frequently list only a person's parents, which contributed, we thought, to an impoverished, straight-ified public image of the Bates "community" that bore insufficient witness to important social, intimate, and erotic lives and networks.

What could we do about that? We discussed one idea. When a current or retired Bates faculty member dies, a colleague offers a tribute to that person at a subsequent faculty meeting in a "Memorial Minute," so called because the text is entered into the meeting's official record, or "minutes." I told Paqui that if I died early, I wanted her to ensure that my Memorial Minute made clear, whether or not I died single, that I had had a rich erotic and personal life, with friends, lovers, and family who might not fit into the ordinary "survived-by" narrative. She agreed, suggesting that the story of blowing out the electricity would be great to include. Of course, to some people vibrators suggest lonely solo operations, but only if one understands masturbation or sexual "aids" as sorry substitutes, used only in the absence of sex with another human being. Besides, other stories could be more erotically peopled, and wouldn't it be great to inject a little heat into the genre of after-life narratives? Rarely does such eulogizing do more than gesture obliquely to erotic life through reference to long-term spousal partners.

Six months later, on that plane, the conversation with Paqui came back to me. This time, I was thinking less about workplace exclusion than about what I would really want said about me. I realized that if I died after Paqui and I retired, someone younger would give my Memorial Minute. I thought of another friend on the faculty who would enjoy the Magic Wand story, immediately understand what Paqui and I had been riled about, and agree to follow my directives. It seemed imperative to contact Rebecca as soon as I got home, just in case. When I started to imagine telling her, however, I started to cry and couldn't stop. By the time I had wept silently from one U.S. coast to another, I was forced to admit something that should have long been obvious. During a sabbatical year spent in participant-observation research about pleasure, I was actually quite depressed—and unknowingly six weeks away from a sequence of blind-sides that I came to shorthand by month: May June July August September: biopsy, biopsy, break-up, sprained ankle, unexpected move. None were so bad, but they kept me reeling.

The Limits of Pleasure

I offer this story for two reasons. The first must come partly from being enculturated in the glass-breaking, horseradish-dispensing Jewish tradition dictating that you must never celebrate or be happy without having evil, injustice, destruction, regret, repentance, sorrow, and mourning right in front of you. I could not transmit seemingly innumerable testimonials, mine included, about how wonderful skating can be without a compulsion to serve the bitter with the sweet. Figure skating is a luxury. Few people have or can conjure the resources. Even if you can, the touted magic often fails. Skaters may disappear into depression or be thinking about ending their lives. Maybe they do it. Physical movement practices don't guarantee health as is often promised, even setting aside the injury, overtraining, and stress that athletic pursuits can cause. The men I knew who dropped dead in or near their fifties from unanticipated heart attacks (more sadness here) include a nationally medaling "senior athlete" and people with regular, moderate routines, including that heart-healthy cardio.

Besides, as my interview with Alyn Libman emphasized, skating is never separable from what you bring to it. Libman is a trans man who started figure skating at five. He was attracted to the challenge of jumping after his mother refused to let him play hockey; girls shouldn't play sports, she said, where you might get your teeth knocked out. Although unwelcome gender dictates appeared long before he figured out he was trans—judges advising him to skate more femininely; clothes he didn't want to wear—he also found something of a safe haven at the rink. He was allowed not to compete to "girl music." He ran into less trouble there than elsewhere for certain masculine-coded, aggressive, risk-taking behaviors. He felt safe in an environment full of gay men from the brutalizing harassment that increasingly characterized his life outside the rink, based on perceptions that he was a dyke, which for a while he thought he was. But that didn't mean that he could thereby ignore or easily humor increasing pressures to present himself as feminine. Nor could he leave the effects of harassment at the rink door. The physical injuries of gay bashing sometimes affected his ability to skate. (This is only one way, of course, that injuries and deprivations attending diverse injustices may affect athletic abilities. Susie Bright quotes her mother describing the permanent damage of a long childhood illness, rheumatic fever, that weakened her heart: "'I used to be the fastest girl on the block—I could outrun everyone, even the boys—but after I was sick I couldn't run anymore.'" Her mother was reticent, Bright suggests, to vocalize having had a disease of poverty. She didn't say, Bright writes, "'My mom died when I was almost thirteen, and we were home alone without food.' It was then that she became so ill and unable to run anymore.")[1]

Besides, Libman, noted in our discussion, the mind-sets of refuge and stress relief can be largely incompatible with the mind-set that is needed for training. As I know, too, from both my own skating and my work with beginning adults, skating may fail to serve as a break for reasons on both sides of the project and across the spectrum of skating and problems. Taking months to accomplish a 3-turn can make skating feel not so different than your frustrating job, which you can't always put behind you anyway.

It Looks Like Fun

Second, my meltdown, while not about skating, was bound up with, and transformed, my thinking about a central topic of the book: the look of pleasure from outside. It was an issue I faced frequently in fieldwork, as I worked to move from seeing toward getting. Sometimes distinctions between them were obvious and hilarious, like the week I skated at a snotty, expensive skating club out of town where I imagined that I had happened upon the scene of a reality show called *Gigolos on Ice*. I knew that what I had actually registered was my rage at how cold those well-preserved ladies and their male dance coaches had been to me. I was angry enough to forget that, should my perception have been accurate, I don't actually look down on sex for hire if all parties are into it. Sometimes the getting was sobering, including my great sadness upon learning a month after someone told me why he loved skating that he had taken his own life. I also dealt with seeing and getting as the person being seen—especially as I tried to discern the costs and assessments of my gender presentation.

Yet it was dealing with one particular source of personal misery that helped me understand something important that I might not have understood otherwise about how thorny relations between seeing and getting can be. Several years after ending a long-term relationship, I'd become convinced that the only people interested in dating me were substantially younger; in some former or otherwise complicated relation to female (trans, genderqueer, intersex); short-haul; and, most recently—for a year and a total of two people, and in a bizarre coincidence for the whitest state in the nation—Asian. I had no problem with those characteristics in one lover or one relationship, or even a few. All are fine, great. I wouldn't have traded away those connections: the joys of variety, the new, and the fleeting, which were precisely what I wanted for a while; the chance to get picked up at the gym or to develop enduring ties with people that might far outlast the realm of dating. I also knew why my recent life could look enviable, given what many people, my age or not, partnered or not, often go without.

But I didn't prefer young, Asian, not-female partners—only the last even hinted at a preference, for a sizable portion of queer masculinity—and I hated possibly looking like I did. At the time, the press was enshrining "cougar," *Time*'s top buzzword of 2007, with its foul implication that only as predators—never as objects of pursuit or even as people whose interest might be happily received—might middle-aged women garner the erotic attention of younger (or really any) people; both the desires of and the desires for not-young women are routinely stigmatized and ridiculed.[2] I didn't want to look pathetic, or, even worse, creepy and disrespectfully fetishistic. I understood why both people of Asian origin or descent that I dated wanted to make sure right away that I didn't have "Yellow Fever." My answer when one, learning about the other, asked, "Wait, do you like Asians?" could only be messy: "NO!" [I don't fetishize

Asians]. "No, YES!" [I'm not a racist who doesn't like Asians]. "But NO, not like that . . . hey, *you* asked *me* out." It reflects the way that historical echoes of bigotry, oppression, and exoticizing inevitably inform cross-racial attachments.

But do they necessarily poison them? I didn't want to disavow or condemn participating in affiliations that crossed boundaries such as age, race, or relation to gender normativity or that challenged traditional notions—now presented as progressive by "marriage equality" movements—that long-term, two-person partnering represents the pinnacle of joy, success, maturity, and morality. I just didn't necessarily want to spend the rest of my personal life representing for the unconventional. I became obsessed with wondering who might otherwise be trying to hook me up with their exciting friend, sister, or self if they weren't misreading my patterns as preferences. I became even more miserable as evidence mounted that even close friends were doing so. The lack of judgmentalism that I'd relished earlier now sometimes seemed to prevent them from really hearing how my life was going for me. By the time I hit a Thanksgiving weekend so spectacularly disastrous in girl-on-the-side odd-girl-outness that it could easily ground a sequel to *Home for the Holidays*, I wanted to smack the next person who said "Go, girl!" to me about the young ones or who sought to remind me from within a long-standing relationship—in the same exact words and in the same exact tone (wistful yet stern, sympathetic yet all-knowing)—that "the trade-offs are profound." Besides, there was no holiday movie turn-around in sight.

Expansive Openness Revisited

I've argued throughout this book for expansive openness to accounts of pleasures—twirling around, crashing into people—that remain opaque as pleasure if they don't pleasure you. I remain a staunch advocate of that position, even more so after, in order to fulfill the "service" requirements of my job, I got myself appointed to the Bates Committee on Athletics in 2008. Among its charges, the AC works on apparent conflicts between athletics and academics, most obviously matters like scheduling but also on perceptions about values and priorities. Some colleagues, or at least it seemed so to me, were prone to see bad ideology when they couldn't fathom why athletes did what they did. One even suggested that enthusiastically endorsing a desire to win was "dangerously close" to "endorsing winning at all costs" as opposed to focusing on students' health and education. To me, that seemed like shocking bigotry, "dangerously close" in logic, I suggested, to the notion that if you let gay people marry each other, the next thing you know we'll be trying to legalize hooking up with children or animals. What suspicious outsiders may view as a likely terminus to a slippery slope can be easily identified as an outlier crime from the inside. It can also be recognized as such from the outside if you advance some goodwill and benefit of the doubt toward pursuits, desires, or people that may seem alien.

My colleague thought my analogy was crap. But I still believe it. As a result of having come late to an athlete identity, I'd been on that mystified outside myself. Now that I have a coach, and I count athletes and coaches among my cohorts, not just pals, I have a different perspective on numerous matters. For example, once you've heard, or told, a lot of gleeful stories like, "did I tell you about the time I tried to play with two sprained ankles?!" it becomes clear that apparent spectacles of evil coaches ordering injured athletes to perform anyway can actually involve a range of situations, including the one in that story where the coach chewed out and benched the player. It's not that evil coaches don't exist or that sports practices never promote questionable values and behaviors. But that's hardly the whole story about coaches any more than is the whole story about professors represented by tales of the evil ones who change up and add requirements at whim, as if only their courses matter.

Yet my off-ice blues kept reminding me about how opaque pleasures can be even if you're open to seeing them, maybe even because you're open to seeing them or even if you're inside them. For example, what do patterns mean? Repetition complicates liking—how it looks, how it feels—and not in consistent ways. Personally, I love being the object of someone's taste for queer femmes, which makes me feel well recognized and possibly in for a great time; I dislike hearing "I like older women," which I generally find both slick and uninteresting (even though I like older women); and I hate suspecting that I'm the latest in a string of exoticized Jews.

Plus, the objects, meanings, and content of wanting and satisfaction are changeable. I thought I wanted black skates for fashion, but really (or was it later?) I just wanted my friend back, and maybe Chicago. Even the most attentive person, being very attentive right then, may not be able to read you. "I want you to know," Ivan Coyote says in "To All the Kick Ass,

Beautiful Fierce Femmes Out There . . . ," "that I know it is not always easy to love me. That sometimes my chest is a field full of landmines and where you went last night you can't go tomorrow. There is no manual, no roadmap, no helpline you can call. My body does not come with instructions, and sometimes even I don't know what to do with it."[3]

Sometimes, attentive people have big, understandable reasons for not quite being there. I could have factored my friends' own desires and sadnesses into their misperceptions if I'd been in any shape to mediate betrayed with empathetic. Our contexts and histories inevitably color our perceptions. Susan Young, for instance, who took up adult figure skating after training in ballet and before she took up boxing, found in the shift to skating a release from problems that some skaters locate right in the middle of it: demands to perform ethereality and tacit support of unhealthily acquired skinniness. She saw instead support for females unabashedly to display muscles, "frank athleticism," and "unbridled aggressive power." It was the push to camouflage all of those that had stood out to me.[4]

26

Politics at Hand

At the Gay Games Opening Ceremony in Chicago, Staceyann Chin performed a "speech/poem," as she called it, that addressed the inequities that a celebratory Gay Games both ignores and depends on ignoring. "The companies that sponsor our events / do not honor the way we live or love / or dance or pray." We celebrate in leisure as "in India / in China / in South America a small child cuts the cloth / to construct you a new shirt / a new shoe / an old lifestyle held upright / by the engineered hunger and misuse of impoverished lives." Whether as athletes, prime movers, or invited performers, she emphasized, we all support or benefit to some degree from mainstream, monied gay movements that often seek to understand and fight antigay prejudice in isolation of other oppressions: *"fuck you-you-fucking-racist-sexist-turd / fuck you for wanting to talk about homophobia / while you exploit the desperation of undocumented immigrants / to clean your hallways / bathe your children and cook your dinner / for less than you and I spend on our tax deductible lunch!"*[5]

Exclusion, Oppression, Expression, Intrusion?

I found her performance to be a highlight of the ceremony. At the rink the next day, however, as I first met the other skaters, I learned that many had reacted to her with disinterest, inattention, and disapproval. (In fact, that was a great lesson about maintaining flexible research agendas because an absolutely unanticipated query, "What did you think of Staceyann Chin's performance?" turned out to be a helpful route to much else that interested me.) Many skaters, especially white, affluent middle-aged men, criticized her for impoliteness, inappropriateness, and lack of civility: Who was that angry woman?—a question I took tacitly to mean sometimes "who is that angry black woman?" Why did she have to use the "F word" especially when this program was televised? This is the wrong time and place for a rant like that.

I thought it was precisely the right time. Her performance hardly represented, as some of her critics implied, the intrusion of downer politics into the scene. For one thing, the first two "acts" of the four-hour (!) ceremony were called "Exclusion" and "Oppression." There were also "Expression" and "Ignition"; the Gay Games, following the Olympics, has a flame. All placed the Games in a political context.

Yet as Karen Lambert notes about the Opening Ceremony at the 2002 Gay Games in Sydney, such ceremonies are designed to create a sense of exhilarating unity, community, and possibility that also often functions as a powerful agent and obscurer of white dominance.[6] Chin's performance punctured that aura. It also provided a counter to some troubling political matters obscured by celebratory glitter and routed through conventions that dominate sports events. One of the most glaring examples, I thought, lay in fawning praise for Chicago's mayor, Richard M. Daley, as a friend of the gays. Yes, it's standard to thank mayoral hosts, and "welcome, hordes of nonheterosexuals," is still no civic stance to take for granted. Yet Daley was in the news at the time for having known about but failed to act against the torture of black men in police custody during his tenure as Cook County's state's attorney, a position he held in the 1980s.[7] Lauding him repeatedly as a liberator illustrated the narrow-focused vision that Chin criticized. The seemingly unmitigated satisfaction in delivering the praise suggested that an impolite response was more than in order.

Star Spangled Rock-Out

Sports events do a lot to naturalize patriotism, along with more localized loyalties, and harness athletic enthusiasm to it. At international skating events, competitors represent their countries. At USFS events, including Adult Nationals, announcers call out skaters' club affiliations, if they have one. I have to admit that skating out to begin my program as the announcer says, "She represents the North Atlantic Figure Skating Club in Falmouth, Maine," in the same intonation I'd heard often on TV, was one of those moments when I felt hailed, if a bit surreally, as a serious skater. The Gay Games follows the Olympics in having athletes process into the Opening Ceremony by country. In Chicago, athletes from the United States also processed by state—thus my skirt instead of shorts appeared gigantic on the Jumbotron as it projected our tiny, three-person Maine contingent. In the Closing Ceremony, also like in the Olympics, athletes enter the stadium together to represent international harmony generated through sport.

I won't itemize the myriad issues involved in presuming and promoting patriotism. But I do think that patriotism is a matter that demands thoughtful reflection about the country that one declares loyalty to, as well as the context and manner of displaying it. I was disturbed, then, at the Closing Ceremony, when the pop rock band Betty, famous for *The L-Word* theme song, rocked out to "The Star-Spangled Banner" dressed in sexy remade stars-and-stripes. Although I didn't yet know it, I was actually seeing something relatively common to nonmainstream sporting events. For example, the authors of *Down and Derby*, who played with the L.A. Derby Dolls, write that, at the Dolls' bouts, "'The Star-Spangled Banner' has been performed by everyone from transgendered celebrity Alexis Arquette to a band of female kazoo players to Gene Simmons [from the band Kiss]. Tonight it's an adorable local singer named Audra Mae with a sparkly smile and a voice like velvet. She belts out the patriotic tune like a modern day Bessie Smith."[8]

As their description indicates, performances of the anthem can marshal the deviant, the fabulous, and the outrageous. They can parade local and national talent. They can invite conventional sentiment or playful variations on fist-pumping enthusiasm. At a local demolition derby in Scarborough, Maine, and a Rose City Rollers event in Portland, Oregon, I saw a driver and skater, respectively, race their track as the anthem played, waving the flag. While the *Down and Derby* account works to legitimate the sport both as unconventional and as sport—we play the anthem, too, but check out how!—playful, queered-up, campy renditions also work to legitimate and sometimes to pressure rocking out to patriotisms, often without regard for the particulars of time and place. To me, as a person opposed to current U.S. military actions among other matters, any performance of the anthem at the Gay Games Closing Ceremony suggested the harmonizing of sport with imperialism, a gesture ill-suited in any case to the theme of harmony across borders emphasized in the Gay Games VII motto, "Where the World Meets."

Sports don't require ceremonies to bring politics to fun. Sports pleasures, like other pleasures, never float free. To the contrary, as numerous critics have emphasized, many pleasures, along with the very concept of leisure time itself, owe much of their development and characteristics to those who benefit from inequities in current regimes of power. It's hardly accidental that discipline, time management, and rules—more conducive than unruly debauchery to worker productivity—loom large in so many activities marked as fun. Nor is it surprising that consumer-driven, lifestyle identities and *So You Think You Can Dance* receive more public attention than anti-imperialist activism. In sports, too, consider the purse strings, although nothing is ever as simple as who holds them. As Richard Gruneau and David Whitson write, and deftly illustrate, in *Hockey Night in Canada: Sport, Identities, and Cultural Politics*, the history of modern sport has always involved struggle with much at stake: "about power and privilege; about whose values count and whose do not; about who gains advantage from certain changes in technology, values, or patterns of social organization, and who is disadvantaged," about "legitimate uses of time and the human body."[9]

I've been writing about these factors in figure skating. One trained toe-point hits most of them. I offer here an example from another sport, snowboarding. In 2009 the beverage company Red Bull built Shaun White his own secret half-pipe course "deep in the back country of Colorado . . . sculpted out of the rugged San Juan mountains" to invent new snowboarding tricks for the 2010 Winter Olympics.[10] Like many highly, here arguably obscenely, capitalized training strategies, it worked. He won both a gold medal and, it turned out, immunity from being disciplined for disrespect after he played air guitar while the anthem played at his medal ceremony. Although NBC deleted White's strumming in replays—at the Olympics, unlike the venues I discussed earlier, there is an expectation of uniformly displayed solemnity—coverage continued to lionize him and he faced no official reprimand or other consequences. It was a far different situation than when John Carlos and Tommie Smith were ejected for their famous Black Power salute at the 1968 Olympics. The dividing line isn't simply about deviating for fun versus politics; the Nazi salute, allegedly for being a nation's official anthem choreography, had stood in 1936.

Red Bull's *Project X* video suggests how Shaun White, if of course much more subtly and less harmfully, might be seen to illustrate raced nationalist ideals as well. As a lone helicopter flies over the mountains to deposit a lone athlete in the snow—virgin apart from Red Bull's intervention—the deep voiceover describes the "superpipe" as the "foundation for a training ground that would test the limits of both man and machine." Technological prowess marries sports individualism to intrepid (white) American frontiersmen and manifest destiny. Kyle Kusz suggests that this is precisely what the rise of extreme sports in the 1990s was about. Amid growing perceptions that white men and white masculinity were embattled, both within and outside sports, white men showed their control over themselves and their environment by risking death in acts of daring at first and still mostly performed by them alone.[11]

Norms in Action

Those are big-picture forces dramatically rendered that apply to athletes at diverse levels of involvement. Sedimented histories of recreation, professionalization, and ideas about who can represent the glory of the nation still affect who gets ice time. Dubious criteria for health care—like personal wealth or a link to "benefits" through work or legitimated affectional ties—ensure that the possible consequences of risk taking are ill distributed. The thrill, the danger, the exhilaration, the satisfaction—they wouldn't be for everyone even if the appeal were universal.

There is also important information to be found in the smaller moments, the day to day. Sara Ahmed argues that the study of emotions can help to show how people "become invested in particular structures," as well as institutions, values, and entities.[12] I had a vivid experience that seemed to crystallize the sometimes baffling connection between investments and emotions as I was watching a scene in the movie RISE. The movie is about a 1961 plane crash that killed the entire U.S. figure skating team on its way to the World Championships, and the rebuilding, or "RISE," of U.S. skating from the ashes of that crash. The concept is visible on the souvenir ticket (figure 14) that people with a ticket stub from the premier could trade the ticket stub in for, receiving a pin in trade, too, after completing an online survey, and, USFS hoped, adding in a donation. I saw the movie at the premiere myself, which involved a giant simulcast on February 17, 2011, involving 525 movie theaters across the country.

14. Commemorative ticket and pin from *RISE*, acquired by sending in my ticket stub from the simulcast premier in February 2011. Photograph by Paul Heroux.

The scene in question here involved the famous coach, Frank Carroll—himself a student of Maribel Vinson Owen, who died in the crash. As Carroll stands at the boards watching his student Evan Lysacek compete, viewers can discern his lips move, counting. While people outside skating might think Carroll was counting (badly) to the music, insiders would recognize that he was counting spin revolutions, making sure that Lysacek had enough in each position to get credit according to the IJS Code of Points. He could hardly have enjoyed the impetus to do so. As I've said before, IJS is widely despised. Carroll has spoken against it, and no one I know likes it, certainly not Ann, my own coach. Yet as I sat there next to her, watching the movie, with another friend she coaches and in a theater filled with people we know who are involved in skating around Maine, I couldn't help turning to her with a smile. Hey, just yesterday she was counting my own revolutions, yelling them out so I wouldn't stop short. It's a good example of how hated tools of body management may also generate a sense of belonging bred of familiarity, insider knowledge, shared misery, and the mixed pleasure and pain to be found in obedience to a strict mistress.

With figure skating, I think, investments often involve gendered norms about appearance, movement, and behavior, more and less explicitly involving class(iness), sexuality, and race. These also feature regularly in narratives or decisions about buy-in. One adult skater I met located her turn toward the serious in entertaining her coach's insistence that she would skate better if she practiced in a skirt. "Of course, he turned out to be right," she told me. Bryan Smith described in *Men's Health* overcoming the mental barrier of the outstretched arms: "'Do I have to do the arm thing?' I asked. 'I'm afraid so,' [my coach] said, adding with a smile, 'if you want to skate like me.'"[13] I saw the reluctance about those arms repeatedly as a volunteer coaching assistant. Especially when you put one arm forward and one behind you to learn crossovers, they can suggest a desire to display lovely manicured nails. For beginning female skaters who identified or presented themselves as butch, or otherwise masculine or nonfeminine, that pose could be like the local availability of white figure skates only, inducing someone to quit early or never get started.

Skating, of course, is only one facet of life where being the right or wrong kind of girl can bring censure, shame, violence, reward, satisfaction, excitement, or comfort. Norms circulate locally, nationally, and across borders. They invite and regulate our participation daily in innumerable contexts: at school, work, and play; as consumers and political actors; with friends, lovers, family members, acquaintances, and strangers. They create, meet, and frustrate our needs and desires with an intensity that is often challenging to explain and, consequently, I think, important to look at in both macro and micro moments of operation.[14]

27

Getting the Goods

As I frequently tell my students, I still follow a rule I learned from one of my English teachers at Evanston Township High School (Mrs. Lawler, Mr. Foote, or Mr. Reque): A conclusion should answer the question "so what?" I thought about "so what" often during this project especially as I formulated descriptions of it for others. For years, I'd imagined myself as a public, unabashed fan of pleasure. I ask students to think about whether high heels really do always signal oppression and whether abstaining from erotic activity can really improve your game, your thinking, or your writing—a superstition about squandering energy that pops up all over from Baudelaire to the derby girl who told me that her prebout ritual involved twenty-four hours of "no." I've argued in my scholarship that we may dehumanize, disrespect, and misinterpret the people we study if we view them apart from, duped by, or simplistic in their pleasures. I've persisted, despite sometimes being viciously attacked for it, in being forthright about when my own embodied pleasures have lubricated my intellectual pursuits. I oppose presenting scholars and critics as disengaged entities floating about their material.

Yet once I became immersed in this project, I discovered that my adamant pro-sex, pro-pleasure stance had more cracks than old patent leather. It depended, apparently, on confidence that others perceived oppression to be my primary concern. I had usually been able to gesture to noble, difficult freedom struggles in a word or two about my research: Ellis Island, gender policing, antiracist pedagogy, censorship, the religious right, the French Revolution, even Barbie, whose potentially toxic effects are so patent as to carry the promise of exposé in the mention of her name. "I'm writing about figure skating" simply doesn't work that way.

Laundry Disservice

Grappling with my own somewhat fraudulent relation to pleasure affected this project in several ways. For a while, both in pursuing and in representing my work, I emphasized the political issues beyond pleasure that studying pleasure could help me address. I was writing, I said, about "the politics of pleasure." In fact, I was.

Yet I also became concerned about what happens to pleasure in directing it to that end, which a comment by Ratowe T. Ampu, in an essay about his stint with the queer African American hip-hop group Deep Dickollective (D/DC), helped me think about. Writing about what he considered lazy academic flattery that failed to look critically at D/DC's relation to masculine privilege, he remarked, "It seems like I've found where street cred . . . meets academia . . . and they launder each other's privilege."[15] Each offers the appearance of legitimacy to the other, helping to hide the dirt.

I find Ampu's concept of laundering very helpful, and I think it can be extended in several ways. The first concerns the function of laundering on politics. While Ampu writes about laundering privilege by failing to deploy critical tools, the use of such tools, although surely better than not using them, may also constitute a form of laundering akin to cause-related marketing. Donate a bit to cancer research and continue to sell cosmetics with carcinogens; notice all the white people at the rink and buy yourself permission to skate your life away.[16] The second concerns the function of laundering on pleasure, which can be distorted or diminished even through using "the politics of pleasure" as an explanatory, justifying phrase. Pleasure and politics; art and science; sex and war; twirling and defense (as in *off*ense versus *def*ense): the first term in each pair has been denigrated in numerous contexts for allegedly feminine attributes. The more I reflected on noxious antifemininity, the more I suspected that while truly interested in the politics of pleasure I was touting that interest to butch up my topic in a way that validated a long history of dubious, gender-weighted dichotomies.

More important, I began to see more clearly as my research progressed what rushing to foreground the politics could short-circuit and, conversely, what dwelling in and on pleasure might accomplish. For example, the coaching encounters I used in the last section to illustrate the policing function of norms can also illustrate using knowledge to abet pleasure. Once I recognized—using my well-honed butchdar, pleasurably gleaned itself—that discomfort about the manicure position could involve something different than the challenge of mastering the unfamiliar, I came up with a few strategies to help skaters who wanted to quit rather than display it. I could explain the practical benefits of the extension, moving it from the category of alien aesthetic to the category of tool. Sometimes a conceptual shift can go a long way. Or I could help them work toward avoiding that extension. It's clear from watching people learn to skate in contexts geared to hockey or speed skating that skaters can stroke forward and do crossovers without it as long as they can do what that arm position facilitates: engaging core muscles, balancing, and, with crossovers, turning one's upper body toward the inside of the curve. Yet in beginning figure skating, those arm extensions, which some tricks and turns definitely do require, are often presented as always necessary until skaters advance enough to be deemed ready to abandon them occasionally, sometimes to our great confusion. Thus, during a class at one of those adult skater training weekends I attended, the famous coach Nikolai Morozov, half-laughing, half-scolding, tried to impress on us that we could now traverse the rink with quite a bit more fluidity and discretion in arm position, varying the one we had all dutifully assumed for him—even if, as in my case, our own coaches had already been drilling the same point.

So What?

A few happy skaters can hardly constitute the sufficient result—political, intellectual, or otherwise—of participant-observation research on pleasure. Yet I want to ask what it means, metaphorically speaking, to skate right past them. What pleasures might be possible to have or to spread if we dwelled in and on them? What else might change? What could work environments be like? Many of them, and academics in general, seem to promote a culture of bonus points for misery: How was your weekend? Ugh, I graded fifty papers. That's nothing: I graded seventy-five and wrote a conference paper. As my good friend and downstairs neighbor, Wendy Chapkis, reminds me repeatedly, we collude in whittling away gains that labor activists fought for when, even with tenure, we fail to challenge the extras-turned-tacit-job-description that result in our seven-day workweeks. Plus, what might be different in the world if more people could say on more occasions "wow, you really like that" with interest rather than judgment? How many ills, like the legion born of sex panic—oh no, the perverts are coming!—would lose their fire?

I don't mean to pose the glories of connection and understanding, across gulfs or otherwise, as always good. Idealizations of community and common bonds can obscure the injustices that those may perpetuate.[17] My figure skating communities, which sometimes feel like family in the best of ways, show easily what may be glazed over. They offer a chance to make community across incompatibilities. But that opportunity requires cash to participate and not-so-infrequent decisions to let not-so-sleeping issues lie. But I do not then yield pleasure as ancillary to social change. As Ahmed suggests, understanding what other people's lives are about—including their pains and their pleasures—is integral to making connections for social justice work that recognize people's histories, humanity, vision, and desires. Visceral pleasures, aesthetic interests, "freedom dreams," and the ecstatic, as Robin D. G. Kelley argues, deserve honor and visibility in our pasts, our presents, and our visions of possible futures.[18]

Nor do I want to dismiss automatically the bits of pleasure and small interventions that may have troubling features and seem insufficient in scope. Yes, Oprah-like largesse carries the wrong, big message. It's a message that is common within the now-dominant practices known as neo-liberalism, which suggest that private funding, self-help strategies, and boosts for a very few people are appropriate correctives for structural problems that the correctives then obscure.[19] One of Oprah's own signature moves, Janice Peck argues in *Age of Oprah: Cultural Icon for the Neoliberal Era*, is to depoliticize what she intervenes in.[20]

Then there's more devil in the details. Mimi Nguyen presents a great model for considering how in her essay on the beautician training brought to Kabul, Afghanistan, in 2003. As she demonstrates, it worked to justify the recent invasion—and mask the complicity of the U. S. in the rise of the Taliban—by portraying the women as victims being rescued into good hair, commercial success, self-esteem, and individual freedom. Yet freedom apparently doesn't include the freedom to enjoy heavy makeup and glitter. The "correct exercise of freedom," it seems, should result in a controlled, modest look, not one that critics of the women's pretraining tastes associated with adolescence and drag queens; artifice, play, and the queer-labeled do not belong.[21] Every makeover segment on

TV—whether turning gang members into secretaries, punks into prom queens, frumpy moms into fashionable wives, or tomboys into ladies—carries a similar promise that freedom comes from acceding to dominant norms. (An amusing example of redirection as "freedom" comes from that class I took about the rigid arms. Morozov tried to cure us of them, not by asking us to use them freely exactly, but by assigning choreographed movements that represented hanging loose. When you cross your leg over just so, swing your arms just like this. To be honest, it proved quite helpful as a path to breaking rigid habits.)

Yet dwelling on pleasures, including my own, made me rethink what it means to toss away opportunities for other people that I used to judge primarily on how tainted they were by bad politics. Should people who depend on largesse for lipstick, beautician training, playing time, or a chance to skate in their own recital not get to have them because it's foul, which it is, to force people to depend on aristocratic hand-downs even for basic needs? Those systematic inequities won't end any time soon, and I don't want to assume that people receiving enculturation in U.S. supremacy, bootstrap individualism, leg-crossing modesty, or, to the contrary, routinized panty flashing will take away precisely that.

What about all those people, seemingly all over, who find ways to sing, dance, twirl, act, write, make art, play music, or put on a show? My friend Lise's kids attended an Iowa public high school that didn't teach Shakespeare in English class but brought in two choreographers from out of state and spent about $4,000 to rent costumes for 100 of the 250 kids to perform *Beauty and the Beast*; they packed the 1,000-seat theater for 4 nights. My dental hygienist coaches baton-twirling teams a few highway exits south in the town where she grew up twirling herself; in 2010 one team twirled to "L'chaim" from *Fiddler on the Roof*. People compete on *America's Got Talent* from various stages of prior training and in a crazy array of acts: the yodeling dominatrix; the groomed-into-hyper-adorable kids; the rural burlesquing moms; the Shakira impersonator; all manner of singers and dancers hailing from poverty, training, shared workplaces, or all three. Who gets to decide what constitutes frivolous misplacement of scarce resources versus support for life- and culture-enhancing activities? Who can know exactly what people take from participating in them?

Who should intervene when, about what, and to what end? Since I started skating, I've made more choices like the one where I picked the sparkly dress for my first ice show instead of protesting further about why the men played the artists and the women played the models. But I can also imagine situations where I might have to decide differently. Eight years later, I was much more alarmed when someone suggested that our spoof of *General Hospital* might involve a (white) skater impersonating Obama, given the then-current focus on his health-care bill. I don't think I could have skated in a program involving something so close to black-face. But now I know how deeply sad I would have been to miss participating in the show in a way that I simply didn't understand back in 1989, during the first decade of AIDS, when my sister pulled her parody of the song *Nine to Five* out of her med-school graduation "follies" after she couldn't get her classmates to drop the gay-bashing skits. I also understand why an antiracist friend decided to make it a teaching opportunity rather than pull her young child out of the Cowboys and Indians number in that same Portland show—at least after the choreographer promised to represent not the Cowboys obliterating the Indians, but becoming friends instead (presumably not with the sinister intentions based on the historical model). While I continue to grapple with politics, pleasure, and laundering, I offer in the conclusion a few suggestions for changes with modest reach in the small domains where I pursued this research.

CONCLUSION *If I Ruled the Rink,*
or Make the Rink by Skating

I'd venture that virtually every avid adult skater has ideas about improving adult skating, skating culture more generally, and the contexts in which skating happens. A privilege of writing this book is to offer some of mine.

Spread the Love

Gliding is heavenly; skating is like sex or it isn't. Whatever grabs you about the act of skating itself, enjoying it depends on the other people around. At every stage of venturing into adult skating, kindness, generosity, and support kept me coming back. There was the woman who introduced herself at a public-skating session and helped me with the crossovers and 3-turns I was learning. There were program directors, coaches, staff, and skaters, at home and as I ventured out, who invited me to make their scenes our scenes or who, when I was passing through, made me feel like a welcome visitor.

None of those things just happen. Many tales of adult skating describe us as the bottom-feeding crumb-seekers barely tolerated in the skating world.[1] In contrast, while I sometimes encountered coldness and disrespect, I often received even more gestures of respect than I wanted, including, at both my home rink and club, solo opportunities usually reserved for advanced kids that I sometimes experienced as exercises in bravery and graciousness more than desired attention. I cherish what they stand for anyway.

A friendly environment requires active work, including sharing insider knowledge that is easy to forget you have. "Aha, the skater wearing the pinnie is *intentionally* skating to the music." "Why do you think I need your help with my 'stroking' and why are you telling me here?" "What do you call it when the coach coaches from behind the rink wall?"

Quinn Miller, who asked that last question, succinctly named the scope and effect of insider knowledge when I asked how he knew it was called something (coaching at or from "the boards"). That's ideology, he said, the way every little feature has terminology that gets thrown around as natural and functions to exclude people who don't know it. Barriers to starting out or staying in a sports environment also include not knowing what to expect, who people around you might be, whether everyone else might be wearing spandex, or, as Miller notes, what you might be able to wear or where you might be able, comfortably, to change into it.[2] A great study by the Canadian Association for the Advancement of Women and Sport about how to promote exercise among women aged fifty-five to seventy offers extensive, extractable ideas pertaining to people of diverse ages, genders, and cultural backgrounds.[3]

Promoting a friendly environment can involve sharing common culture and working to change it. Amy Entwistle, an adult skater, wrote a guide called *Ice Etiquette* for the Central Carolina Skating Club that offers a saner way to conceptualize "right of way" on the ice. Try to defer, as is custom, to skaters performing their program or having a lesson, but yield to the skater "who doesn't see the potential for a collision." Meanwhile, cut people a break for a lapse or bad day and teach others by telling rather than by terrifying them with near collisions. Skaters new to practice ice, for instance, usually need to learn that the corners are the opposite of out of the way: lutzes, dance patterns, and Moves all end up there.[4] But the virtual certainty that skaters new to practice ice will seek refuge at the edges is one more example that skate culture, like all culture, is learned.

Mind the Cash

One thing that impressed me when I hung out with women hockey players in the locker room was their keen sense of disparate incomes and collective effort to make travel to away games and tournaments affordable to people who wanted to participate. In contrast, my skating club offers solos in its annual ice show to people who, in effect, buy them by paying for a certain number of sessions on club freestyle ice. Buying the ice, however, is described as "supporting the club," as if loyalty were solely the issue. Even awards to graduating seniors include hours skated on club ice among the criteria. Granted, the club needs to tug at guilt and heartstrings like any other cash-strapped organization that depends on disposable income; it also provides opportunities to sell or trade skates and dresses. But collective brainstorming about sharing resources at various skating venues could take more people further. Good work to provide opportunities and resources could be further emulated.[5]

Some other aspects of skating culture might use rethinking with attention to resource issues as well. A friend from another area told me about a dilemma she faced upon observing a child taking ice dance lessons from a coach who couldn't keep time to the music, which neither the child nor her parents could perceive. While skating etiquette, for some good reasons, forbids recruiting students away from their coaches, my friend desperately wanted to tell the child's mother, a friend no less, that she was wasting money on incompetent instruction. Or consider the coach whose students come and go, depending on the vagaries of the fishing season that their family income depends on. Are there local or larger institutional ways to address problems whereby the livelihood of coaches can be derailed by everything from a harvest to skater injuries to their own lack of sick days to the drop in hours when hockey season commandeers our freestyle ice?

Free Gender

Not all skaters think a lot about gender on the ice. Maybe they don't have to; they fit right in. Maybe they don't care so much about their own gender expression. As a close friend and filmmaker, Jed Bell, creatively put it, in dismissing my unhappy suspicion that abandoning hockey required more reasons than hating the outfit, gender isn't just about *what* but also about *how much*: "Some people have a lot of gender; if you're one of those people, the outfit is crucial to being properly expressed."[6] Maybe they take the rightness or inclusiveness of rink gender norms for granted. For example, enthusiasts about the up-and-coming discipline of synchronized skating, which is often touted for keeping skaters in the sport who might not be destined for glory as freestyle or dance competitors, never seem to notice that it's unavailable to people skating as female who cannot live in their skin under the requisite, usually feminine, matching hair, dresses, and makeup.

Sports should offer as many participants as possible the opportunity to express their gender the way they want to. Granted, individual sports often have restrictions and possibilities specific to their sport. With flying pucks, hockey has good reason to require clunky overall padding. It might not have offered Uzi Sioux what derby did: the opportunity to be simultaneously "tough, aggressive, independent" and feminine, helping her to "separate the tough girl [she wants] to be from the tough guy [she] used to have to try to be," before she transitioned from male to female.[7] But too many other sports have clothing conventions or requirements that serve no purpose. Does Olympic lifting, as Toby Beauchamp, a lifter and gender scholar, asks, really require that leotard-esque number?[8]

Figure skating ought to enable many forms of expression. But too often, I think, the unspoken principle that I noted at Adult Nationals underlying the divide between the technical program and the interp adheres instead. Skaters are welcome to impersonate gender identities, for occasions designated as entertainment, that they are not welcome to occupy as genuine to themselves in competitive programs or even, sometimes, simply in practice. Cindy Crouse, an adult skater, told me about finding "gender-appropriate clothing required" added to her rink's practice-ice contract forms after she brought a male skating friend with her once who routinely practices in a dress. Nothing had (yet) existed on the books to toss him off the ice, but, clearly, only because implicit gender laws had not yet been violated.[9]

Limits should be imposed by safety, not decorum or conformity: no Isadora Duncan strangulator scarves; no spikes that could spear you if you fall; no giant pieces of loose glitter that become shiny little death agents if they fall to the ice when you sweat. Encourage people to dress and move in ways that make them feel happily alive, which involves more than degrees of masculinity or femininity. I struggle a lot myself with a tendency to be snarky about what I consider poser-ish or age-inappropriate. While I'll never regret gloating at the limited competitive prospects of the sneering teens at that one rink I visited, I do regret silently laughing along when one said to the other about another woman my age, "Stop wearing your daughter's skating dresses, Mrs. Jones." I'd been entertaining that mean-spirited thought myself instead of being impressed that she was rocking a look that made her happy—and as if that bluish black in my hair only incidentally dyed the gray out.

Anti-snark is something everyone can do right now. We can also recognize and work to change the numerous skating contexts that demand, or appear to demand, adherence to certain gender norms. I say "apparent" because sometimes people have more options than they realize. A skater

I interviewed at my own rink told me that she would never join the adult number in our annual show because she wouldn't wear those dresses. She hadn't noticed that our rink director, who choreographs the number, will provide a pants-wearing alternative for refusers, and I understand why she didn't. Like I did at the Gay Games, newcomers survey a scene created partly through long histories of self-selection and exclusionary practices that have already taken out many gender nonconformers: when confronted by "the arm thing," as Bryan Smith put it, or, by the prospect of wearing the first assigned costume. Or maybe by the prospect of not being able to wear someone else's costume: The skater I was interviewing told me that a young boy sitting near her at the last show expressed disappointment that only the girls seemed to get flashy costumes.

Free Sexuality

I did not attribute current or future gender and sexuality to the child in question, but I do want to situate the lack of flash he noticed among common responses in skating culture to stereotypes about male skaters being likely gay and effeminate. Too often, they resemble the one that Skate Canada's "Tough Campaign" was widely seen to assume: It's not true, it's not true. In the best take on this issue that I've read in a children's novel, *Crossovers*, written by another adult skater, LeAnne Hardy, the heterosexual male protagonist learns to claim, proudly and publicly, both figure skating as his sport, despite its reputation, and the femmy gay skater as his friend.[10] That's progress. Now let's create a culture where those femmy gay kids, femmy nongay kids, nonfemmy gay kids, and nonfeminine people of any sexuality skating as female can proudly, visibly, and publicly occupy a protagonist status without worrying about censure.

Maybe a collective "get over it" attitude is growing. Johnny Weir won the *Skating Magazine*'s Reader's Choice Award for Skater of the Year in 2008 and 2010. At AN 2011, Thom Mullins got a great audience reception for an interp that queered up the message of the Gay Games 2006 group number to Aguilera's "Beautiful," which I mentioned in the introduction. In that number, we'd worn shirts bearing words often hurled as slurs that the sight of our giant rainbow ribbon ultimately replaced. Mullins similarly started off with writing across the front of his costume bearing words that might be used hurtfully, in this case "You Queer Skating Fag." But the dance remix he was using of the original somber ballad suggested more of a fuck-you self-naming that he later made explicit. Having ripped off the words halfway through his program, which turned out to have been on a scarf-like panel Velcro-ed to his shirt, Mullins used that cloth for flourish and then he turned it around at the end to reveal "Yes, and I am beautiful" on the other side. Cheesy, maybe, but fierce. Take us as we are and want to be, including those of us well represented by rainbow ribbons and those of us who don't fit the "just like you" image and polite terminology that "gay rights" campaigns courting a straight or straight-acting public often use to portray us.

Free Sex

USFS allowed the trans skater Alyn Libman to participate in collegiate competition as a male. That's great. Still, nowhere in the rulebook or on the website, years later, could I find any policy statement on who does and can occupy the categories of Girls, Boys, Ladies, and Men.[11] Instead of quietly dealing with athletes on a case-by-case basis, both USFS and ISI should proactively formulate policies designed to emphasize inclusion. Such policies should be easy to locate for transgender athletes and their allies, and for anyone reading rulebooks and websites to run across.

Publicized policies can educate, encourage support, and deter preju-dice and noncompliance. Thus, in 2006, on a related matter, the Gay Games pairs partners Johnny Manzon-Santos and Alan Lessik, with help from the National Center for Lesbian Rights (NCLR) had recourse to Cali-fornia's civil rights act and the Berkeley municipal code when they were "harassed, discriminated against, and kicked out of their home rink for skating together" as they practiced their same-sex pairs program for the Gay Games.[12] That they were harassed out of a rink in Berkeley, the al-leged bastion of progressivism, for a routine that contained nothing more salacious than holding hands, should give pause. The duo was then in-strumental in persuading ISI to expand its nondiscrimination policy. The policy now includes sexual orientation and gender identity and expres-sion. Importantly, it can be accessed through a link at the bottom of every page after the splash page. USFS needs to catch up.[13]

But take addressing sex categories a step further and ask several other questions. Why should USFS and its parent ISU require pairs and dance teams to be constituted by one male and one female, generally in one male costume and one female costume each attached to the supposedly corresponding body that then performs gender-appropriate moves?[14] Think about how many more people could participate in dance or pairs otherwise, especially given the dearth of male skaters.

Why do solo skaters compete separated into male-labeled and female-labeled categories? While valid arguments may exist for maintaining sex segregation in some sports and at some levels of sport—although perhaps not as many as common wisdom might suggest[15]—figure skating offers ample evidence that sex segregation is not always the ally of fairness even apart from questions regarding gender assignment, gender identity, and gender norms. At Adult Nationals, so few men compete that sometimes men of three age groups compete against each other. The overall disparities between someone who is twenty-two and someone who is forty-nine must surely be more than between a male and a female in most categories—if such disparities indeed exist to the benefit of males. Foes of dropping sex segregation in sports often cite the cost to females, who are presumed to be at a disadvantage. But males don't necessarily perform better. At the 2011 Junior Nationals, for instance, where the top Juvenile and Intermediate kids compete, the top Intermediate Lady outscored the top Intermediate Man by fifteen points.[16] Serious scoring differences don't emerge until the very top levels, but partly, as Adams points out, because inequities built into the system, including shorter maximum program times and component scores calculated at 80 percent of what men receive, prevent women from scoring as highly. At the 2010 Olympics, Adams persuasively argues, the women's champion, Kim Yu-na, could have outscored Lysacek, the winner of the men's event, under a fairer system.[17] Even under the current system, however, sex segregation could be dropped for skaters in many contexts. Very importantly, that change would remove obstacles for skaters who change, don't occupy, or don't want to occupy a sex category. It might also help transform pressure and training to "skate like a girl" or "skate like a boy," which can affect, subtly or not, tricks, moves, gestures, choreography, music, and dress.

This is not to argue that meaningful sex and gender differences don't exist and demand attention. For instance, a study of concussions in high school athletes indicated that "males . . . were more likely to report amnesia and confusion/disorientation (cognitive symptoms) than were females [while] females reported drowsiness (neurobehavioral symptom) and sensitivity to noise (somatic symptom) more than did males."[18] But to assess alleged differences and act on those conclusions, we need to tease out unexamined habits of bias that may be tangled in the mix. Some concussion symptoms may be misdiagnosed as evidence of feminine emotionality, especially in people understood to be feminine or female. Concussion-related depression may remain unattended for similar reasons, especially in athletes for whom the label "feminine" may be considered antithetical or shameful.[19] Research about "males" and "females" may be conducted or used with a presumption that all athletes participating as "male" or "female" have the same anatomy and physiology. As resistance and activism grow against the barriers that now prevent trans and other gender nonconforming people from participating fully in organized physical activities, those presumptions become increasingly important to dismantle also.

Rigidly linking gender or sex to biology, as Dean Spade makes clear in his very helpful guide called "Some Very Basic Tips for Making Higher Education More Accessible to Trans Students and Rethinking How We Talk about Gendered Bodies," can lead to coaching strategies and instruction that ill-serve numerous people. A yoga modification designed to accommodate protruding breasts, for instance, may not most helpfully be suggested as a modification for "women" in a group of people where some men, trans or not, might have the protrusions and some women, trans or not, might not yet, not ever, or no longer have them.

Or consider the argument of Denise Wall, a dance teacher and the mother of SYTYCD stars Travis Wall and Danny Tidwell, that male dancers need to be trained by people who are experts in training them specifically as boys. Such trainers, she says, can aid boys' development in several ways: by giving males distinct choreography and costumes, because "guys need to dance like guys"; by recognizing physiological differences like effects of growth spurts that are particular to boys; and by being mindful that boys may get in the way of their own extensions because they are "trying to be butch," and thus gripping instead of lengthening.[20] The items on that wish list seem alternately to reinforce, to have little to do with, or to combat restrictive gender training. Where Wall combats restrictive gender training, her insights could be taken much further. For instance, if she is correct that a masculine gender identity or the desire to present a masculine gender expression—which is how I interpret her comment about "trying to be butch"—affects the ability to extend one's legs, then that observation, which would not apply to all males, would actually help in training any dancer with masculine identities and desires, whether male, female, intersex, genderqueer, trans, not trans, or any of those, or more, in combination.

What If They Gave a Skating Competition . . .

What if they gave a skating competition and nobody sandbagged? Or the rules were clear and easy to access? Within skating, those proposals sound as naïve as the common slogan of my antiwar childhood, "What if they gave a war and nobody came?" They shouldn't. The belief that division by sex should be the default in sports, if problematic, is understandable; it's underpinned by centuries of law and custom across innumerable realms. In contrast, sandbagging and opaque scoring make little obvious sense either outside of skating or to many people within it. It shouldn't be so hard to change Well-Balanced Program guidelines so that they require skaters to compete against people of comparable, and not masked, ability. Nor should it be so hard to write clear rules.

And what if they gave a competition that reflected a skating culture rewarding diverse movement traditions, body types, and relations to ability? I remember a conversation with Johnny Manzon-Santos soon after I attended Figure Skating in Harlem's "A Gift from Africa" show. I had wanted to see how skating might look different in a context that didn't center a classical, European tradition of movement and music, which was decentered in the show's very theme. But another spectacle of difference, I told him, based on economic disparity, made my original question hard to address: kids skating courtesy of family wealth, rather than a 501(c) 3 nonprofit, had far more lesson and practice time to refine each trick, stroke, and turn. (That's why FIH is touted for helping kids get to college, not the Olympics.) He added that addressing the question also poses the challenge of discerning between the niceties and necessities. Do an extended leg and pointed toe simply align the skater with balletic norms, or do they facilitate checking out of a jump? What I've come to understand more since that conversation is the extent to which the aesthetics actually create the necessities. Thus, the aerodynamic body types and alignment that multiple-revolution skating jumps require come from and contribute to the reality that scoring standards embed aesthetic, cultural, racial, and ethnic ideals, although not in predictable and stable ways.

Those ideals also affect day-to-day experience in practice, recreation, and competition, including how people are triaged up or out of them.[21] In her exit montage on *Dancing with the Stars* in 2010, Margaret Cho talked about having quit dancing as a young child after someone called her "the fattest ballerina." Johnny Weir praised Real Housewife Bethenny Frankel on *Skating with the Stars* a few weeks later, but before their feuding about the quality of her skating made the tabloids, for having the perfect skinny skater's body.[22] Too many people have stories like this, which hardly tell the whole story about how people come to more and less alien styles of movement that they have more and less consciously learned to identify with, adopt, display, or hide. As Miliann Kang details in her wonderful ethnography on Korean manicurists, people from nondominant cultural traditions discipline their bodies to conform to dominant standards in countless ways.[23]

Concepts of athletic excellence also depend on conceptions of ability, disability, advancement, and degeneration. This point was brought home to me in the summer of 2010 at a performance of the Axis Dance Company, which presents "physically integrated dance" with dancers in various relations to standard definitions of "disabled." As David Kociemba well describes in "'Proud Mary'": *Glee*'s Very Special Sham Disability Pride Anthem," Axis choreography, in contrast to the unimaginative and otherwise problematic choreography for *Glee* dancers in wheelchairs, "treats the assistive technology as a part of the body, which allows for greater complexity. The dancers use the handles for lifts. The wheels aid jumps. There are dips, tilts and spins. One dancer twirls another in the air slowly, chair and all. The choreography is not afraid to use the floor either."[24] What struck me especially was watching the muscled, indelicate, rough interaction involving some of the dancers in wheelchairs, including in their interactions with dancers not in wheelchairs. It smashed assumptions I hadn't known I had that people with certain physical limits require gentle engagement rather than what some of the Axis dancers got instead: a seat-belt-equipped chair that enabled intense and gorgeous dance versions of rough-housing. Despite the thrill of rough contact I witness and share in other contexts, I'd unconsciously written off its availability and desirability to them.

In adult figure skating, I think of these issues in terms of not just who can get on the ice and how, but also the persistence of standards that especially reward skills that age impedes learning or retaining. We're more likely to keep advancing in spins and footwork than we are to land that elusive axel or double jump. Yet jumps we have, want, had, or lost can command a lot of attention. My friend Mary has virtually opposite skating strengths than mine, and we have sometimes joked about how she can't always even recognize the turns in my footwork. Yet it goes without saying that I recognized her lutz-loop combination before I could do anything close to approximating it and we both know that, at least in scoring, her skills serve her better. She's also clearly also the better skater overall, and I don't offer this example to introduce specific alternatives to current practices. While I might have some thoughts about reweighting, altering, or inventing elements and criteria, I am primarily invested in a vision akin to that in the 2006 movie *Stick It*, where the gymnasts take over their meet with better music and a refusal to accept downgrades for wayward bra straps, and in promoting thoughtfulness about what practices and standards, never neutral or inevitable, do, don't, and might offer to whom.

Race to the Center

It's easy to let race slide away into song, dance, and celebration. The television series *Hellcats*, for instance, which debuted on the cw in 2010, was inspired by Torgovnick's study *Cheer!* But you'd never know by watching the Hellcats struggle to secure resources for Nationals that systemic racial inequities, as Torgovnick so well details, often factor into who receives support. *Bring It On*, in contrast, makes clear that economic point about differently capitalized institutions, but in a context in which the accessories of human connection and identity belong primarily to the white kids—the only ones who have visible families, romance, sexual orientations, and, with few exceptions, even names.[25]

Skating cultures, too, often just go for the production with minimal or reluctant attention to race and racism. Attention often awaits outstandingly thoughtless programs, with highly visible protestors: like the 2010 "Aboriginal" dance skated by the Russian dance team of Oksana Domnina and Maxim Shabalin, complete with imbecilic expressions, browned skin, and ape postures. Yet thinking about race and racism would benefit skating and skaters within and outside skating. I heard about a coach who, rightly, told parents not to apply "Oriental eye" makeup on their white kids. The next step, maybe, is to reconsider choreographing little children—or bigger children or grown-ups—bowing in groups to a King of Siam or soloing as harem denizens, Vietnamese sex workers, or Poca-hontas. What, too, might such roles imply depending on who occupies them and how? Turning such roles into sources of education and conversation could help skaters and people in charge of them make informed decisions.

Spectacles of skating can also occasion informative discussion. I wonder, for instance, if Lindsey Vonn, the super-blond skier, versus a figure skater as usual, was the "darling" of the 2010 Winter Games because skating's top contenders came from Asia. Did raced feminine ideals of "darlings" as white inform that situation? Did it inform the NBC Sports coverage of the U.S. Ladies team, which featured Rachel Flatt largely to the exclusion of Mirai Nagasu? Although Flatt just had beaten Nagasu in the U.S. Nationals, their skating resumés suggested that Nagasu, who wound up placing higher, was an equal contender.

When I've mentioned a costume choice or choreographic gesture that seemed years behind even minimal changes for the better in common habits of respect, I sometimes hear in response, "What do you expect, they spend their lives/grew up at a rink?" Why couldn't those years in the rink occasion education about cultural practices and habits of respect? I don't think that it's wrong by definition to take inspiration from cultural traditions that you don't claim as part of your own personal history. But I do think that processes of doing so should avoid replicating a standard colonial model whereby (predominantly white) people in power take what they want from wherever and whomever they can. At minimum, I would argue, respect requires attention to people who inhabit cultures that interest you about what they want to offer, share, hold for themselves, and prohibit. Learn what they consider disrespectful or damaging and why. For example, in 2010 as the Maine Indian Tribal-State Commission prepared to introduce legislation to ban Native American team nicknames, mascots, and imagery from Maine schools, the commission's chair, Jaimie Bissonette Lewey, explained that even if white people claim to maintain those traditions as gestures of respect, their concept of honor blatantly disregards the wishes of supposed honorees. It also forces those honorees, regardless of the home team's intention, to "endure opposing teams yelling 'scalp them.'"[26]

The next important step regarding cultural appropriation and exchange, I believe, involves a variation on the principle of ethical fieldwork: Don't take from communities you study without giving back, which leads me to my final point.

Take It Outside

As I said earlier, my embarrassment about studying figure skating had some questionable effects and sources. But I'm not embarrassed for wanting to be visible as a person who can be counted on to participate in anti-oppression struggles across categories of race, gender, sexuality, economics, and nation—and not just regarding democratized access to pleasures. Whatever your beliefs and commitments—which I'm also not embarrassed to hope I may have affected here—there is not one single way to effect change about them in the rink only. We need to get out there and do the work. And still, then again . . .

If I Can't Skate

Emma Goldman, it turns out, did not actually say, "If I can't dance, I don't want to be in your revolution." But she did express that sentiment attributed to her on once ubiquitous T-shirts. As she recounts in her memoirs,

> At the dances I was one of the most untiring and gayest. One evening . . . a young boy took me aside. With a grave face, as if he were about to announce the death of a dear comrade, he whispered to me that it did not behoove an agitator to dance. Certainly not with such reckless abandon, anyway. . . .
>
> I grew furious at the impudent interference of the boy. . . . I did not believe that a Cause which stood for a beautiful ideal, for anarchism, for release and freedom from conventions and prejudice, should demand the denial of life and joy. . . . If it meant that, I did not want it. "I want freedom, the right to self-expression, everybody's right to beautiful, radiant things."[27]

And sparkle.

NOTES

Introduction

1. Carter, *Off the Deep End*.

2. Adam Carolla on *Dancing with the Stars*, April 8, 2008. That advice appears repeatedly on the Internet, sometimes credited to Eleanor Roosevelt without further specification.

3. "Pretty and witty and gay" is in the lyrics for the movie version of "I Feel Pretty." The original version for the stage production had the line as "Pretty and witty and bright," which was changed for the 1961 movie. According to the Internet Movie Database's trivia for *West Side Story*, "bright" was changed to "gay" because the scene of the song was changed from nighttime to daytime for the movie, and the primary goal was to switch the rhyming word "tonight" to "today." See http://www.imdb.com. This apparently then-trivial switch got new attention in 2006 when a Nike ad using the song chose the version that had the word "bright," setting off, because of the now well-known movie version, a debate about whether that choice was homophobic.

4. Meshell Ndegeocello's "If That's Your Boyfriend (He Wasn't Last Night)," on *Plantation Lullabies* (Maverick Records, 1993). Queen Pen, *Girlfriend* (1997) on *My Melody* (Interscope Records, 1997).

5. On the history of roller derby, including an early version with male entrepreneurs and skaters competing in female and male pairs, and the recent development first as a banked-track and then a flat-track sport for women, see Coppage, *Roller Derby to Rollerjam*; Joulwan, "Melicious."

6. "Titanium Unleashed! Enter Now to Win a Stick," an e-mail ad sent through USAH Information for Mission eNews, sent November 13, 2007.

7. Adams, *Artistic Impressions*, 107.

8. Ibid., passim.

I. Seeing and Getting

1. Dodge, *Hans Brinker, or The Silver Skates*, 209.

2. Owen, *Primer of Figure Skating*, 131.

3. WTF: What the fuck?

4. The IRB exists at every academic institution to enforce research guidelines that are devised to ensure the safety and anonymity of "human subjects."

5. On the relationship of fan attachments to scholarly study, see Jenkins, McPherson, and Shattuc, "The Culture That Sticks to Your Skin," 3–26, 7.

6. Sedgwick, "Privilege of Unknowing," 23.

7. In that case, they can now compete on the relatively new "Competitive Test Track," which prohibits using elements tested above the competition level. The creation of the test track can be considered a nod to how out-of-control sandbagging has gotten, a gesture toward the "compete and have fun" ethos, and a smart, revenue-generating way to keep skaters engaged in the sport who lack the resources, talent, or drive to be its stars.

8. Conversation with Lorrayne Carroll, Portland, Maine, August 19, 2009. The Senior Games took place in Palo Alto, California, from August 1–15, with the "Celebration" on August 8.

9. I base this comment partly on watching the streaming video archive at Icenetwork.com for every event in the 2008 Adult Nationals competition.

10. At the skaters' meeting on April 12, 2008, at AN, the chief referee, Lynn Goodman, explained these issues, using the sit spin as an example.

11. E-mail communication with the author, March 5, 2008.

12. E-mail communication with the author, August 7, 2008.

13. Only those jumps (and the unpleasant, minimal-credit half-loop, which can precede only a salchow) take off from the same back outside edge that a skater lands every other jump on.

14. E-mail communication with the author, August 7, 2008.

II. Skating Is Like Sex

1. Because it was once part of the entry "Pleasure" provided by Dictionary.com, where I originally found it, a Google search of the whole phrase returns numerous hits.

2. Bornstein, *Hello, Cruel World*, 65.

3. Ibid., 139–40.

4. Ibid., 187.

5. See, on this matter, Griffin's groundbreaking work *Strong Women, Deep Closets*.

6. Gambs, "Myocellular Transduction," 118.

7. Gray, *Out in the Country*, 92, 19.

8. I attended the game on September 16, 2010. The event also offered a great local example of sport as an opportunity to display cross-cultural goodwill and national identity. First the Japanese and then the U.S. national anthems were played, each followed by collective stick-banging on the ice, and then the Portland women

skated over to the men with little gift bags that had teal tissue paper sticking out, a gesture made, I thought, to honor what were understood to be Asian gift-giving traditions and perhaps aesthetics. It certainly contrasted with hockey indelicacy and ruggedness.

9. Stewart, *Ordinary Affects*, 15.

10. Gordeeva, *My Sergei*, 215, 219–20.

11. Laskowski, "Figure Skaters for Christ."

12. Kirby, *A Perfect Landing*, 64.

13. Ibid., 100–101.

14. Lewis, *Dreams on Ice*.

15. Kociemba, *A Surprise Finish*, 116–19.

16. Lewis, *A Perfect Match*, 11, 113–24.

III. Hooks

1. Ash, "The Tie: Presence and Absence," 166–67. The professor and custodian example is mine.

2. Ash, "Memory and Objects," 219.

3. "Custom Boot Packages," Harlick Skating Boots, http://www.harlick.com.

4. "Customs and Specials," Riedell Skates, http://www.riedellskates.com.

5. Kestnbaum, *Culture on Ice*, 104–5.

6. Owen, *Primer of Figure Skating*, 20. Another indication of the changing trend in process appears in the 1936 movie *Wife versus Secretary*. At an ice skating company party, the one woman who can do tricks wears white skates and a knee-length skirt. The other women wear black skates and longer dresses.

7. Ibid., 17–19, 20.

8. While the white skate and black skate divide reigns in international competition, I would not generalize about gendered norms regarding different kinds of skates—which also depend on where hockey reigns—or about other ways that skaters engage with standards of masculinity or femininity, which have varied regionally and over time, affected by numerous issues, including sexuality (what's too queer), racism, orientalism, and classed standards of refinement.

9. E-mail communication with the author, August 18, 2011.

10. Capezio offers "Nude" and "Suntan"; Danskin, "Classic Light Toast" and "Light Toast."

11. I attended the performance on March 23, 2007. A group photograph of the performers in costume appears on the FIH website at http://www.figureskating inharlem.org. In contrast, the tights functioned more successfully as costume accessory for the bright yellow costumes worn in a disco number performed in 2002 to "I Will Survive," which was introduced by Gloria Gaynor herself.

12. Kestnbaum, *Culture on Ice*, 119. As Kestnbaum notes, the ruling was known

as the "Katarina rule" after Katarina Witt, whose costume during the same season had only feathers for the skirt. Some people think the unitard contributed to the disappointing artistic marks Thomas received, which has also been linked to the program's overall style, in particular to what Kestnbaum described as her "high-energy step sequence involving angled limbs, shoulder isolations, and syncopated rhythms . . . [that] invoked images of contemporary urban dance derived from African American culture, congruent with Thomas's own racial heritage if not her personal experience." Kestnbaum, using also the example of Harding skating to "the down-and-dirty pop culture rhythms of rapper Tone Loc and ZZ Top," suggests that women's scores were never enhanced by reaching toward pop-culture roots that strayed from elite, white-rooted traditions, although similar music choices sometimes marked men as innovators (141–42).

13. For example, Owen offered advice to people who couldn't afford coaching: study illustrations, ask fellow skaters, and imitate those instructors one couldn't afford to pay (*Primer of Figure Skating*, 91–92).

14. Hence, the scene in each episode of *Tim Gunn's Guide to Style* (Bravo, 2007) in which, after the style trainee's desperate need for guidance is revealed, she gets fitted for new bras that will undergird new elegance. Again, money makes gender talk.

15. Alison Bechdel, e-mail communication with the author, February 20, 2008. I contacted her after reading *Fun Home: A Family Tragicomic* (2006), in which I saw a certain resonance to issues of loss I consider here. *Dykes to Watch Out For* has been running since 1983.

16. Harper, *Man Tricks*, 11–12.

17. U.S. Department of Labor, Title IX, Education Amendments of 1972: Title 20 U.S.C. Sections 1681–88. Among many locations, the text, with informative accompanying material, can be found in the helpful sourcebook *Women and Sports in the United States: A Documentary Reader*, edited by Jean O'Reilly and Susan Cahn.

18. Personal conversation, March 2, 2008.

19. Miller, "I Can't Sell Something Called Jock Bra," 134–35.

20. Ibid., 135.

21. Serano, *Whipping Girl*, 315.

22. Miller, "I Can't Sell Something Called Jock Bra," 135.

23. Thanks to Ryan Conrad, whose words and work on this topic have influenced my thinking.

24. Miller, "I Can't Sell Something Called Jock Bra," 134.

25. *Today*, March 27, 2008.

26. Brownworth, "Life in the Passing Lane," 71.

27. Ibid., 70.

28. Ibid., 68, 72.

29. SkateOut, http://32degrees.us, accessed March 25, 2007.

IV. Ladies

1. In "'A Radiant Smile from the Lovely Lady': Overdetermined Femininity in 'Ladies' Figure Skating," Abigail Feder-Kane describes many features of the athletic/artistic divide, including the reward for concealing athleticism beyond what the general skating dictum to make it look easy requires. The divide is also a recurring theme in Cynthia Baughman's 1995 anthology, *Women on Ice: Feminist Essays on the Tonya Harding/Nancy Kerrigan Spectacle*.

2. On this topic, see Lenskyj's important *Out of Bounds*.

3. Numerous popular and scholarly works exist on this topic that was made famous in George Butler's and Charles Gaines's 1985 film *Pumping Iron II: The Women*. See also Kaye, *Iron Maidens*.

4. Caudwell, "Femme-Fatale," 152.

5. As Lannin recounts, for instance, the history of girls' and women's basketball includes everything from different rules than the ones for males, like restricted dribbling and guarding, to uniforms with midriff tops to beauty contests in tournaments. See *A History of Basketball for Girls and Women*, 32–33, 57, 64.

6. Doyle, "Modern Minstrels: Sexist Jokes about Women Athletes," from her blog *From a Left Wing*, October 6, 2008.

7. E-mail communication with the author, March 4, 2008.

8. The 2004 policy of the IOC (International Olympic Committee), which many sports federations have adopted, requires transgender players to have had genital surgery and a prescribed amount of time on hormones. Before the IOC policy passed, U.S. Figure Skating had used its own criteria to permit Alyn Libman, a female-to-male trans figure skater who, as a child, had competed as female to compete as male in collegiate competition. See Rona Marech, "Olympics' Transgender Quandary: Debate Rages on the Fairness of New Inclusion Rule," *San Francisco Chronicle*, June 14, 2004. The IOC policy is far from ideal for many, many reasons, including identical policies for male-to-female and female-to-male athletes, because only the former are presumed to have an advantage in their new category before hormonal changes. I discuss the issue further in essay 20, "Gifts of Nature, Freaks of Culture."

9. Holy Rollers website, http://www.txrd.com/holyrollers/. The Texas Lonestar Rollergirls (TXRD) is the league centrally responsible for the reemergence of roller derby in the past ten years. Many players cite the A&E television series about them (*Roller Girls*, 2006) as their own inspiration for founding or joining teams. However, because TXRD still plays on a banked track rather than a flat track, the league is largely removed from the current derby movement

10. *So You Think You Can Dance*, Season 5, May 27, 2009. The outfit of the dancer, Wislande Letang, can be found at *Top Idol*'s May 29, 2009, blog post, "SYTYCD in Miami: Cat Deeley Rules, But Oh Yes, We've Even Found Ourselves a Young Widow," http://topidol.wordpress.com.

11. Prouse, *Tonya Tapes*, 255. The book presents material drawn from interviews conducted between 1999 and 2001, and then in 2007 (19) but doesn't differentiate which material comes from which interview. The deductions as well as other costume issues related to USFS and public censure are discussed in Yamaguchi, *Figure Skating for Dummies*, 153–54.

12. Foote, "Making Sport of Tonya," 11. Foote interestingly also points out that while people frequently propose class as the subtext of media coverage about Harding, the topic was always front and center, if frequently stuck in "hackneyed scripts" (5).

13. Ibid., 11.

14. Yamaguchi, *Figure Skating for Dummies*, 157.

15. Maifair, *Go Figure, Gabriella Grant*; Kirby, *A Perfect Landing*; Kirby, *A Surprise Finish*; Lewis, *Dreams on Ice*.

16. One widely circulated text with the images was Nancy Armour, "Perception a Myth—in Figure Skating and in Life," July 14, 2009, Google News, http://www.google.com/hostednews/ap, accessed July 22, 2009. While the piece is no longer available on Google News, the article still circulates and photographs may be easily found. The skating image is an AP file photograph taken by Amy Sanceto on February 20, 1998, during the Winter Olympics in Nagano. The mug shot is from July 6, 2009, and is credited to the Hudson County Prosecutor's Office.

17. U.S. Figure Skating, *2012 Official U.S. Figure Skating Rulebook*, 304, 306.

18. Six "features" raised the level of difficulty for the 2009–10 season; a skater needed four features for the maximum "Level 4" spiral sequence. Three are one spiral in a "total split position," one "difficult variation of position," and one "significantly different" difficult variation. International Skating Union, *Communication* no. 1557, April 15, 2009, 5.

19. International Skating Union, *Communication* no. 1611, May 4, 2010, 10; International Skating Union, *Communication* no. 1619, section 1, 1.

20. Post by Debi Thomas, March 2, 2010, "Fans for Downgrading Grabbing Your Skate" Facebook group, http://www.facebook.com.

21. Post by JoAnn Schneider Farris, May 26, 2010, "Fans for Downgrading Grabbing Your Skate" Facebook group, http://www.facebook.com. I surmised the source of this information from a post on Schneider Farris's blog, May 23, 2010, called "I'm Going to a US Figure Skating National Technical Panel Seminar!" *Jo Ann's Figure Skating Blog*, http://figureskating.about.com.

22. Manley, "Interview with Ron Ludington."

23. John Manzon-Santos, e-mail communication with the author, July 20, 2009. He was talking about the Catch-22 in skating that in order to be noticed and supported by USFS, which rarely happens anyway, skaters need to display achievements that are expensive to acquire.

24. Jonathan Sachs, "Sasha Cohen Falls Short of Qualifying for 2010 Winter

Olympic Skating Team," January 24, 2010, *Examiner.com*, http://www.examiner
.com.

25. Spelling, *sTORI Telling*, 271.

26. McMains, *Glamour Addiction*, xv, 30–31, 42.

27. So can skipping a critical move relatively common in feminist studies of aging women that embrace or dwell on the "grotesque" or monstrous. I don't find it so illuminating or liberating although books like Frueh's *Monster/Beauty* persuasively argue that it can be.

28. In *Coming on Strong*, Cahn notes that the disjuncture between athleticism and femininity is part of what has pushed women into "aesthetic" sports such as figure skating, besides also misrepresenting the athleticism of those sports (223–24).

29. Shogan, *The Making of the High-Performance Athletes*, 50–55.

30. Martin, "Another Lesbian Jock," 36, 38.

31. Ibid., 37.

32. Plimpton, *Open Net*, 60.

33. Neither I nor Califia nor several editors could put our hands on the essay itself but we all remembered it and I confirmed the account with Califia in several e-mail exchanges, including on August 14 and 15, 2011.

34. The Canadian ice dancers Tessa Virtue and Scot Moir won a bronze medal in the 2009 World Championships, and they used a Pink Floyd song for their free dance, which had costumes also signaling unconventionality—no skating dress for her either.

35. Wald, "Just a Girl?" 606.

36. Killer Quick, *Maine Roller Derby Media Handbook*, 4.

37. Rule 4740 of the 2012 USFS rulebook states, "Use of skating skills to develop a theme and interpret music, and effectiveness of the costumes will be reflected in the marking." U.S. Figure Skating, *2010 Official U.S. Figure Skating Rulebook*, 220. The wording leaves some latitude about the relative weight of the skill level and the skills' interpretive function, but more advanced skating often wins out, and the audience applause for good jumps and spins is another reflection of some carryover criteria.

38. Ibid., 185.

39. Serano, *Whipping Girl*, 110.

40. Manley, "Interview with Debi Thomas"; Prouse, *Tonya Tapes*, 122–23.

41. Liz Rose and Taylor Swift, "You Belong with Me," on the album *Fearless*, 2009.

42. Pictures and a video of the Stones number in another competition are available on Chanel's *IceNetwork* INcrowd page at http://www.icenetworkincrowd.com.

43. Rowell, *The Women Who Raised Me*, 50, 74–77, 157, 187.

44. Ibid., 138, 188.

45. Gia Kourlas, "Where Are All the Black Swans?" *New York Times*, May 6, 2007.

46. E-mail communication with the author, February 23, 2010.

47. Lop-Her, "Campaign for Real Booty: Punchy O'Guts."

48. Lop-Her, "Campaign for Real Booty: DayGlo Divine."

49. "Campaign for Real Booty," *Big Derby Girls Don't Cry*, February 21, 2008, http://bigderbygirls.blogspot.com.

50. McMains, *Glamour Addiction*, 152.

51. Ibid., 153. McMains cites Arthur Murray, *How to Become a Good Dancer: With Dance Secrets by Kathryn Murray* (New York: Simon and Schuster, 1959), 219.

52. Oliver and Shapiro, *Black Wealth/White Wealth*.

53. Adams, *Artistic Impressions*, 172–73.

54. Jere Longman, in a *New York Times* piece ("Figure Skaters of Asian Descent Have Risen to Prominence," January 23, 2010) analyzing the phenomenon, notes that skaters of Asian descent comprised one-third of the "Senior Ladies" competing at the 2010 Nationals.

55. Faulkner, *I Skate!*, 36–37. Interestingly, Berig, musing on the qualities needed to succeed in skating, counts not being "too tall or too fat"—she weighed only fifty-four pounds at the time—along with musicality, concentration, athleticism, and the ability to "project personality," a complicated mix of variously changeable and trainable features, along with one of the least mutable, height (52, 58).

56. In *Figure Skating: A History*, Hines details the early battles in the history of figure skating between the idea of tracing sometimes extremely complex figures (see, for instance, his diagrams on p. 74) and the shift to jumps, spins, and choreography. Compulsory figures were eliminated from international competition after the 1990 World Championship. Hines quotes the famous coach Carlo Fassi predicting that once they were eliminated, fourteen- and fifteen-year-old girls would dominate the sport (235). He wasn't wrong. Analysts of the phenomenon generally cite the combined factors that not being slowed down by mastering figures allows girls to master advanced jumps before hips and breasts of puberty might derail them, at least temporarily.

57. Tator, Henry, and Mattis, *Challenging Racism in the Arts*, 141–58. Evidence of how troubling the musical is appears in the decision of the Toronto Board of Education, after activism by the group Asian ReVision—in the city where Kim later trained to skate *Miss Saigon*, under the coaching of the Canadian 1988 Olympic silver medalist Brian Orser—to mandate supplementary curriculum for all classes seeing the play. The chapter includes an excerpt from the Board of Education packet with an impressive list of study questions.

58. The biography page for Carolyn-Ann Alba at Icenetwork.com, http://web .icenetwork.com, mistakenly lists the Salome program a year earlier, although I watched the skate on that network. See also "Kristine Musademba" under *IceNetwork: Skaters*, http://web.icenetwork.com (both accessed June 27, 2010). On the

skaters' backgrounds, see Scott M. Reid, "A New Ice Age," *Orange County Register*, December 3, 2004, and Liz Clarke, "Behind Smiles, Sequins, Nothing but Hard Work," *Washington Post*, January 20, 2008.

59. Michelle Kwan, Long Program at U.S. Figure Skating National Championships, January 2006, http://www.youtube.com.

60. Molina-Guzmán, *Dangerous Curves*, 59–70. For another excellent account of how race and sexuality affect media coverage and the ability to maneuver, see Jamieson, "Reading Nancy Lopez."

61. Molina-Guzmán, *Dangerous Curves*, 68–73.

62. Shimizu, *Hypersexuality of Race*, 16.

63. Fung, "Call in the Tropes!," 9. José Esteban Muñoz's *Disidentifications* considers the pleasures and survival strategies that engaging with dominant representations can make possible.

64. Shimizu, *Hypersexuality of Race*, 17–21.

65. Ibid., 25.

V. Masculine Wiles

1. Kevin Thomas, "Growth Pains for Girls' Hockey," *Portland Press Herald*, November 3, 2009, http://www.allbusiness.com.

2. Rudolph, "Rule Changes," 36; Mastrangelo, "Eye and Face Injuries in High School Hockey," 52; Biasca, Wirth, and Tegner, "Head Injuries and Facial Injuries in Ice Hockey."

3. I looked up his stats on the NHL website, www.nfl.com, and on www.hockeydb.com, a hockey database.

4. Rudolph, "Rule Changes," 36.

5. Quoted in Bernstein, *The Code*, 169.

6. Thanks to Jarrett Freedman for pointing this out and for his help with hockey material throughout, among much helpful research assistance.

7. Mike Chambers, "The Frozen Four Descends on Denver. Stop! In the Name of Loving to Win," *Denver Post*, April 9, 2008.

8. As per NHL rule 60, "accidental contact . . . committed as a normal windup or follow through of a shooting motion" is permissible, but a "wild swing" at a "bouncing puck" is forbidden. Rule 60: High-Sticking," http://www.nhl.com. A new 2010 rule adding penalties for "a lateral, back-pressure or blind-side hit to an opponent where the head is targeted and/or the principal point of contact" reflects an official reluctance simply to ban hits to the head. See Paul Hoogcamp, "Should the NHL Ban All Shots to the Head?" TSN, March 26, 2010, http://www.tsn.ca.

9. Toby Keith, "As Good as I Once Was," lyrics by Toby Keith and Scotty Emerick, *HonkyTonk University* (Universal Music, 2005).

10. Buccigross, "Imagine This Story."

11. Ibid.

12. Farber, "Man of His Word."

13. Ibid.

14. On representations, reactions, and teaching regarding DeVine's absence, see Brody, "Boyz Do Cry"; Nero, "Teaching Note"; Halberstam, *In a Queer Time and Place*, chapters 2 and 3, especially 29 and 91. In an argument related to the point I make here, Halberstam argues that the movie also rehabilitates Brandon Teena as fundamentally a normative lesbian, thus making him palatable as a martyr by removing his trans gender, besides banishing the complexities of the matter, including competing models of white masculinity and the white supremacist affiliations of the killers.

15. Mahiri and Van Rheenen, *Out of Bounds*, 42–45, 64–65, and throughout.

16. Thangaraj, "Ballin' Indo-Pak Style," 377.

17. "The Audacity of Hoops."

18. Bernstein, *The Code*, 133.

19. *Battle of the Blades*, CBC Television, season 1, week 7, November 15, 2009. CBC prevents audiences within the United States from watching whole episodes, but there are many clips on YouTube.

20. *Battle of the Blades*, CBC Television, season 1, week 1, October 4, 2009. Michael Fenkell, for instance, in "We Will Certainly Miss Bob Fighting Legend Bob Probert" (*Detroit Red Wings Examiner*, July 6, 2010, http://www.examiner.com), writes, "Everyone that you talk to that knows the man personally, says he was one of the kindest and most loved people off the ice."

21. Lapointe, "Bob Probert, a Life of Violence, Sadness."

22. Here is another example. In Maine, tributes to Charlie Howard, who got thrown off a bridge in Bangor at the age of twenty-three in 1984, often omit the "flamboyant" side that Wikipedia nonetheless now details to include his fondness for makeup, women's accessories, and belting out "I Am What I Am" from *La Cage Aux Folles*. "Charlie Howard," Wikipedia, http://en.wikipedia.org (accessed July 16, 2010).

23. Buccigross, "Imagine This Story of Acceptance between Brian and Brendan Burke"; Farber, "Man of His Word."

24. *Billy Elliot*, dir. Stephen Daldry; *Billy Elliot the Musical*, book and lyrics by Lee Hall.

25. The ad aired on February 3, 2007, and can be seen on http://www.youtube.com.

26. Messner, "When Bodies Are Weapons," especially 206–8. Among many other sources on masculinities and sport, see Burstyn, *Rites of Men*; McKay, Messner, and Sabo, *Masculinities, Gender Relations, and Sport*; and Birrell and Cole, *Women, Sport, and Culture*.

27. Mission Hockey advertisement, *USA Hockey Magazine*, October, 2007, 3. Prompted by e-mails I received from USA Hockey on November 14 and 5, 2007, respectively, about titanium in my shaft, I also watched web ads for the Mission

sticks and the Easton Stealth S17; these ads are no longer available. "Sticks," Bauer website, http://www.bauer.com. TeXtreme is manufactured by oXeon, which advertises on its website (www.oxeon.se) that x:60 was used in the overtime goal that won the Stanley Cup for the Blackhawks.

28. HockeyMonkey.com, October 21, 2010. This can still be found at http://www.youtube.com.

29. Cammalleri's suspension three weeks before the video came out for "slashing" a rookie on the New York Islanders offers an example of this phenomenon, although coverage of the incident also reflects the complicated rules about fighting that I discussed earlier. See, for instance, the AP story "Mike Cammalleri Ejected for Slashing," October 3, 2010, http://sports.espn.go.com.

30. Etue and Williams, *On the Edge*, 166–69; "Girls' Hockey Teams Vie for Ice Time," CBC News, November 15, 2009, http://www.cbc.ca. *On the Edge* offers a great account of the way diverse inequities in resources affect hockey play for females, as does Theberge's *Higher Goals*. Although both were written based on studying hockey in the 1990s, many of the issues remain. At a meeting in April 2008, for instance, the Greater Portland Women's Ice Hockey League revealed the possibility of securing a third hour of ice, which would occur on Friday evenings; even at this not so appealing time, it had been hard to come by.

31. Christopher, *Cool as Ice*, 134. Christopher died in 1997, but the books in the series are still published under his name.

32. MacLeod, *Waiting to Score*, 197.

33. Dale Christopher, e-mail communication with the author, November 16, 2007.

34. See, for example, John Fischer, "Fighting Homophobia in Hockey Must Come from the Fans as Well as the League," *[New Jersey] Devils Issues and Views*, July 7, 2010, http://www.inlouwetrust.com. It responds to an earlier post that day by Derek Zona on an Edmonton Oilers site, "Homophobia and Discrimination in Hockey—Why the NHL and NHLPA Need to Step Up," *The Copper and Blue*, http://www.coppernblue.com. Zona, in turn, refers to a piece by Brendan's brother, Patrick, a law student and scout for the Flyers. See Burke, "Brendan Burke's Coming Out."

35. "Pronger Not Discussing *Trib* Illustration," ESPN.com, June 9, 2010.

36. Scott M. Reid, "Let Figure Skating's Cold War Begin," *Orange County Register*, February 17, 2010.

37. Stojko, "The Night They Killed Figure Skating." Stojko was referring partly to the large loss of points for a quad that a skater attempts but does not achieve, making it a safer bet simply to skip it.

38. Thompson, "A Message."

39. Christopher Lawson, "Sequins? What Sequins? Canada's New Spin on Triple Loops: Figure Skaters Have a Tough Time Pitching the Sport's Muscle; 'Show the Masculinity.'" *Wall Street Journal*, April 3, 2010. The photo shoot was later de-

scribed differently, however, in Skate Canada's 2009 *Annual Report*, which only used the word "tough" in the phrase "tough economic times." It called the shoot part of the "Dream Big, Reach Higher" campaign making celebrities of skaters and "positioning . . . our athletes as 'people.'"

40. Patrick White, "Figure Skating Gets Tough," *Globe and Mail*, February 3, 2009; Ziegler Jr., "Can Canada Make Figure Skating Tough?" In his blog post, Ziegler embedded a video, "CBC Saskatoon: Tough Skate," CBCSports.ca, which is no longer available.

41. "Skating," *Elvis Stojko*, http://www.elvisstojko.net.

42. Karlinsky and Harper, "Figure Skating Gets Macho Makeover."

43. Steve Buffery, "Elvis Stojko: If You're Very Lyrical and You're Really Feminine and Soft, Well, That's . . . NOT Men's Skating," *Toronto Sun*, May 3, 2009.

44. See, for instance, Buzinski, "Elvis Stojko: I Don't Hate Gays." Among other issues, Buzinski criticized Stojko's use of "sexual preference" ("cringe") instead of "sexual orientation," which allows for various understandings about whether sexual identities and leanings are chosen or innate.

45. "Olympic Gold Medalist Shows His True Colors," *Gender Test* THIS, 7 August 7, 2010, http://gendertestthis.wordpress.com. The comment during the Olympics appeared on RDS television in Quebec on February 17, 2010. A transcript can be found on the Facebook page, "Le CQGL demande des excuses à Mailhot et Goldberg pour propos homophobes!," http://fr-ca.facebook.com.

46. NBC Olympic coverage, February 24, 2010.

47. Adams, *Artistic Impressions*, 89, and the whole chapter "Manliness and Grace: Skating as a Gentleman's Art," 81–104.

48. Bergling, *Sissyphobia*. See also Anderson, *In the Game*; Pronger, *Arena of Masculinity*.

49. Thompson, "A Message."

50. Amaechi, "Making Sport More Human and Humane"; Amaechi and Bull, *Man in the Middle*, 134.

51. Kim, "'The Gayest Sport in America.'" Kim maintained the site *Rainbow Ice: Lesbian, Gay, Bisexual, and Transgendered Issues in the Sport of Figure Skating*, http://www.plover.com/rainbowice/.

52. Jackson, *On Edge*, 157–58.

53. Bryan Safi, "That's Gay: Johnny Weir," *Current* TV, February 25, 2010, http://current.com.

54. Caple, "Johnny Weir Is a Real Man." This description appears in Tommy Craggs's "occasional series," on the blog *DeadSpin* and is called "Today in Euphemizing Johnny Weir's Gayness."

55. Weir, *Welcome to My World*. His flamboyance and issues raised about it in figure skating are a recurring theme in the Sundance Channel series *Be Good Johnny Weir*, which premiered in 2010.

56. Amaechi and Bull, *Man in the Middle*, 140–41.

57. Abrams, "Nigel Lithgoe Tweets Off." Lithgoe, in Stojko style, defended himself by saying he hated effeminate dancing, not gays, nicely distinguishing between sex and gender but with no acknowledgment that gender bashing fuels gay bashing.

58. *So You Think You Can Dance*, season 8, Fox Television, Summer 2010: exit of Billy Bell, July 29, 2010; Mia Michaels's comment to Lauren Froderman and the Alex and tWitch routine, June 30; Alex and tWitch, June 30; Finale, August 12.

59. *Stars on Ice*, Portland, Maine, April 9, 2011.

60. The bout took place on September 8, 2007.

61. I allude here to a once-famous book, and book title, in lesbian culture by JoAnn Loulan (with Sherry Tho), *The Lesbian Erotic Dance: Butch, Femme, Androgyny, and Other Rhythms* (San Francisco: Spinster Books, 1990).

62. "About," www.butch/femme.com.

63. On *transmasculine*, see Sinclair Sexsmith, "The Term 'Transmasculine.'" Sexsmith credits the term to the Transmasculine Community Network, but the hyperlink led to a site concerned with technology. Comments by the group's founder, S. Leigh Thompson, who identifies it as on possibly permanent hiatus, can be found as a comment, posted on September 30, 2009, posted to "Crafting Language: Transmasculine," on the blog *Adventures in Gender*. "Mission," *The Brown Boi Project*. See also "About" on the Butch Voices website.

64. The song is actually called "There! Right There!" written by Laurence O'Keefe and Neil Benjamin, 2007.

65. This event took place in Scarborough, Maine, on September 14, 2007.

66. We went to the skate park on October 2, 2007.

67. Williams, "Fruitboots." There are numerous other discussions, written and otherwise, on the topic.

68. "About Us," *Maine Roller Derby*, http://www.mainerollerderby.org (accessed April 7, 2011). This site still exists on the web under the .org address but www .mainerollerderby.com, the site that is current, no longer uses it.

VI. Having the Wherewithal

1. "Membership Process," Philadelphia Skating Club and Humane Society website, http://www.pschs.org.

2. Gladwell, *Outliers*, 40–41.

3. Ibid., 42.

4. Ibid., 21–25.

5 Ibid , 33

6. Dear Abby (Jeanne Phillips), "Woman Searches for Reason to End Her Guiltless Affair," *Portland Press Herald*, December 15, 2007.

7. Sam Fussell well describes this aspect of bodybuilding in *Muscle*, especially chapter 9, "The Vocational Opportunities,"145–58.

8. She said this repeatedly in interviews and in the prologue of her book *Age Is Just a Number*: "Ok, let me pause right here and say it: I'm totally fine with aging except for the recovery time. Is it really necessary to take 48 hours to recover from a 24-second sprint?" (5).

9. "Evan Lysacek Is Vera Wang's New Skating Muse."

10. Stars on Ice, twenty-fifth annual show, Portland, Maine, April 8, 2011.

11. Brennan, *Inside Edge*, 188–90.

12. "About Us," Dartfish, http://www.dartfish.com.

13. Marty Myers and Ashley Teatum, "Clarks Summit's Rippon Sets Sights on Olympic Bid in 2010," *Times-Tribune.com*, December 25, 2007, http://www.thetimes-tribune.com.

14. "About Us," Authentic Change, http://www.authenticchange.com. Authentic Change was incorporated in 2006. The workshop, "Peak Performance," occurred on June 30, 2007, at the annual Adult Figure Skating Training Camp weekend at the Ice House in Hackensack, New Jersey.

15. I can tell from talking to serious recreational or competitive adult skaters in other skating areas that their big "here's a sign of how serious I am" skate outlays run between $300 and $500, although Riedell now makes higher-end derby boots that are comparable in cost to figure skating boots.

16. Bartlett, "Ask the Expert."

17. "875 TS," on the Riedell Skates website, http://www.ice.riedellskates.com (accessed on August 26, 2010).

18. MacDougall, *Born to Run*, 169–72.

19. "Buying Crystals for Figure Skating Dresses," *Ice Mom's Adventures in Figure Skating*, October 15, 2008, http://icemom.blogspot.com. Ice Mom now has a larger blog with regular contributors and it offers a lot of interesting discussion about the cost and culture of skating at Icemom.net.

20. *So You Think You Can Dance*, season 4 (June 5, 2008).

21. "*So You Think You Can Dance*, Milwaukee Auditions, Vegas Callbacks" on the blog *Television! You Black Emperor*, June 8, 2008, http://tybe.blogspot.com.

22. Blog post by "Daniel," "So You Think You Can Dance: It's Vegas, Baby!" *Television without Pity*, undated entry on recent June 5, 2008 episode, http://www.televisionwithoutpity.com.

23. Blog and media coverage of the finale repeatedly characterized them that way, echoing a comment from the host, Cat Deeley, that season 4 would be the first to crown one.

24. A nice thread on the *Television without Pity* forums from June 2008 called "Joshua Allen: Hip Hopper . . . Avec Brisé" also noted that he was being singled out for cross-training that is embedded in the training of most dancers labeled "contemporary," who study jazz, hip-hop, ballet, and more at the studios they train at. The thread begins at http://forums.televisionwithoutpity.com.

25. *So You Think You Can Dance*, season 4, August 6, 2008.

26. Audition of Paige Jones, *So You Think You Can Dance*, season 4, June 5, 2008.

27. Audition of Anthony Bryant, *So You Think You Can Dance*, season 4, August 6, 2008.

28. "Virginia Beach Man Proves He Can Dance," *HamptonRoads.Com*, August 17, 2007, http://hamptonroads.com.

29. Mogulescu, "Most Culturally Radical Show on TV."

30. Gia Kourlas, "So He Knows He Can Dance: A Prince among Paupers," *New York Times*, July 11, 2007 (correction added July 17, 2007).

31. Power, "An Interview with Joshua Allen from SYTYCD."

32. *America's Next Top Model*, cycle 9, November 29, 2007.

33. *Institute for the Study of the Neurologically Typical*.

34. Bruce Grierson, "The Incredible Flying Nonagenarian," *New York Times*, December 25, 2010. The article has a fascinating account of both general aging and the particulars of Kotelko's situation, attending to matters ranging from physiology to her late start.

35. See the profile of Luce Bandit in Barbee and Cohen's *Down and Derby*, 219–21.

36. Conversations with Gary Gurney in Portland, Maine, in 2010 and 2011.

37. In *Sport, Technology, and the Body*, Magdalinski notes how prevalent is the language of being good in discussing food management, for instance.

38. C. Montague Cobb, "Race and Runners," *Journal of Health and Physical Education* 7, no. 1 (Jan. 1936): 3–7, 52–56, p. 56, quoted in Bass, *Not the Triumph but the Struggle*, 70–71.

39. Jere Longman, "Figure Skaters of Asian Descent Have Risen to Prominence," *New York Times*, January 23, 2010.

40. Quoted by Jason Maoz in "Court Jews: Pro Basketball's Forgotten History," *The Jewish Press*, June 27, 2007, and in the movie *The First Basket: A Jewish Basketball Documentary*.

41. The history of testing in the Olympics is well situated by Schweinbenz and Cronk in "Femininity Control at the Olympic Games."

42. Griffin and Carroll, *On the Team*, co-sponsored by the National Center for Lesbian Rights (NCLR), the Women's Sports Foundation (WSF), and, within WSF, It Takes a Team! Education Campaign for Lesbian, Gay, Bisexual, and Transgender Issues in Sports, October 4, 2010.

43. Teetzel, "On Transgendered Athletes," 243–45.

44. Devlin, "Genetic Freaks."

45. "Proof That Muralitharan Does Not Chuck," *The Cricket Show*, available on the *Island Cricket* website, uploaded on December 14, 2008, http://www.islandcricket.lk. The video appeared on YouTube a month before but the interview itself is not dated. The person who posted it to *Island Cricket* stated in a comment that it was

filmed in 2004, the same year that another former cricketer turned sportswriter, this time for Britain, had another such video test conducted. That year makes sense because the third big controversy about his delivery took place then. See the comment by "Hilal" on the Dilmah Cricket Network Forum, December 2, 2009, http://dilmahforum.cricinfo.com; and Mark Nicholas, "Brace Yourselves for New Footage That May Prove Murali's Not Bending the Law," *Sydney Morning Herald*, July 8, 2004.

46. For a history and analysis of the phenomenon, see Coco Fusco, "Other History of Intercultural Performance," in her *English Is Broken Here*, 39–63.

47. McCullough, "Body Like a Rocket."

48. The 2011 skating movie *RISE*, which I discuss in the section "Politics at Hand," shows historical footage of a pairs team skating up to an announcer to say how much they enjoy L&M cigarettes.

49. Magdalinski, *Sport, Technology, and the Body*, 85 and throughout.

50. Teetzel, "On Transgendered Athletes," 245.

51. McCullough, "Body Like a Rocket."

52. Rowell, *The Women Who Raised Me*, 188.

53. Avril Lavigne, "Sk8er Boi," *Let's Go*, 2002.

VII. Blade Scars/Biopsy Scars

The source of this section's epigraph was a performance by Flutterbox, 2008, at Mass MoCA, which was formerly available on the museum's website, where I heard it.

1. Killer Quick, "How to Spot a Derby Girl." It appeared in numerous Maine Roller Derby event programs and in numerous places on the web, including *Whip It Good*, March 28, 2008, http://www.mainetoday.com/blogs.

2. In the revised edition of the rulebook posted on the WFTDA website, dated May 26, 2010, 9.2.6.1.2, it states "Injury—Referees will only call off a jam in the case of a serious injury or an injury that could endanger another skater." Guidelines under 10.3 specify that under some circumstances, except never when they are bleeding, injured players may return to play during the same bout.

3. Audre Lorde, *The Cancer Journals* (San Francisco: Aunt Lute Press, 1997 [1980]), 60, cited in Jain, "Cancer Butch," 508.

4. See Cheryl Wall, *Worrying the Line*, 48–49, on Audre's connection with Eudora in the novel as contributing to a narrative of feminist connection and cross-generational "mythical matrilineage." Lorde quotations from *Zami*, 164, 169, 168, 175, respectively.

5. I refer to the term "bootylicious," from the song by that name, written by Rob Fusari, Beyoncé Knowles, and Faltone Moore, which appeared on the group's 2001 album *Survivor* (Columbia Records).

6. "You Might be a Figure Skater if . . . ," http://www.facebook.com; "Figure

Skating Will Eventually Kill Me . . . or at least give me arthritis," http://www
.facebook.com/ (capitalization of the page titles reflects how they appear on the site).

7. "Other Things That Might Suggest You're a Figure Skater," "You Might be a
Figure Skater if . . ." http://www.facebook.com. Accessed October 28, 2009.

8. *Help Tequila Mockingbird*, http://www.helptequila.com/, accessed February 1,
2008. The text was updated several years later to indicate her progress: "Tequila
has returned home and works daily in therapy to regain her strength and physical
abilities. She has regained some movement in all of her limbs and due to sheer
perseverance and hard work, she is using the walking machine and swimming
with the assistance of her physical therapists. As she approaches the two-year anni-
versary of her accident, she is positive about the direction of her recovery and
thanks all who have helped her along the way. There is still work to be done and
she still needs your help" (accessed November 13, 2009).

9. Mary Waldron, "Lawyer by Day . . . Part One," *Law Crossing*, July 30, 2007.

10. Eric Herman, "'Anomaly': Lawyer by Day, Skater by Night Doesn't Blame
Sport for Injury." *Chicago Tribune*, September 10, 2007.

11. Tequila maintained this attitude when she was interviewed several years
later for Barbee and Cohen, *Down and Derby*, 122–25.

12. Theberge, *Higher Goals*, 128–29, 134–35.

13. The "Panthers Hockey Operations" bio page on the team's website listed, for
the 2009–10 season a trainer and physical therapist who had both been on staff for
multiple years by then. http://panthers.nhl.com.

14. An official representative of WFTDA insurance clarified this point on Facebook, pointing out that "skating only with WFTDA coverage is skating extremely
under-insured." Comment on the entry "WFTDA, USARS reach agreement on insurance coverage," on the WFTDA Facebook page.

15. Jenni Carlson, "Derby Players Pitch In; Roller Derby Skating Accident
Brings Paralysis," *NewsOK*, November 8, 2009, http://www.newsok.com.

16. Torgovnick, *Cheer!* 165.

17. Ibid., xxii, 54, and throughout.

18. Ibid., 162–63.

19. Ibid., 85.

20. On needing Oprah, see also Holliday, *The Larry Holliday Story*, which discusses the financial challenges of an African American figure skater (122).

21. "NCAA Catastrophic Injury Insurance Program Benefit Summary for the
Period 8/1/09 through 7/31/10," pp. 3–4, http://www.ncaa.org. Starting in 2006–7,
the NCAA had required cheerleading squads to be covered by their catastrophic insurance and to be under the supervision of a "safety-certified coach or advisor."
"Future Coverage Adds Supervision Component."

22. USA Swimming, EAHI, 2010. The national governing bodies of many Olympic sports indicate related and easily accessed criteria on their websites. But specific information about what EAHI covers is password-protected, offered online by

the U.S. Olympic Committee to only eligible or already covered athletes. "Elite Athlete Health Insurance," *Team USA* website, http://teamusa.org (accessed November 11, 2009). However, the United States Ski and Skateboarding Association (USSA) indicates that the plan has a $25,000 sports injury deductible. "USOC Elite Athlete Health Insurance," USSA website, http://www.ussa.org. The organization also indicates that "all named A-B-C national team members of Olympic and Paralympic ski and snowboard disciplines will be provided Secondary Sport Accident coverage, Excess Catastrophic Medical coverage and Emergency Medical Evacuation coverage." Ibid.

23. Greg Bluestein, "A Hit and Missed Paperwork Alter Player's Life," *Los Angeles Times*, February 26, 2006, sec. A, p. 13; Steve Wyche, "Ex-Bulldog Suing Georgia Athletics," *Atlanta Journal-Constitution*, December 22, 2004, sec. E, p. 3.

24. Scott M. Reid, "A New Ice Age," *Orange County Register*, December 3, 2004.

25. See Environmental Justice Resource Center, *Environmental Justice*.

26. See, for instance, Mishori, "Who Gets Sick in America—and Why." As Barbara Ehrenreich points out, early detection devices and practices should not be considered to be 100 percent advantageous as they are often presumed to be: Some small tumors that only mammograms detect can already be spreading; some people wind up with false diagnoses or treatment that they might not have needed. "Welcome to Cancerland," 43–53.

27. The expression "Mrs." first appeared in the season premiere of *America's Got Talent*, June 23, 2009, and in several subsequent episodes. "Bio: Sharon Osbourne," *America's Got Talent Season 4*, http://www.nbc.com.

28. See, for instance, Beyondmarriage.org, *Beyond Same-Sex Marriage: A New Strategic Vision for All Our Families and Relationships*, executive summary (beyondmarriage.org) and full statement (http://beyondmarriage.org/full_statement .html, July 26, 2006). As the authors emphasize, elevating the conjugal-couple household also "does a tremendous disservice to the many other ways in which people actually construct their families, kinship networks, households, and relationships," including single-parent families, extended families sharing domestic space, living situations involving a person and that person's caregiver, and other ways that people share domestic space to share care, expenses, and warmth. As the statement suggests, "think *Golden Girls*."

29. Bailey, Kandaswamy, and Richardson "Is Gay Marriage Racist." See also Dean Spade and Craig Willse, "I Still Think Marriage Is the Wrong Goal," http:// makezine.enoughenough.org/prop8.html, which includes the short statement with that title, first published in the aftermath of the November 4, 2008, election, as well as many excellent sources on the topic. As members of the radical queer group LAGAI ask, about the 1,138 federal benefits and responsibilities that marriage confers, "Why should we fight for 1,138 rights for some people, instead of all rights for all people?" See Kate and Deeg, "Marriage Is Still the Opiate of the Queers."

30. For a great guide to thinking about referring to body parts ordinarily presumed to be gendered, see Dean Spade, "Some Very Basic Tips for Making Higher Education More Accessible to Trans Students and Rethinking How We Talk about Gendered Bodies."

31. Ehrenreich, "Welcome to Cancerland," 43–53, 49, 46–48, and throughout.

32. Ibid., 47–48.

33. Jain, "Cancer Butch," 501–38, 504.

34. See essay 8, "Form-Fitting: The Bra in Three Stories."

35. Sedgwick, "White Glasses," 262.

36. Ibid., 256–57, 262.

37. Jain, "Cancer Butch," 512–13.

38. See essay 8, "Form-Fitting: The Bra in Three Stories."

39. Jain, "Cancer Butch," 514.

40. Ibid.

41. Ibid.

42. Ibid., 515.

43. Jain, "Cancer Butch," 504; Ehrenreich, "Welcome to Cancerland," 49; Sedgwick, "White Glasses," 262.

44. "Before and After Looks," on the website for *Look Good . . . and Feel Better*, http://www.lookgoodfeelbetter.org. On carcinogens in cosmetics and other issues concerning the politics of pink-ribbon campaigns, see *Think Before You Pink*.

45. Kittredge, "Dazed and Concussed," 2. See also her "Twenty-One Guys, Forty-Four Skates, and Me."

46. Kittredge, "Losing My Manhood."

47. Ibid., 1.

48. Ibid., 6–7.

49. Ibid., 7–8.

VIII. The Politics of Pleasure

1. Telephone interview with Alyn Libman, March 24, 2008. Interviews with Libman can also be found in the press, including: Fields-Mayer, "Gender Jump"; Robert Bergin, "Meet Alyn Libman," *The Daily Californian*, August 24, 2006. Bright, *Big Sex Little Death*, 49.

2. Gilbert Cruz, "Top Ten Buzzwords," from *Top Ten Lists of 2007*, *Time*, http://www.time.com.

3. Coyote, "To All the Kick Ass, Beautiful Fierce Femmes Out There . . ."

4. Young, "From Ballet to Boxing," 49–51.

5. Staceyann Chin, Performance, Gay Games VII Opening Ceremony, July 15, 2006, text at http://www.staceyannchin.com/archives.

6. Lambert, "2002 Sydney Gay Games," 331–34. See also Caroline Fusco, "Cultural Landscapes of Purification," for an excellent discussion about how sporting

spaces themselves, from buildings through locker rooms, the focus of her study, are racialized to the dominance of white people.

7. John Conroy, "The Police Torture Scandal: A Who's Who, Part 3, Who Knew," *Chicago Reader*, June 15, 2006, http://www.chicagoreader.com. As Conroy's piece, published a month before the Gay Games started, indicated, the results of the "four-year, multimillion dollar" investigation were imminent and big news.

8. Barbee and Cohen, *Down and Derby*, 2–3.

9. Gruneau and Whitson, *Hockey Night in Canada*, 53. As they show, nothing in hockey, from its current rules to the turtle pace of women's access to ice time, can be characterized as a product of evolution.

10. Red Bull, *Project X*, http://www.shaunwhite.com/projectx.

11. Kusz, *Revolt of the White Athlete*, 70–73, 102–3.

12. Ahmed, *Cultural Politics of Emotion*, 12. Although, in the sentence I quote, Ahmed refers specifically to investment in structures, her book, including the pages surrounding this quote, addresses diverse investments: in ideas of the nation, in particular nations, in heterosexual-style couplings, and more.

13. Smith, "Miracle on Ice."

14. Thanks to Eithne Luibhéid for our work together on elaborating the function of norms; the language of this paragraph is shared.

15. Ampu, "What I Learned," 112–26.

16. Among many offenders, Avon, in particular, is well known for this contradiction. See *Think Before You Pink*.

17. See Joseph, *Against the Romance of Community*, and the great study by Kath Weston and Lisa B. Rofel ("Sexuality, Class, and Conflict in a Lesbian Workplace") of a lesbian-owned mechanic shop where the ideal of "lesbian community" got in the way of fair labor practices.

18. See Kelley's *Yo Mama's Disfunktional*, 36–41, and *Freedom Dreams*, 10–11 and throughout. Duggan's *Twilight of Equality?*, 87–88, brought me to study Kelley's work in this context.

19. For an excellent account of neoliberalism, see Duggan's *Twilight of Equality?*

20. Peck, *Age of Oprah*, 222.

21. Nguyen, "The Biopower of Beauty," 377–78.

Conclusion

1. For example, Han, "Confessions of a Middle-Aged Figure Skater."

2. Quinlan Miller, "Commercial Break: Yoga, Trans Elixer," *Come All Without . . .* YouTube Channel, December 21, 2010, http://www.youtube.com.

3. Canadian Association for the Advancement of Women and Sport, *Focus Group Report*. See also Sykes, *Queer Bodies: Sexualities, Genders, and Fatness in Physical Education* for an excellent account of how childhood education in sports needs to and might be changed to value and support the participation of people

who don't conform to interconnected norms of race, gender, sexuality, and relations between fatness and fitness.

4. Entwistle, *Ice Etiquette*.

5. Organizations working to mitigate the cost of skating have diverse purposes. Figure Skating in Harlem uses skating to promote education and life skills along with skating. Ice Bridges (http://www.icebridges.org) raises financial support for advanced but economically disadvantaged skaters. MySkatingMall.com facilitates private resale of skating equipment and such to support skating clubs, teams, or charitable projects. In addition, I've run across various people, at my club and skating community and elsewhere, who have personally taken on projects like collecting and giving away used skates.

6. Conversation with Jed Bell, December 2008.

7. Sioux, "Talk Derby to Me," 217.

8. Conversation with Toby Beauchamp, Chicago, March 26, 2011.

9. Chrystal Ice House, Chrystal Lake, Illinois, practice ice contract, winter/spring 2011.

10. Hardy, *Crossovers*.

11. Rona Marech, "Olympics' Transgender Quandary: Debate Rages on the Fairness of New Inclusion Rule," *San Francisco Chronicle*, June 14, 2004; U.S. Figure Skating, *Official 2011 U.S. Figure Skating Rulebook*.

12. National Center for Lesbian Rights, "NCLR Settles Suit against Gay Skaters."

13. The 2011 USFS mission statement still announces an intention to avoid discrimination only on the bases of "race, color, religion, age, gender or national origin," although it offers a broader guideline in various other places, like under "Respect for Participants and Dignity" in the *Coaches Code of Ethics, Standards, and Conduct*: "Coaches are aware of cultural, individual and role differences, including those due to age, gender, race, ethnicity, national origin, religion, sexual orientation, disability, language and socioeconomic status. Coaches try to eliminate the effect on their work of biases based on those factors, and they do not knowingly participate in or condone unfair discriminatory practices." It's a good start. Now make such policies easily visible, deem them rulebook-worthy, and consider the implications of where such topics are addressed now. I found that coaching directive in the USFS *Risk Management Guide*. Risk management is the umbrella category under which certain administrators, at my institution and elsewhere, now also want to conceptualize nondiscrimination compliance. It's sad. And wrong. USFS Mission Statement, in the *2011 Rulebook*, Article 2H, p.1, and on the USFS website at http://www.usfigureskating.org; U.S. Figure Skating, *Coaches Code of Ethics, Standards, and Conduct*, in the *2007–2008 United States Figure Association Risk Management Guide*, http://www.usfigureskating.org/content/RiskManagementGuide .pdf (accessed December 23, 2010).

14. In a conversation at AN 2011, Cindy Crouse directed me to the 2006 Adult competition in Obertsdorf, Germany, in which a Gold-level dance team got two

costume deductions for wearing "opposite-sex" clothes, even though the result was one male-costumed and one female-costumed skater. Switching parts can also get one docked, and the rareness of women lifting men, not always out of the question size- and strength-wise, testifies also to rigid divisions.

15. For a thorough account of the debate and good arguments for dropping the notion that sex segregation should be the default, see McDonagh and Pappano, *Playing with the Boys.*

16. See 2011 U.S. Junior Figure Skating National Championships, results, IceNetwork.com, http://www.usfigureskating.org.

17. Adams, *Artistic Impressions*, 230–32.

18. Frommer, et al., "Sex Differences in Concussion Symptoms of High School Athletes," 82; Sander, "Female Athletes Concussion Symptoms May Be Overlooked."

19. Frommer, 77; Sander; Carl Ehrlich, "A Relentless Opponent Stalks the Locker Room," *New York Times*, November 12, 2010. Although these sources do not explicitly discuss gender stereotyping, the likelihood that gender stereotyping factors into the types of misdiagnosis and nondiagnosis that they discuss is clear.

20. Wall, "Denise Wall on Raising Dancin' Boys."

21. In "Cultural Expressions of African American Female Athletes in Intercollegiate Sport," Stratta offers an instructive comparison in her ethnographic study of African American athletes at a "predominantly white institution," noting everything from the burden of being expected to explain or represent their race to the opportunity, or lack of it, to contribute to warm-up music playlists.

22. *Dancing with the Stars*, ABC, October 5, 2010; *Skating with the Stars*, ABC, November 22, 2010. For a classic text on the demands of skating and dance training, see Ryan, *Little Girls in Pretty Boxes.*

23. Kang, *Managed Hand.* For instance, Korean manicurists often rested in a squatting position off-duty in the backrooms, but they avoided "body arrangements that suggested premodernity and ethnic otherness" in front of customers (148–49).

24. Kociemba, "'Proud Mary'": *Glee*'s Very Special Sham Disability Pride Anthem."

25. Thanks to my students in several iterations of Interdisciplinary Studies 250 for wise comments on this aspect of the film. *Glee*, as Lucas Hilderbrand points out in "Stage Left," is quite the mixed bag on race, too.

26. Heather Steeves, "Panel Seeks Ban on Indian Mascot Names at School," *Bangor Daily News*, December 14, 2010. For an excellent approach to considering appropriation in cultural, political, social, and historical contexts, see "The Properties of Culture and the Politics of Possessing Identity," in Coombe, *Cultural Life of Intellectual Properties*, 208–47.

27. Goldman, *Living My Life*, 56, quoted in Shulman, "Dances with Feminists."

BIBLIOGRAPHY

Abrams, Natalie. "Nigel Lithgoe Tweets Off against GLAAD's 'Homophobic' Accusation." *E! On-Line*, May 22, 2009, http://www.eonline.com.

Adams, Mary Louise. *Artistic Impressions: Figure Skating, Masculinity, and the Limits of Sport*. Toronto: University of Toronto Press, 2011.

Ahmed, Sara. *The Cultural Politics of Emotion*. New York: Routledge, 2004.

Amaechi, John. "Making Sport More Human and Humane: Thoughts on LGBT Athletes, Coaches, and Sport Industry Professionals." Presented at the Sports, Culture, and Sexuality Conference, Ithaca College, Ithaca, N.Y., March 19, 2009.

Amaechi, John, with Chris Bull. *Man in the Middle*. New York: ESPN Books, 2007.

America's Got Talent. NBC. WSCS, Portland, Maine, June 23, 2009.

America's Next Top Model. The CW. WPXT, Portland, Maine, November 29, 2007.

Ampu, Ratowe T. "What I Learned from Being G Minus in the World of Homohop Commerce." In *Nobody Passes: Rejecting the Rules of Gender and Conformity*, edited by Mattildha Bernstein Sycamore, 112–26. Emeryville, Calif.: Seal Press, 2006.

Anderson, Eric. *In the Game: Gay Athletes and the Cult of Masculinity*. SUNY Series on Sport, Culture, and Social Relations. Albany: State University of New York Press, 2005.

Ash, Juliet. "Memory and Objects." In *The Gendered Object*, edited by Pat Kirkham, 219–24. New York: St. Martin's, 1996.

———. "The Tie: Presence and Absence." In *The Gendered Object*, edited by Pat Kirkham, 162–71. New York: St. Martin's, 1996.

"The Audacity of Hoops." *Real Sports with Bryant Gumbel*, Segment Prod. Ezra Edelman and Joe Perskie. HBO, April 15, 2008, http://www.youtube.com.

Bailey, Marlon M., Priya Kandaswamy, and Matt Richardson. "Is Gay Marriage Racist: A Conversation." In *That's Revolting: Queer Strategies for Resisting Assimilation*, edited by Mattildha Bernstein Sycamore, 87–96. New York: Soft Skull, 2008.

Barbee, Jennifer, and Alex Cohen. *Down and Derby: The Insider's Guide to Roller Derby*. New York: Soft Skull, 2010.

Bartlett, Chris. "Ask the Expert: Chris Bartlett Talks about Figure Skate Blade Sharpening." Interview by Icemom. June 16, 2010, www.icemom.net.

Bass, Amy. *Not the Triumph but the Struggle: The 1968 Olympics and the Making of the Black Athlete*. Critical American Studies Series. Minneapolis: University of Minnesota Press, 2002.

Battle of the Blades. CBC Television. Season 1, October 4, 2009, Bob Probert segment, http://www.youtube.com; Season 1, November 15, 2009, Claude Lemieux segment, http://www.youtube.com.

Baughman, Cynthia, ed. *Women on Ice: Feminist Essays on the Tonya Harding/Nancy Kerrigan Spectacle*. New York: Routledge, 1995.

Bechdel, Alison. *Fun Home: A Family Tragicomic*. New York: Houghton Mifflin, 2006.

Be Good Johnny Weir. Season 1. Sundance Channel, 2010.

Bergling, Tim. *Sissyphobia: Gay Men and Effeminate Behavior*. New York: Southern Tier Editions, 2001.

Bernstein, Ross. *The Code: The Unwritten Rules of Fighting and Retaliation in the NHL*. Chicago: Triumph, 2006.

Biasca, Nicola, Stephan Wirth, and Yelverton Tegner. "Head Injuries and Facial Injuries in Ice Hockey Role of the Protective Equipment." *European Journal of Trauma*, no. 4 (2005): 369–74.

Billy Elliot. Dir. Stephen Daldry. Universal Focus, 2000.

Billy Elliot the Musical. Book and lyrics by Lee Hall. London debut, 2005; Broadway, 2008.

Birrell, Susan, and Cheryl L. Cole, eds. *Women, Sport, and Culture*. Champaign, Ill.: Human Kinetics, 1994.

Blades of Glory. Dir. Josh Gordon and Will Speck. Dreamworks, 2007.

Bolin, Anne, and Jane Granskog, eds. *Athletic Intruders: Ethnographic Research on Women, Culture, and Exercise*. SUNY Series on Sport, Culture, and Social Relations. Albany: State University of New York Press, 2003.

Bornstein, Kate. *Hello, Cruel World: 101 Alternatives to Suicide for Teens, Freaks, and Other Outlaws*. New York: Seven Stories, 2006.

Brennan, Christine. *Inside Edge: A Revealing Look into the Secret World of Figure Skating*. New York: Doubleday, 1997.

Bright, Susie. *Big Sex Little Death: A Memoir*. Berkeley, Calif.: Seal Press, 2011.

Bring It On. Dir. Peyton Reed. Universal Studios, 2000.

Bring It On: All or Nothing. Dir. Steve Rash. Universal Studios Home Entertainment Family Productions, 2006.

Brody, Jennifer DeVere. "Boyz Do Cry: Screening History's White Lies." *Screen* 43 (Spring 2002): 91–96.

The Brown Boi Project. http://www.brownboiproject.org/.

Brownworth, Victoria A. "Life in the Passing Lane: Exposing the Class Closet." In *Queerly Classed*, ed. Susan Ruffo. Boston: South End, 1997.

Buccigross, John. "Imagine This Story of Acceptance between Brian and Brendan Burke." ESPN.com, November 24, 2009, http://sports.espn.go.com.

Burke, Patrick. "Brendan Burke's Coming Out and Death Showed His Brother and Family the Welcoming Side of Hockey. Now Their Arms Are Open for Other Gay Athletes." *Outsports.com*, June 21, 2010.

Burstyn, Varda. *The Rites of Men: Manhood, Politics, and the Culture of Sport.* Toronto: University of Toronto Press, 1999.

Butch Voices. http://www.butchvoices.com.

Buzinski, Jim. "Elvis Stojko: I Don't Hate Gays." *Outsports.com*, May 15, 2010.

Cahn, Susan K. *Coming on Strong: Gender and Sexuality in Twentieth-Century Women's Sport.* New York: Free Press, 1994.

Canadian Association for the Advancement of Women and Sport. *Focus Group Report: Physical Activity and Women 55–70.* April 2007, http://www.caaws.ca.

Caple, Jim. "Johnny Weir Is a Real Man." *ESPN.com*, January 12, 2010, http://sports.espn.go.com.

Carter, W. Hodding. *Off the Deep End: The Probably Insane Idea That I Could Swim My Way through a Midlife Crisis—and Qualify for the Olympics.* Chapel Hill: Algonquin, 2008.

Caudwell, Jayne. "Femme-Fatale: RE-thinking the Femme-inine." In *Sport, Sexualities and Queer/Theory*, edited by Jane Caudwell, 143–58. London: Routledge, 2006.

———. *Sport, Sexualities and Queer/Theory.* Routledge Critical Studies in Sport. London: Routledge, 2006.

Christopher, Matt [actually written by Paul Mantell]. *Cool as Ice.* New York: Little, Brown, 2001.

Coombe, Rosemary J. *The Cultural Life of Intellectual Properties: Authorship, Appropriation, and the Law.* Post-Contemporary Interventions. Durham: Duke University Press, 1998.

Coppage, Keith. *Roller Derby to Rollerjam: The Authorized Story of an Unauthorized Sport.* Santa Rosa, Calif.: Squarebooks, 1999.

Coyote, Ivan. "To All the Kick Ass, Beautiful Fierce Femmes Out There . . ." Performance. San Francisco, April 10, 2010, http://www.youtube.com.

Cragg, Tommy. "Today in Euphemizing Johnny Weir's Gayness." *DeadSpin*, January 18, 2010, http://deadspin.com.

Cutting Edge, The. Dir. Paul Michael Glaser. MGM, 1992.

Dallas Cowboy Cheerleaders: Making the Team. CMT. Portland, Maine, 2007.

Dance Moms. Season 1, Episode 7, "She's a Fighter." Lifetime. Portland, Maine, August 25, 2011. Episode 8, "Love on the Dance Floor," September 1, 2011.

Dancing with the Stars. Season 6, Episode 8. ABC. WMTW, Portland, Maine, April 8, 2008; Season 11, Episode 6, October 5, 2010; Season 11, Episode 19, 2010.

De Regniers, Beatrice Schenk. *How Joe the Bear and Sam the Mouse Got Together.* New York: Parents' Magazine, 1965.

Devlin, Jane. "Genetic Freaks: Semenya and Yao. One Gets Humiliation, the Other Gets an NBA Contract. Why?" *Huffington Post*, August 24, 2009.

Dodge, Mary Mapes. *Hans Brinker, or, The Silver Skates: A Story of Life in Holland*. New York: Grosset & Dunlap.

Doyle, Jennifer. "Modern Minstrels: Sexist Jokes about Women Athletes." *From a Left Wing: The Cultural Politics of Soccer*, October 6, 2008, http://fromaleft wing.blogspot.com.

Duggan, Lisa. *The Twilight of Equality? Neoliberalism, Cultural Politics, and the Attack on Democracy*. Boston: Beacon Press, 2003.

Ehrenreich, Barbara. "Welcome to Cancerland: A Mammogram Leads to a Cult of Pink Kitsch." *Harper's Magazine*, November 2001, 43–53.

Entwistle, Amy. *Ice Etiquette*. Central Carolina Skating Club website, January 20, 2006, http://www.centralcarolinasc.com/IceEtiquette.aspx.

Environmental Justice Resource Center, Clark Atlantic University. *Environmental Justice in the United States: Threat to Qualities of Life, Fact Sheet*. Published for the Second National People of Color Environmental Leadership Summit. Washington, D.C., 2002, http://www.ejrc.cau.edu.

Etue, Elizabeth, and Megan K. Williams. *On the Edge: Women Making Hockey History*. Toronto: Second Story, 1996.

"Evan Lysacek Is Vera Wang's New Skating Muse." *New York Magazine*, January 29, 2010.

Farber, Michael. "Man of His Word." Sports Illustrated Vault, March 1, 2010, http://sportsillustrated.cnn.com.

Faulkner, Margaret. *I Skate!* Boston: Little, Brown, 1979.

Feder-Kane, Abigail M. "'A Radiant Smile from the Lovely Lady': Overdetermined Femininity in 'Ladies' Figure Skating." In *Reading Sport: Critical Essays on Power and Representation*, edited by Susan Birrell and Mary G. McDonald, 206–33. Boston: Northeastern University Press, 2000.

Fields-Mayer, Thomas. "Gender Jump." *People Magazine*, March 17, 2003.

"Figure Skating Gets Macho Makeover: Attempts to Brand Sport as 'More Masculine' Spark Outrage in Gay Community." ABC News, April 30, 2009, http://abcnews.go.com.

The First Basket: A Jewish Basketball Documentary. Dir. David Vyorst. Laemmle/Zeller Films, 2008.

Foote, Stephanie. "Making Sport of Tonya: Class Performance and Social Punishment." *Journal of Sport & Social Issues* 27, no. 1 (2003): 3–17.

Frommer, Leah J. et al. "Sex Differences in Concussion Symptoms among High School Students." *Journal of Athletic Training* 46, no. 1 (2011): 76–84.

Frueh, Joanna. *Monster/Beauty: Building the Body of Love*. Berkeley: University of California Press, 2001.

Fung, Richard. "Call in the Tropes! Miss Saigon Undergoes Analysis." *Fuse* 17, no. 2 (1993/94): 7–9.

Fusco, Caroline. "Cultural Landscapes of Purification: Sports Spaces and Discourses of Whiteness." *Sociology of Sport Journal* 22 (2005): 283–310.

Fusco, Coco. *English Is Broken Here: Notes on Cultural Fusion in the Americas*. New York City: New Press, 1995.

Fussell, Samuel Wilson. *Muscle: Confessions of an Unlikely Bodybuilder*. New York: Poseidon, 1991.

"Future Coverage Adds Supervision Component." NCAA *News*. NCAA website, July 18, 2005.

Gambs, Deborah. "Myocellular Transduction: When My Cells Trained My Body-Mind." In *The Affective Turn: Theorizing the Social*, edited by Patricia Ticineto Clough, with Jean Halley Durham, 106–18. Durham: Duke University Press, 2007.

Gladwell, Malcolm. *Outliers: The Story of Success*. New York: Little, Brown, 2008.

Goldman, Emma. *Living My Life*. New York: Knopf, 1934.

Gordeeva, Ekaterina. *My Sergei: A Love Story*. New York: Time Warner, 1996.

Gottesman, Jane. *Game Face: What Does a Woman Athlete Look Like?* New York: Random House, 2001.

Gray, Mary L. *Out in the Country: Youth, Media, and Queer Visibility in Rural America*. New York: New York University Press, 2009.

Griffin, Pat. *Strong Women, Deep Closets: Lesbians and Homophobia in Sport*. Champaign, Ill.: Human Kinetics, 1998.

Griffin, Pat, and Helen Carroll. *On the Team: Equal Opportunity for Transgender Student Athlete*. October 4, 2010, http://www.nclrights.org.

Gruneau, Richard, and David Whitson. *Hockey Night in Canada: Sport, Identities, and Cultural Politics*. Toronto: Garamond, 1993.

Halberstam, Judith. *In a Queer Time and Place: Transgender Bodies, Subcultural Lives*. Sexual Cultures. New York: New York University Press, 2005.

Han, Christina. "Confessions of a Middle-Aged Figure Skater." *Marie Claire*, July 14, 2010.

Hardy, LeAnne. *Crossovers*. Charleston: BookSurge, 2009.

Harper, Nick. *Man Tricks: Everything Men Need (or Just Want) to Know*. Naperville, Ill.: Sourcebooks, 2007.

Hilderbrand, Lucas. "Stage Left: *Glee* and the Textual Politics of Difference." *Flow*, December 4, 2009, http://www.flowtv.org.

Hines, James R. *Figure Skating: A History*. Urbana: University of Illinois Press; and Colorado Springs: World Figure Skating Museum and Hall of Fame, 2006.

Holliday, Norma Jean. *The Larry Holliday Story*. Denver: Outskirts Press, 2008.

Ice Castles. Dir. Donald Wrye. Columbia, 1978.

Ice Princess. Dir. Tim Fywell. Disney, 2005.

Institute for the Study of the Neurologically Typical. Last modified March 18, 2002, http://isnt.autistics.org/index.html.

International Skating Union. *Communication* nos. 1611, 1619, and 1557. News, ISU website. http://ww2.isu.org.

Jackson, Jon, with James Pereira. *On Edge: Backroom, Dealing, Cocktail Scheming,*

Triple Axels, and How Top Skaters Get Screwed. New York: Thunder's Mouth Press, 2005.

Jain, S. Lochlain. "Cancer Butch." *Cultural Anthropology* 22, no. 4 (2007): 501–38.

Jamieson, Katherine M. "Reading Nancy Lopez: Decoding Representations of Race, Class, and Sexuality." In *Reading Sport: Critical Essays on Power and Representation*, edited by Susan Birrell and Mary G. McDonald, 144–65. Boston: Northeastern University Press, 2000.

Jenkins, Henry, Tara McPherson, and Jane Shattuc, "The Culture That Sticks to Your Skin: A Manifesto for a New Cultural Studies." In *Hop on Pop: The Politics and Pleasures of Popular Culture*. Durham: Duke University Press, 2002.

Joseph, Miranda. *Against the Romance of Community*. Minneapolis: University of Minnesota Press, 2002.

Joulwan, Melissa. "Melicious." *Rollergirl: Totally True Tales from the Track*. New York: Touchstone, 2007.

Kang, Miliann. *The Managed Hand: Race, Gender, and the Body in Beauty Service Work*. Berkeley: University of California Press, 2010.

Kate and Deeg. "Marriage Is Still the Opiate of the Queers." April 2004, http://www.lagai.org/.

Kaye, Kristin. *Iron Maidens: The Celebration of the Most Awesome Female Muscle in the World*. New York: Thunder's Mouth, 2005.

Kelley, Robin D. G. *Freedom Dreams: The Black Radical Imagination*. Boston: Beacon, 2002.

———. *Yo Mama's Disfunktional! Fighting the Culture Wars in Urban America*. Boston: Beacon, 1997.

Kestnbaum, Ellyn. *Culture on Ice: Figure Skating and Cultural Meaning*. Middletown, Conn.: Wesleyan University Press, 2003.

Killer Quick (Maureen Wissman). "How to Spot a Derby Girl." *Whip It Good*. March 28, 2008, http://www.mainetoday.com.

———. *Maine Roller Derby Media Handbook*, unpublished, 2007.

Kim, Lorrie. "'The Gayest Sport in America': So How Come No Figure Skaters Are Out?" *Outsports.com*, February 9, 2006, http://www.outsports.com.

Kirby, Lynn. *A Perfect Landing*. Nashville: Thomas Nelson, 1998.

———. *A Surprise Finish*. Nashville: Thomas Nelson, 1999.

Kittredge, Katharine. "Dazed and Concussed." Unpublished essay, 2002.

———. "How to Make Love to a Mid-Life Hockey Player (Hint: Very Carefully)." Unpublished essay, n.d.

———. "Losing My Manhood and Losing My Mind: A Female Hockey Player's Experience with Post Concussion Syndrome." Presented at the Sports, Culture, and Sexuality Conference, Ithaca College, Ithaca, N.Y., March 20, 2009.

———. "Twenty-One Guys, Forty-Four Skates, and Me: Female-Adventures in Masculine Sport." *Women in Sport and Physical Activity Journal* 11 (no. 1, Spring 2002): 163–72.

Kociemba, David. "'Proud Mary': *Glee*'s Very Special Sham Disability Pride Anthem." *In Medias Res*, April 9, 2010.

Kusz, Kyle. *Revolt of the White Athlete: Race, Media and the Emergence of Extreme Athletes in America*. Intersections in Communications and Culture; Vol. 14. New York: Peter Lang, 2007.

Lambert, Karen. "The 2002 Sydney Gay Games: Re-Presenting 'Lesbian' Identities through Sporting Space." *Journal of Lesbian Studies* 13, no. 3 (2009): 319–36.

Lannin, Joanne. *A History of Basketball for Girls and Women: From Bloomers to Big Leagues*. Minneapolis: Lerner Sports, 2000.

Lapointe, Joe. "Bob Probert, a Life of Violence, Sadness." *Fanhouse*, July 5, 2010, http://www.fanhouse.com.

Laskowski, Brigitte Gitta. Figure Skaters for Christ website. Last modified August 6, 2006, http://www.fs4christ.com/.

Lenskyj, Helen. *Out of Bounds: Women, Sport and Sexuality*. Toronto: Women's Press, 1986.

Lewis, Beverly. *Dreams on Ice*. Minneapolis: Bethany House, 1998.

———. *A Perfect Match*. Minneapolis: Bethany House, 1999.

Lop-Her, Cindy. "Campaign for Real Booty: DayGlo Divine." *Big Derby Girls Don't Cry*. June 20, 2008, http://bigderbygirls.blogspot.com.

———. "Campaign for Real Booty: Punchy O'Guts," *Big Derby Girls Don't Cry*. June 13, 2008, http://bigderbygirls.blogspot.com.

Lorde, Audre. Zami. *A New Spelling of My Name*. Freedom, Calif.: Crossing Press, 1982.

MacDougall, Christopher. *Born to Run: A Hidden Tribe, Superathletes, and the Greatest Race the World Has Never Seen*. New York: Alfred A. Knopf, 2009.

MacLeod, J. E. *Waiting to Score*. Lodi, N.J.: WestSide Books, 2009.

Magdalinski, Tara. *Sport, Technology, and the Body: The Nature of Performance*. London: Routledge, 2009.

Mahiri, Jabari, and Derek Van Rhéenen. *Out of Bounds: When Scholarship Athletes Become Academic Scholars*. New York: Peter Lang, 2010.

Maifair, Linda Lee. *Go Figure, Gabriella Grant*. Grand Rapids, Mich.: Zondervan, 1997.

Malin, Jo, ed. *My Life at the Gym: Feminist Perspectives on Community through the Body*. Albany: State University of New York Press, 2010.

Manley, Allison. "Interview with Debi Thomas." *Manleywoman Skatecast*, Episode 30, August 24, 2009, http://www.manleywoman.com.

———. "Interview with Ron Ludington." *Manleywoman Skatecast*, Episode 19, September 30, 2008. http://www.manleywoman.com.

Martin, April. "Another Lesbian Jock." In *SportsDykes: Stories from on and off the Field*, edited by Susan Fox Rogers, 35–38. New York: St. Martin's, 1994.

Mastrangelo, Frank A. "Eye and Face Injuries in High School Hockey: Cutting

Down the Risks." In *Safety in Ice Hockey*, edited by C. R. Castaldi and Earl F. Homer, 52–54. Philadelphia: ASTM, 1989.

McCullough, Sarah Rebolloso. "Body Like a Rocket: Performing Technologies of Naturalization." *thirdspace: a journal of feminist theory & culture* 9, no. 2 (2010). http://www.thirdspace.ca.

McDonagh, Eileen L., and Laura Pappano. *Playing with the Boys: Why Separate Is Not Equal in Sports*. New York: Oxford University Press, 2008.

McDonald, Mary, ed. *Reading Sport: Critical Essays on Power and Representation*. Boston: Northeastern University Press, 2000.

McKay, Jim, Michael Messner, and Donald F. Sabo, eds. *Masculinities, Gender Relations, and Sport*. Thousand Oaks, Calif.: Sage, 2000.

McMains, Juliet E. *Glamour Addiction: Inside the American Ballroom Dance Industry*. Middletown, Conn.: Wesleyan University Press, 2006.

Messner, Michael. "When Bodies Are Weapons: Masculinity and Violence in Sport." *International Review for the Sociology of Sport* 25, no. 3 (1990): 203–18.

Miller, Hinda. "I Can't Sell Something Called Jock Bra." In *Game Face: What Does a Female Athlete Look Like?* edited by Geoffrey Biddle, 134–35. New York: Random House, 2001.

Mishori, Ranit. "Who Gets Sick in America—and Why." *Parade*, June 28, 2009, 8–10.

Mogulescu, Miles. "The Most Culturally Radical Show on TV (and Sometimes One of the Cheesiest) Is on Fox," *Huffington Post*, July 14, 2010, http://www.huffingtonpost.com.

Molina-Guzmán, Isabel. *Dangerous Curves: Latina Bodies in the Media*. New York: New York University Press, 2010.

Muñoz, José Esteban. *Disidentifications: Queers of Color and the Performance of Politics*. Cultural Studies of the Americas. Minneapolis: University of Minnesota Press, 1999.

National Center for Lesbian Rights. "NCLR Settles Suit against Gay Skaters." Press release. NCLR website, May 10, 2006.

Nero, Charles. "Teaching Note on Jennifer DeVere Brody's 'Boyz Do Cry': Screening History's White Lies." *Screen* 43 (Spring 2002): 91–96. *Radica Teacher* 67 (2003): 43–44.

Nguyen, Mimi Thi. "The Biopower of Beauty: Humanitarian Imperialisms and Global Feminisms in an Age of Terror." *Signs* 36, no. 2 (Winter 2011): 359–84.

Oliver, Melvin L., and Thomas M. Shapiro. *Black Wealth/White Wealth: A New Perspective on Racial Inequality*. New York: Routledge, 1995.

O'Reilly, Jean, and Susan K. Cahn, eds. *Women and Sports in the United States: A Documentary Reader*. Boston: Northeastern University Press, 2007.

Owen, Maribel Vinson. *Primer of Figure Skating*. New York: McGraw-Hill, 1938.

Peck, Janice. *Age of Oprah: Cultural Icon for the Neoliberal Era*. Boulder: Paradigm, 2008.

Plimpton, George. *Open Net*. New York: W. W. Norton, 1985.

Power, PZ. "An Interview with Joshua Allen from SYTYCD: He's So Much More Than Dancing," *National Muscle*, June 2009. Republished on *PZ Power.Com*, http://www.pzpower.com.

Project X: The Secret Half Pipe. Prod. Red Bull. 2009, http://www.shaunwhite.com.

Pronger, Brian. *The Arena of Masculinity: Sports, Homosexuality, and the Meaning of Sex*. New York: St. Martin's, 1990.

Prouse, Lynda D. *The Tonya Tapes: The Tonya Harding Story in Her Own Voice*. New York: World Audience, 2008.

Pumping Iron II: The Women. Dir. George Butler. Cinegate, 1985.

RISE. Dir. Lisa Lax and Nancy Stern Winters. Lookalike Productions, 2011.

Roller Girls. Prod. Gary Auerbach and Julie Auerbach. A&E, 2006.

Rowell, Victoria. *The Women Who Raised Me: A Memoir*. New York: William Morrow, 2007.

Rudolph, M. "Rule Changes and Their Effect on Safety in Ice Hockey." In *Safety in Ice Hockey*, edited by C. R. Castaldi and Earl F. Homer, 35–36. Philadelphia: ASTM, 1989.

Ryan, Joan. *Little Girls in Pretty Boxes: The Making and Breaking of Elite Gymnasts and Figure Skaters*. New York: Warner, 1996.

Sander, Libby. "Female Athletes Concussion Symptoms May Be Overlooked." *Chronicle of Higher Education*, December 7, 2010.

Schweinbenz, Amanda Nicole, and Alexandria Cronk. "Femininity Control at the Olympic Games." *thirdspace: a journal of feminist theory & culture* 9, no. 2 (2010). http://www.thirdspace.ca.

Sedgwick, Eve. "Privilege of Unknowing: Diderot's *The Nun*." In *Tendencies* by Sedgwick, 23–51. Durham: Duke University Press, 1993.

———. "White Glasses." In *Tendencies* by Sedgwick, 252–66. Durham: Duke University Press, 1993.

Serano, Julia. *Whipping Girl: A Transsexual Woman on Sexism and the Scapegoating of Femininity*. Emeryville, Calif.: Seal Press, 2007.

Sexsmith, Sinclair. "The Term 'Transmasculine.'" *Sugarbutch Chronicles*, April 11, 2008, http://www.sugarbutch.net.

Shimizu, Celine Parreñas. *The Hypersexuality of Race: Performing Asian/American Women on Screen and Scene*. Durham: Duke University Press, 2007.

Shogan, Debra A. *The Making of High-Performance Athletes: Discipline, Diversity, and Ethics*. Toronto: University of Toronto Press, 1999.

Shulman, Alix Kates. "Dances with Feminists." *Women's Review of Books* 9, no. 3. (December 1991). Posted at "The Emma Goldman Papers," Berkeley Digital Library, 2002, http://sunsite.berkeley.edu/Goldman/Features/dances_shulman .html.

Sioux, Uzi. "Talk Derby to Me." In *Gender Outlaws: The Next Generation*, edited by Kate Bornstein and S. Bear Bergman, 213–17. Berkeley, Calif.: Seal Press, 2010.

Skate Canada. *Skate Canada: 2009 Annual Report*. www.skatecanada.ca.

Skating with the Stars. ABC, WMTW, Portland, Maine, November 22, 2010.

Smith, Bryan. "Miracle on Ice." *Men's Health*, January 28, 2009.

So You Think You Can Dance. Fox. WPFO, Portland, Maine, Season 4, June 5, June 8, and August 6, 2008; Season 5, May 27, 2009; Season 8, June 30, July 29, and August 12, 2010.

Spade, Dean. "Some Very Basic Tips for Making Higher Education More Accessible to Trans Students and Rethinking How We Talk about Gendered Bodies," in "No More Special Guests: Teaching Trans Now," ed. Shana Agid and Erica Rand, special issue, *Radical Teacher* 92 (2012): 57–62.

Spelling, Tori, with Hilary Liftin, *sTORI Telling*. New York: Simon Spotlight Entertainment, 2008.

Stewart, Kathleen. *Ordinary Affects*. Durham: Duke University Press, 2007.

Stick It. Dir. Jessica Bendinger. Touchstone Pictures, 2006.

Stojko, Elvis. "The Night They Killed Figure Skating." *Yahoo! Sports*, February 19, 2010.

Stratta, Terese M. Peretto. "Cultural Expressions of African American Female Athletes in Intercollegiate Sport." In *Athletic Intruders: Ethnographic Research on Women, Culture, and Exercise*, edited by Anne Bolin and Jane Granskog, 79–106. Albany: State University of New York Press, 2003.

Sykes, Heather Jane. *Queer Bodies: Sexualities, Genders, and Fatness in Physical Education*. New York: Peter Lang, 2011.

Tator, Carol, Francis Henry, and Winston Mattis, eds. *Challenging Racism in the Arts: Case Studies of Controversy and Conflict*. Toronto: University of Toronto Press, 1998.

Teetzel, Sarah. "On Transgendered Athletes, Fairness and Doping: An International Challenge." *Sport in Society* 9, no. 2 (April 2006): 227–51.

Thangaraj, Stanley. "Ballin' Indo-Pak Style: Pleasures, Desires, and Expressive Practices of 'South Asian American' Masculinity." *International Review for the Sociology of Sport* 45, no. 3 (2010): 372–89.

Theberge, Nancy. *Higher Goals: Women's Ice Hockey and the Politics of Gender*. SUNY Series on Sport, Culture, and Social Relations. Albany: State University of New York Press, 2000.

Think Before You Pink. Founded in 2002. Breast Cancer Action, http://www.think beforeyoupink.org/.

Thompson, S. Leigh. "Crafting Language: Transmasculine." *Adventures in Gender*, February 19, 2009, http://xploragen.blogspot.com.

Thompson, William. "A Message from the CEO William Thompson." Skate Canada website, May 6, 2009.

Torgovnick, Kate. *Cheer!* New York: Touchstone, 2008.

Torres, Dara, with Elizabeth Weil. *Age Is Just a Number: Achieve Your Dreams at Any Stage in Your Life*. New York: Broadway, 2009.

U.S. Department of Labor. Title IX, Education Amendments of 1972: Title 20 U.S.C. Sections 1681–88.

U.S. Figure Skating. *Coaches Code of Ethics, Standards, and Conduct.* In the USFS *Risk Management Guide.* 2007–8 [unpaginated], http://www.usfigureskating .org/content/RiskManagementGuide.pdf.

———. *The 2010 Official U.S. Figure Skating Rulebook.* Colorado Springs: U.S. Figure Skating, 2009.

———. *The 2011 Official U.S. Figure Skating Rulebook.* Colorado Springs: U.S. Figure Skating, 2010.

———. *The 2012 Official U.S. Figure Skating Rulebook.* Colorado Springs: U.S. Figure Skating, 2010.

Wald, Gayle. "Just a Girl? Rock Music, Feminism, and the Cultural Construction of Female Youth." *Signs* 23, no. 3 (Spring 1998): 585–610.

Waldron, Mary. "Lawyer by Day . . . Part One." *Law Crossing,* July 30, 2007, http:// www.lawcrossing.com.

Wall, Cheryl A. *Worrying the Line: Black Women Writers, Lineage, and Literary Tradition.* Chapel Hill: University of North Carolina Press, 2005.

Wall, Denise. "Denise Wall on Raising Dancin' Boys Part Three," interview by Nina Amir. On *My Son Can Dance: One Mom's Musings about Boys in the Dance World,* March 7, 2010, http://mysoncandance.wordpress.com.

Weir, Johnny. *Welcome to My World.* New York: Gallery, 2011.

Weston, Kath, and Lisa B. Rofel. "Sexuality, Class, and Conflict in a Lesbian Workplace." In *Long Slow Burn: Sexuality and Social Science,* by Kath Weston, 115–42. New York: Routledge, 1998.

"Who Are We?" *Butch-Femme.com/.* 2002–5, http://www.butch-femme.com.

Wife versus Secretary. Dir. Clarence Brown. MGM, 1936. Warner Home Video, 2006.

Williams, Jordan. "Fruitboots: Moldy Gender Issues That Are Ripe for Analysis," unpublished essay, March 2009.

Women's Flat Track Derby Association. WFTDA *Standardized Flat Track Derby Rules,* Updated May 26, 2010, WFTDA website.

Yamaguchi, Kristi, with Christy Ness and Jody Meacham. *Figure Skating for Dummies.* Foster City, Calif.: IDB Books, 2007.

Young, Susan. "From Ballet to Boxing: The Evolution of a Female Athlete." In *My Life at the Gym: Feminist Perspectives on Community through the Body,* edited by Jo Malin, 43–60. Albany: State University of New York Press, 2010.

Ziegler Jr., Cyd. "Can Canada Make Figure Skating Tough?" *Outsports,* February 3, 2009, http://outsports.com/jocktalkblog.

INDEX

Note: Page numbers in italics refer to illustrations.

Adams, Mary Louise, 11, 156, 255
addiction narratives, 174
Adult Nationals (AN): club affiliation announcements, 236; confusion on rules, 36–37; dresses in, 23; gender policing at, 117–24, 252; in Lake Placid (2008), 7; medical registry, 192–93; mutual support at, 31, 125–26; sandbagging at, 26–30; scoring systems, 34; sex segregation and, 255; technical vs. interpretive programs, 120–21; whiteness at, 127
adult skating: adult figure skater, meaning of, 1–2; dominant feminine norms in, 111–16; friendly environment of, 249–50; obstacles to level playing field, 30–31; "proprietary data," 37–39; standards and age, 258–59
Adult Skating Committee, 36–38
Adult Training Camp, 60–61, 178, 244
affinity and identity, 58–59
Afghanistan, 245
African Americans, 76, 128–32, 146, 188, 284n21
age: adult skating standards and, 258–59; adults who skated when younger, 30–31; boys' hockey and age groups, 172; clothing appropriateness and, 252; condescension and, 29; "cougars," 231; gender expression and, 112; limits on body, 186–87; propriety standards, 116; recovery time and,

176, 276n8; spins and, 34. *See also* adult skating
Agid, Shana, 186
Aguilera, Christina, 5, 253
Ahmed, Sara, 239, 245, 282n12
Alba, Carolyn-Ann, 133, 270n58
Allen, Debbie, 180–83
Allen, Joshua, 180–84, 276n24
Amaechi, John, 156, 158
Amateur Hockey Association of the United States (AHAUS), 140–41
American Hockey League (AHL), 140–41
America's Got Talent (TV), 213, 246
America's Next Top Model (ANTM), 184–85
Ampu, Ratowe T., 243
Anderson, Pamela, 104
animals, dressing like, 121
arm extensions, 241, 244, 246
Armour, Nancy, 268n16
Armstead, Agatha, 128, 132
Arquette, Alexis, 237
"artistic" vs. "athletic," 97–99, 159
"Artists and Models" group number (2002), 91–92
Ash, Juliet, 71–72
Asian-descent skaters, 132–34, 139–40, 188–89
Asperger's syndrome, 184–85
athleticism: artistry placed in contrast with, 97–99, 159; "feminine mandate" and, 113–14; femininity opposed

athleticism (*continued*)
to, 112; inside vs. outside view, 232–34; roller derby and, 120
Audra Mae, 237
axel jumps, 27

Bäckström, Nicklas, 141
ballet, 57, 104, 128–30, 148, 176, 180–84, 194–95
ballet buns, 22, 125
Banks, Tyra, 185
"Barette Manifesto" (Serano), 82
Barnsley, Paula, 172
Bass, Amy, 188
Bates College, 212, 227–28
Bates Committee on Athletics, 232–33
baton twirling, 246
Battle of the Blades (TV), 147, 272n19
Bauer, Wendy, 125
Baughman, Cynthia, 267n1
Beauchamp, Toby, 252
"Beautiful" skating programs, 5, 253
Bechdel, Alison, 77–78, 266n15
Be Good Johnny Weir (TV), 273n55
Bell, Billy, 158
Bell, Jed, 251
Bell, William, 128
Bergling, Tim, 156
Berig, Karen, 133, 270n55
Bernstein, Ross, 147
Betty (band), 237
Beverly Hills, 90210 (TV), 44, 111
Billy Elliot (film), 148
biopsies, 9, 201–3, 210–18
Blackhawks, Chicago, 151
blades, 17–19, 179. *See also* skates
Blades of Glory (film), 10, 66
Bobek, Nicole, 106
body, bodies: aging limits on, 186–87; arm extensions, 241, 244, 246; big butts, 129–31; biopsy scars and breast cancer, 201–3, 210–18; blade scars, 199–201; brain, brawn, and whiteness, 146; enhancement vs. repair or restoration, 193; extension, extreme, 106–7, *109*; "fat girl deduction," 124; natural ability, attribution of, 190–95; normative tools of body management, 240; physicality, gender, and hockey, 57–59; race and body shapes, 129–32; scoring and body types, 257; shift in thinking about, 9; titanium and, 9–10. *See also* breasts; injury
Boitano, Brian, 2
Bonaly, Surya, 97
books for children, 65, 65–66, 106, 150–51, 253
boot covers, 90
Bornstein, Kate, 43–45
Boss, Stephen "tWitch," 159, 182
boxing, 162
Boys Don't Cry (film), 146, 272n14
bras, 79–84
Breakaways hockey team, 57
breasts: binding of, 82; biopsies and cancer scare, 9, 201–3; bras, 79–84; cleavage, 104; culture of breast cancer, 215–18; eroticism and gender identity and, 216–18; as term, 214
Brennan, Christine, 177
Bright, Susie, 230
Bring it On (film), 259
Bring it On 3 (film), 120
Brown Boi Project, 162
Brownworth, Victoria, 86–87
Bryant, Anthony, 183
Bryant, Decory, 209
Buccigross, John, 144, 148
Burke, Brendan, 144–48, 151
Burke, Brian, 144–48, 151
Burke, Patrick, 273n34
butch and butchness: arm extension and, 241, 256; "athletic" as, 97–98; boys, dance training, and, 256–57; breast cancer and, 217; butch/femme scale, 165; clothing and, 75; feminine visibility and, 99; Gay Games and, 5; gender terminology and, 52; ideo-

logical positions and, 115; markers of, 160–63; orientation assumptions, 214; pressure to butch up, 98, 159. *See also* masculinity

"butchdar," 161–63

Buttle, Jeff, 65

Button, Dick, 134

butts, 129–31

buy-in narratives and decisions, 240–41

Buzinski, Jim, 273n44

Byrd, James, Jr., 146

Cahn, Susan K., 269n28

Califia, Patrick, 115

Cammalleri, Mike, 149, 273n29

Canadian Association for the Advancement of Women and Sport, 250

cancer and breast biopsies, 9, 201–3, 210–18

Caple, Jim, 157

Carlos, John, 238

Carolla, Adam, 4

Carroll, Frank, 240

Carter, W. Hodding, IV, 3

Catholic Church, 145

Caudwell, Jayne, 98

Cee, Maggie, 130

ceremonies in sports, 235–37

Chanel, Joan, 126

Chapkis, Wendy, 244

cheerleading, competitive, 207–8

Chicago Blackhawks, 151

children's books, 65, 65–66, 106, 150–51, 253

Chin, Staceyann, 235–36

Cho, Margaret, 258

choice. *See* risk, choice, and "perilicious"

Christopher, Matt, 151, 273n31

Cindy Lop-Her, 130

class: Adams on, 11; "athletic" label and, 97; Foote on, 268n12; shoes, gender, and, 85–88; "white trash" judgments, 105

cleavage, 104

clothing and costumes: at Adult Nationals, 23, 120–21; "age-inappropriate," 252; beginners and, 74; body shape and, 130; bras, 79–84; butchdar and, 160–63; class and, 105; deductions for "opposite-sex" clothing, 284n14; derby garb, 103–4, 200; "gender-appropriate" policies, 252; Harding downgrade for, 105; hockey garb, 52–54; illusion fabric, 21, 23; ISU rules, 76; Juvenile Girls, dresses for, 21; Juvenile Girls and gender issues, 23; Nine Inch Nails/Pink Floyd program (Rand), 117–20, *118*; "Piece of My Heart" program (Rand), 99, *100*; pinnies, 170; race and, 119–20; shoes, gender, and class, 85–88; for technical vs. interpretive programs, 120–21; of Teresa Henderson, 60, 63, *64*; ties, 71–72; tights, 75–76; unitards, 76. *See also* skates

club affiliation announcements, 236

"club ice," 169–70

coaches, coaching: arm extensions and, 241, 244, 246; body and brain, 47–48; condescension by, 29; "from the boards," 249–50; information access and, 38; policing function of norms and, 240–41; "putting you on the ice," 29–30; USFS nondiscrimination directive, 283n13

Cobb, C. Montague, 188

Cohen, Sasha, *109*, 109–10

Colonial Adult Winter Challenge, 121

color of skates, 73–78, 89–93

community across incompatibilities, 245

"competing up," 26, 27

Competitive Test Track, 264n7

concussions, 219–21, 255–56

condescension, 29

Conroy, John, 282n7

Cool as Ice (Christopher), 151

cost of skating. *See* money and cost

costumes. *See* clothing and costumes

"cougars," 231

Coyote, Ivan, 233–34

Cricket Show, The (TV), *191*, 191–92, 277n45

Criscitiello, Ra, 80–81

cross-dressing, 121

Crossovers (Hardy), 253

crotch display, codes of, 105–10

Crouse, Cindy, 252, 283n14

cultural appropriation, 260–61

Cutting Edge, The (film), 66

Daley, Richard M., 236

Dallas Cowboy Cheerleaders: Making the Team (TV), 104

dance: "disability" and, 258; gender performance and, 111–12; skank-sexy distinction in, 104; *So You Think You Can Dance* (TV), 104, 158–59, 180–84, 267n10; tailbone-tucking and race in, 131; training and boys, 256–57

Dance Moms (TV), 134

DanceSport, 111–12

Dancing with the Stars (TV), 4, 98, 258

Dartfish technology, 177–78

DayGlo Divine, 130

Dean, Christopher, 34

Deep Dickollective (D/DC), 243

deep-insideness, 49–51

DeGeneres, Ellen, 159

demolition derby, 163, 237

derby. *See* roller derby

DeVine, Phillip, 146

Devlin, Jane, 190

"disability," 258

Domi, Tie, 147

Domnina, Oksana, 259

Doyle, Jennifer, 101

"Dr.," 211

Dragon, Annette, 54–55

Dreams on Ice (Lewis), 65, *65*, 106

dresses. *See* clothing and costumes

dykes/lesbians: bras and, 79–80; cliché

of female sports teams and, 45; Gay Games and, 5–6; participation in skating, failure to discuss, 150, 155; terms and identity, 52. *See also* butch and butchness; femme and femme-ness

Dykes to Watch Out For (Bechdel), 77, 266n15

Eastern Conference Hockey League (ECHL), 140–41

Ehrenreich, Barbara, 215, 280n26

Elite Athlete Health Insurance (EAHI), 208–9, 279n22

emotions and investment, 239–41

enhancement vs. repair or restoration, 193

Entwistle, Amy, 250

equipment. *See* skates

ethnic typecasting, 133–34. *See also* race and ethnicity

excellence, athletic concept of, 258–59

extension, extreme, 106–7, *109*

extreme sports, 239

Faber, Michael, 145

Facebook, 107, *108*, 204–5

Fairbanks, Mabel, 132

Family Ice Center, Falmouth, Maine (FIC), 169, 175

"Fans for Downgrading Grabbing Your Skate" Facebook group, 107, *108*

Farris, JoAnn Schneider, 107

Fassi, Carlo, 270n56

"fat girl deduction," 124

Feder-Kane, Abigail, 267n1

femininity and "ladies": "athletic" vs. "artistic," 97–99; bras and, 80–84; crotch display, codes of, 105–10; judging and gender policing in adult skating, 117–25; "ladies" label, 100–102; mutual support in adult skating, 125–27; normativity and, 111–16; pressure to conform, 123–24; race and, 128–35;

skankiness vs. sexiness, 103–5, 110; strength, difficulty, and, 48; visibility of femininity, 99, *100*; "wiles," 142. *See also* gender

femme and femmeness: "artistic" vs. "athletic" and, 97–99; butch/femme scale, 165; Gay Games and, 5; gender terminology and, 52; ideological positions and, 115; misogyny and, 115; as object of desire, 233–34; orientation assumptions, 214

Fenkell, Michael, 272n20

fieldwork, 20–25, 37, 39

figures, compulsory, 133, 270n56

Figure Skaters for Christ website, 64–65

figure skaters, figure skating. *See names of specific people, events, and topics*

Figure Skating in Harlem (FIH), 8, 75–76, 257, 265n11, 283n5

Fischer, John, 273n34

flamboyance, 158, 272n22

Flatt, Rachel, 260

Fleming, Peggy, 215

Foote, Stephanie, 105, 268n12

foot size, 85–86

Frankel, Bethenny, 258

Freedman, Jarrett, 141

freedom, redirection as, 245–46

friend-as-informal-coach role, 29

friendship, unexpected, 60–63, 67

Froderman, Lauren, 158–59

Fung, Richard, 135

Fun Home (Bechdel), 77, 266n15

Furio, Neill C., 199

Fusco, Caroline, 281n6

Galindo, Rudy, 107, 156–57

Gallico, Paul, 189

Gambs, Deborah, 49

Game Face photography exhibit, 81

garter belts, 54

Gay Games, 2–6, 26–28, 114, 235–37, 253

gay men and gayness: figure skating, masculinity, and, 153–59; hockey, masculinity, and, 144–52. *See also* masculinity

Gaynor, Gloria, 265n11

gender: bi-gendered identity, 222; bras and, 79–84; "breast" and, 214–18; coerced vs. consensual, 98; free expression of, 251–52; at Gay Games, 4–6; hierarchical privileging of butch or trans, 122; hockey garb and, 52–54; "how much," 251; as inherent truth to uncover, 50–51; Juvenile Girls category and, 22–23; "Mrs." and, 210–14; naturalization and, 194–95; off-ice conformity, 121; pairs and dance teams rules, 254–55; sexuality vs., 155; skate color and, 73–78, 91–92; transcending stereotypes, 48; transgender, 22–23; visibility of, 99, *100*; "you throw like a girl," 112. *See also* femininity and "ladies"; masculinity

Gendered Object, The (Ash), 71–72

General Hospital spoof program, 123, 247

"genetic lottery," 190

"Gift from Africa" ice show (Figure Skating in Harlem), 8, 75–76, 257, 265n11

Gladwell, Malcolm, 170–72

Glee (TV), 44, 258, 284n25

gliding, 49–50

God, 60–67

Godfrey, Kristin, 125

Godsey, Keelin, 98

going stealth, 44

Goldman, Emma, 261

Goldman, Jason, 4

Goodman, Lynn, 264n10

Gordeeva, Ekaterina, 64

Graton, Marilyn, 11

Gray, Mary, 50

Greater Portland Women's Ice Hockey League (GPWIH), 8, 56–57, 273n30 grievance procedure for scores and results, 26

Grinkov, Sergei, 64

Grinvalski, Kathy (Jacked Rabbit), 160–63, *161*, 165

Gruneau, Richard, 238, 282n9

Gumbel, Bryant, 146

gym class, 56

gymnastics, 259

hair: age and, 252; ballet buns, 22, 125; butch/femme and, 160–61; chest hair, 149; femininity and, 114; hockey and, 50; religion and, 63; unconventional, 117, 121, 127

Halberstam, Judith (Jack), 272n14

Halloween, 121

Harding, Tonya, 7, 97, 105, 124, 266n12

Hardy, LeAnne, 253

harem-girl character, 133–35

Harlick, 73

health care and insurance, 204–5, 207–9

Hellcats (TV), 259

Hello, Cruel World (Bornstein), 43–45

Henderson, Teresa, 60–63, 64, 67

Henie, Sonja, 73–74

Herzig, Rebecca, 12

heteronormativity, 122–24, *123*

Hilderbrand, Lucas, 284n25

Hines, James R., 270n56

hockey: affinity and, 57–59; age groups in boy's hockey, 172; Brian and Brendan Burke and antiqueer sentiments in, 144–48, 150–52; experience of women's hockey, 52–56; face-masks, tough guys, and masculinity, 139–42; Greater Portland Women's Ice Hockey League, 8, 56–57; high-sticking, 139, 141, 271n8; hockey sticks as phallic weapons, 149–50; intimacy, physicality, and exchange, 59; Japan-U.S. game, 57; resource inequities, 150, 273n30; risk, choice,

and the "perilicious," 206, 207, 219–22; rough contact and femininity, 112; skates, 75

Holy Rollers, 103, 267n9

"homophobia," as term, 144, 158

honorifics, 211–12

Howard, Charlie, 272n22

Ice Bridges, 283n5

Ice Castles (film), 21, 24

Ice Etiquette (Entwistle), 250

Ice Mom, 276n19

Ice Princess (film), 20–21

Ice Skating Institute (ISI), 27

ice time, 175–76, 239

identity: affinity and, 58–59; deep-insideness and, 50–51; explanatory weakness of, 71; shift from act to, 221. *See also* gender

"I Feel Pretty" (*West Side Story*), 5–6, 263n3

illusion fabric, 21, 23

information, proprietary, 36–38

injury: admitting, and pride in, 203; from bad gender fits, 122; broken collarbones, 204; concussions, 219–21, 255–56; extreme extensions and, 107; health care and insurance for, 204–5, 207–9. *See also* risk, choice, and the perilicious"

inline skating, 163–64

Institutional Review Board (IRB), 22, 264n4

insurance, medical, 207–9

International Judging System (IJS), 32–36, *33*, 240

International Olympic Committee (IOC), 267n8

International Skating Union (ISU): costume rules, 76; new scoring system, 32–34, *33*; transgender policies, need for, 254–55

interpretive programs ("interps"), 120–21, 252, 253

intersex athletes, 101, 190
Ito, Midori, 97

Jacked Rabbit (Kathy Grinvalski), 160–63, *161*, 165
Jackson, Jon, 156
Jain, S. Locklain, 216–18
Japan-U.S. hockey game, 57
Jews and men's basketball, 189
Jock Bra/Jog Bra, 81–83
Johnson, Robin, 30
Jolie, Angelina, 134
Jordan, Glenn, 101
judging. *See* scores and scoring
jumps: axels, 27; body shape and, 131, 257; confusion on rules, 36–37; equipment and, 179; scoring aligned with body types for, 257
Junior Nationals, 255
Juvenile Girls category, 21–22

Kang, Miliann, 258
Katerina rule, the, 266n12
Keith, Toby, 142
Kellams, Mike, 152
Kelley, Robin D. G., 245
Kerrigan, Nancy, 105
Kestnbaum, Ellyn, 73, 265n12
Killer Quick (Maureen Wissman), 120, 199–200
Kim Yu-Na, 133–34, 255, 270n57
Kittredge, Katharine, 219–22, *220*
Kobayashi, Jay, 121
Kociemba, David, 258
Korean manicurists, 258, 284n23
Kotelko, Olga, 186, 277n34
Kusz, Kyle, 239
Kuszmich, Heather, 184
Kwan, Michelle, 121, 133–34, 179

"ladies." *See* femininity and "ladies"
Lake Placid, 7
Lambert, Karen, 236
Lapointe, Joe, 147

Laskowski, Brigitte Gitta, 64–65
laundering, 243
Lavigne, Avril, 194–95
Lemieux, Claude, 147
lesbians. *See* dykes/lesbians
Lessik, Alan, 254
Letang, Wislande, 267n10
Lewey, Jaimie Bissonette, 260
Libman, Alyn, 229–30, 254, 267n8
"Life in the Passing Lane" (Brownworth), 86–87
Lind, Erika, 75
Lindahl, Lisa, 81–82
Lindhardt, Maureen, 125
Lithgoe, Nigel, 158, 181–83, 275n57
Longman, Jere, 188–89, 270n54
Look Good . . . and Feel Better program, 218
Lopez, Jennifer, 131, 134
Lorde, Audre, 202–3
Ludington, Ron, 107, 108
Lysacek, Evan, 34, 153, 155, 157–58, 177, 240, 255

MacDougall, Christopher, 179
MacLeod, J. E., 150–51
MacNeil, Trevor, 148
Magdalinski, Tara, 193, 277n37
Maine Indian Tribal-State Commission, 260
Maine Roller Derby (MRD), 8, 101, 130, 160, 164–65
makeover segments on TV, 245–46
makeup, stage, 124
Manley, Allison, 107
Man Tricks (Harper), 80
Manzon-Santos, Johnny, 108–9, 254, 257, 268n23
marriage, 213, 280nn28–29
Martin, April, 112–13
masculinity: arm extensions and, 241; bra trick and, 80; figure skating and, 153–59; free sexuality and, 253–54; hockey and, 139–42, 144–52; Kitt-

masculinity (*continued*)
  redge and, 222; roller derby and
  markers of, 160–65; skate parks and,
  163–64; "wiles," 142. *See also* butch
  and butchness
Matthew Shepard and James Byrd, Jr.
  Hate Crimes Prevention Act, 146
McCullough, Sarah Rebolloso, 192–94
McMains, Juliet, 111–12, 131
McSorley, Marty, 141
memorial narratives, 228–29
memory, 86–88, 92–93
men. *See* gay men and gayness; masculinity
"menstrual complications," reporting
  of, 192–93
Messner, Michael, 149, 222
Metzger, Deena, 202
Miami University of Ohio RedHawks,
  144
Michaels, Mia, 158
Miller, Hinda, 81–83
Miller, Quinn, 250
Mission hockey sticks, 149
Miss Saigon, 133, 135, 270n57
Moir, Scot, 269n34
Molina-Guzmán, Isabel, 134
money and cost: addiction narratives
  and, 174; advantages of, 24; estimates and bottom lines, 177–79;
  of ice time, 175–76; insurance and,
  207–9; Regionals and, 24; in roller
  derby, 276n15; sex characteristics
  and, 76–77; skates and, 77, 178–79;
  "supporting the club," 250–51; talent
  and, 170; testing, 175; unaffordability
  of coaching and, 266n13
Morozov, Nikolai, 244, 246
movies about skating, 20–21. *See also
  under titles of specific films*
"Mrs.," 210–14
Mullins, Thom, 253–54
Muñoz, José Esteban, 271n63

Muralitharan, Muttiah "Murali," *191*,
  191–92
Murray, Arthur, 131
Murray, Kathryn, 131
Musademba, Kristine, 133–34
muscle memory, 92–93
muscles, 160, 162
music: adapting to, 12; ethnic stereotypes and, 133–34; gender norms and,
  230; ice venues and, 170, 175; interpretive programs and, 120; judges'
  familiarity with, 119; Pink Floyd/Nine
  Inch Nails program, 117; pop culture
  and, 266n12; Rowell and, 132; solo
  programs and, 3; Stojko on, 155
My Sergei (Gordeeva), 63–64
MySkatingMall.com, 283n5

Nagasu, Mirai, 260
national anthem, 237
National Center for Lesbian Rights
  (NCLR), 254
nationalism, 236–39
Nationals (U.S. Figure Skating
  Championships), 8
Native American team names and mas-
  cots, 260
"natural" vs. unnatural advantages, attri-
  bution of, 190–95
NCAA, 208, 279n21
neoliberalism, 245
New England Regionals, 24
Nguyen, Mimi, 245
Nicks, Stevie, 114
"Night They Killed Figure Skating, The"
  (Stojko), 153–56
Nine Inch Nails/Pink Floyd program
  (Rand), 117–19, 121
nondiscrimination compliance, 283n13
normality and normativity, 111–16, 239–
  41. *See also* gender
North Atlantic Figure Skating Club (Fal-
  mouth, Maine), 236

Obama, Barack, 146
Olympics: age and, 3–4, 176; clothing conventions in lifting, 252; Gay Games and, 2; Gordeeva and, 64; hockey at, 141, 152; ice rinks and, 7; 10C, 267n8; masculinity and, 153, 155; sex segregation and, 255; sex verification testing at, 190; snowboarding and capitalization at, 238–39; swimming and swimsuits at, 193; Thomas and, 76; USOC, 208, 279n22; Weir and, 124, 157; whiteness and, 260
Orser, Brian, 156, 270n57
Osbourne, Sharon, 213
Out in the Country (Gray), 50
Outright/Lewiston-Auburn, 79
Ovechkin, Alex, 141
Owen, Maribel Vinson, 17, 74, 76, 132, 240, 266n13
Owens, Jesse, 188

Panthers, Florida, 207
panty flashing, 106–10
participant observation, 20–25
patriotism, 236–37
Patty O'Mean (Crystal Vaccaro), 204
Peck, Janice, 245
Perfect Landing, A (Kirby), 65, 65
Perfect Match, A (Lewis), 65, 66
"perilicious." *See* risk, choice, and "perilicious"
Phelps, Michael, 193
Philadelphia Skating Club and Humane Society, 169
Pink Floyd/Nine Inch Nails program (Rand), 117–19, 121
pink kitsch, 215–16
pinnies, 170
pleasure: affinity and, 58–59; deep-insideness, 49–51; definitions vs. openness, 43; enjoyment of others, 57–58; God and, 60–67; hooked on skating, 10–11; inside vs. outside view

of, 232–34; joining and sports teams, 43–45; limits of, 229–30; memorial narratives and, 228–29; norms, policing function of, 239–41; politics of, 242–47; power, privilege, and, 238–39; risk and outside vs. inside view and, 222–23; seeing, getting, and, 230–32; sex, skating compared to, 46; skating as world apart, 47–48; sports ceremonies, nationalism, and, 235–37; vibrator story, 227–28; wind on skin and speed, 46–47
Plimpton, George, 114
Plushenko, Evgeny, 153, 155
politics of pleasure, 242–47. *See also* pleasure
pop-culture music, 266n12
Portland Ice Arena (PIA), 169–71, 175
Post Concussion Syndrome (PCS), 219–20
power: gender and, 72; not "getting" it and, 25; pleasure and power regimes, 238–39; risk and, 209; Stojko on, 155; values, identity, and, 58; wiles and, 142
Probert, Bob, 147
Pronger, Chris, 152
Pumping Iron (film), 267n3
Punchy O'Guts, 130
Putin, Vladimir, 153
"putting you on the ice," 29–30

quad jumps and masculinity, 153

race and ethnicity: Adult Nationals and, 127, 188–89; Asian-descent skaters, 132–34, 139–40; "athletic" label and, 97; attachments across, 231–32; color of skates and tights and, 75–76; cultural appropriation, 260–61; extreme sports and, 239; Gay Games and, 236; honorifics and, 212; hypersexualized racial stereotypes and, 135; Jews

race and ethnicity (*continued*)
  and men's basketball, 189; Olympics
  and, 260; skating cultures and, 259–
  60; *So You Think You Can Dance* (TV)
  and, 181–83; swimming and, 193–94;
  talent narratives and, 188–89; white-
  dominated feminine norms and,
  128–32; whiteness and masculinity,
  146–47
"Radiant Smile from a Lovely Lady, A"
  (Feder-Kane), 267n1
Red Bull, 238–39
Regionals (USFS regional championships), 8, 21–22, 24
religion, 60–67
representation, bind of, 135
representing, 184–85
results, contested, 26
Retton, Mary Lou, 107
Rice, Jerry, 98
Riedell, 73, 90–91, 178
right of way on the ice, 250
Rippon, Adam, 178
Rippon, Kelly, 178
RISE (film), 239–40, 240, 278n48
risk, choice, and "perilicious": biopsy
  scars and breast cancer, 201–3, 210–
  18; blade scars and, 199–201; competitive cheerleading and, 207–8;
  figure skating and, 199, 203, 204–5,
  209; health care, insurance, and,
  204–5, 207–9; hockey and, 206, 207,
  219–22; injury and, 203; NCAA and,
  208; pleasure and inside vs. outside
  views of, 222–23; roller derby and,
  199–200, 204, 205–7, 220–21; Title
  IX and, 221; USA swimming and,
  208–9
Roberts, Julia, 134
Robinson, Craig, 146
rockers, 18
Rofel, Lisa B., 282n17
rolfing, 179, 187
roller derby: attire, 103–4, 200; "booty
  block," 130; image of, contrasted with
  figure skating, 200; Maine Roller
  Derby (MRD), 8, 101, 130, 160, 164–
  65; race and, 119–20; risk, choice,
  and "perilicious" and, 199–200, 204,
  205–7, 220–21; rough contact and
  femininity and, 112; sweetheart/ani-
  mal trope and, 164–65; transgender
  players and, 252
Roller Girls (TV), 267n9
Rose City Rollers, 237
Rosenthal, Stephanie, 119
Rowell, Victoria, 128–29, 130–31, 132,
  193
Ruggiero, Angela, 152
Ruiz, Jose, 184
rules, confusion over, 32, 34–39, 257.
  See also scores and scoring

Safi, Bryan, 157–58
Salome program (Kwan), 133–34
Salt Lake City Sports Complex, 7
Sanceto, Amy, 268n16
sandbagging, 21, 26–31, 257, 264n7
Save the Last Dance (film), 182
scars, 199, 201
scores and scoring: costume deductions
  in, 32, 163, 284n14; counting spin
  revolutions, 240; "fat deduction," 124;
  grievance procedure for, 26; International Judging System (IJS) and,
  32–34, 33, 240; rules for, 257; spirals
  and crotch display and, 106–7; Well-
  Balanced Program (WBP) charts and,
  21, 34–37, 257
Sedgwick, Eve, 25, 71, 216–18
"seeing it" and "getting it," 20–25,
  230–32
Semenya, Caster, 190
Serano, Julia, 82, 122
sex, skating compared to, 46
sex segregation in sports, 190, 254–55
Sexsmith, Sinclair, 275n63
sexuality: derby girls and, 103–4; free

expression of, 253–54; at Gay Games, 4–6; gender vs., 155; heteronormativity, 122–24, *123*; hockey garb and, 52–54; "skank" and, 103–5, 110; "sports sexuality spectrum," 157. *See also* dykes/lesbians; gay men and gayness

sex verification testing, 97, 190

Shabalin, Maxim, 259

Shankman, Adam, 181

Shastri, Ravi, 191–92

Shepard, Matthew, 146

Shimizu, Celine Parreñas, 135

shoes, 85–88, 93

Shogan, Debra, 112

Simmons, Gene, 237

SimulCam, 177–78

Sin City Skates, 205–6

"sissyphobia," 156

"Sk8er Boi" (Lavigne), 194–95

skankiness vs. sexiness, 103–5, 110

skateboarders, 163–64, 194

Skate Canada, 154, 156, 253, 273n39

skate parks, 163–64

skates: blade technology, 17–18; boot covers, 90; breaking in, 77; color of, 73–78, 89–93; cost of, 77, 178–79, 276n15; for hockey, 75; jump performance and, 179; lacing up, 71, 92–93; muscle memory and, 92–93; replacement of, 77; sharpening of, 18–19, 179

skating clubs, 169–70, 236

skating culture, 249–61

Skating with the Stars (TV), 258

Slater, Michael, 191

Smith, Bryan, 241, 253

Smith, Emmitt, 98

Smith, Tommie, 238

Snickers ad, 149

snowboarding, 238–39

Sopel, Brent, 151

So You Think You Can Dance (TV), 104, 158–59, 180–84, 267n10

Spade, Dean, 256

speed, 46–47

Speedo LZR Racer, 193–94

speed skating, 58

Spelling, Tori, 111, 114

spins: confusing guidelines for, 34–37, 109–10; counting revolutions of, 240; crotch display and, *109*; jump revolutions and, 153; sit spins, 34

spirals and spiral sequences, 106–7, 268n18

sports bras, 80–84

sports ceremonies, 235–37

sports teams, 44–45, 101, 260. *See also* hockey

Squires, Mary, 165, 202

Stacey, Michelle, 171

"Star-Spangled Banner, The," 237

Stewart, Kathleen, 58–59

Stick It (film), 259

Stojko, Elvis, 153–56, 179, 273n44

Stratta, Terese M. Peretto, 284n21

StroMotion, 177–78

success. *See* talent and success

Summitt, Pat, 101

Surprise Finish, A (Kociemba), *65*, 66

Swift, Taylor, 125–27

swimming, racialization of, 193–94

synchronized skating, 187, 251

tailbone-tucking, 129–31

Takahashi, Daisuke, 159

talent and success: aging and variables, 186–88; costs and, 170, 174–79; equipment and performance and, 179; public skating vs. club ice, 169–70; race, ethnicity, gender, and naturalization of ability, 188–95; training time and, 170–72; TV talent contests and training narratives, 180–85

technical programs, 120, 135, 252

Teena, Brandon, 146, 272n14

Teetzel, Sarah, 190, 193

"10,000-hour rule," 170–72

Tequila Mockingbird, 206, 279n8, 279n11
Texas Lonestar Rollergirls (TXRD), 103
Thangaraj, Stanley, 146
Theberge, Nancy, 206–7
Thomas, Debi, 76, 107, 124, 129, 266n12
Thompson, S. Leigh, 275n63
Thompson, William, 154, 156
throwers in track and field, 97–98
Tidwell, Danny, 183, 256
ties, 71–72
tights, 75–76
Tim Gunn's Guide to Style (TV), 266n14
Title IX, 221
Title Nine (clothing company), 80–81
toe picks, 18, 66
toepoint, 109, 159, 184, 257
Torgovnick, Kate, 207–8, 259
Torres, Dara, 3–4, 176, 276n8
Torville, Jane, 34
"tossies," 125, *126*
"Tough" campaign (Skate Canada), 154, 253
training: Adult Training Camp, 60–61, 178, 244; capitalized strategies of, 238–39; in childhood, adults and, 2, 187; for dance, boys and, 256–57; for dance, Rowell and, 129–30; figures and, 133; gender and, 112; in hockey, 8; "home-grown" skaters and, 24; inside vs. outside view of, 222–23; money and, 8–9, 24; narratives of, in TV talent contests, 180–85; "nature" and, 189, 193–94, 222; refuge and stress relief mindsets and, 230; results and, 170–72; time experience of, 17, 176
transmasculine, 162, 275n63
trans/transgender athletes and issues: chest surgery and, 217; free expression and, 252; inclusion policies, need for, 254–55; IOC policy and, 267n8; Juvenile Girls and, 22–23;

"ladies" label and, 101–2; Libman interview, 229–30; perceived athletic ability and, 190; privileging of, 122; skate color and, 75; Spade's "Some Very Basic Tips," 256
Tunie, Tamara, 75–76
Turner, Lana, 128
TV makeover segments, 245–46
TV talent contests and training narratives, 180–85. *See also titles of specific shows*

United States Olympic Committee (USOC), 208, 279n22
United States Ski and Skateboarding Association (USSA), 279n22
USA Hockey Magazine, 149
USA swimming, 208–9, 279n22
U.S. Figure Skating (USFS): club affiliation announcements, 236; costume rules of, 120–21; mission statement and nondiscrimination policies of, 283n13; race and, 132; transgender policies in, need for, 254–55
U.S. Figure Skating Championships (Nationals), 8
U.S. Figure Skating Regional Championships (Regionals), 8, 21–22, 24
Uzi Sioux, 252

Vaccaro, Crystal (Patty O'Mean), 204
vibrator story, 227–28
Victoria's Secret, 84
Virtue, Tessa, 269n34
Vonn, Lindsey, 260

Waiting to Score (MacLeod), 150–51
Wald, Gayle, 119
Wall, Denise, 183, 256–57
Wall, Travis, 183, 256
Wang, Vera, 105, 158, 177
warrior narratives about cancer, 202–3, 217

Weir, Johnny, 34, 124, 154, 155, 157–58, 253, 258, 273n55

Weiss, Michael, 177–78

Welcome to My World (Weir), 158

Well-Balanced Program (wbp) charts, 21, 34–37, 257

West, Kanye, 127

Weston, Kath, 282n17

West Side Story, 5–6, 263n3

White, Shaun, 238–39

"white-girl butt," 129–32

whiteness. *See* race and ethnicity

"white trash" judgments, 105

Whitson, David, 238, 282n9

Wife versus Secretary (film), 265n6

"wiles," 142

Wilkes, Debbie, 154

Williams, Jordan, 163–64

wind on skin, feel of, 46–47

Winfrey, Oprah, 245

winning, desire for, 232–33

Wissman, Maureen (Killer Quick), 120, 199–200

Witt, Katerina, 266n12

Women on Ice (Baughman), 267n1

Women's Flat Track Derby Association (wftda), 200, 206, 278n2, 279n14

Women Who Raise Me, The (Rowell), 128–29

Wong, Alex, 159

Yao Ming, 190

yoga, 176, 256

"You Belong with Me" (Swift), 125–27

Young, Susan, 234

Zayak, Elaine, 124

Zednik, Richard, 207

Zona, Derek, 273n34

Erica Rand is Professor of Art and Visual Culture and of Women and Gender Studies at Bates College. She is the author of *The Ellis Island Snow Globe* (Duke, 2005) and *Barbie's Queer Accessories* (Duke, 1995).

Library of Congress Cataloging-in-Publication Data
Rand, Erica
Red nails, black skates : gender, cash, and pleasure
on and off the ice / Erica Rand
p. cm.
Includes bibliographical references and index.
ISBN 978-0-8223-5197-9 (cloth : alk. paper)
ISBN 978-0-8223-5208-2 (pbk. : alk. paper)
1. Figure skating—Social aspects. 2. Figure skaters.
3. Sex role. I. Title.
GV852.3.S63R36 2012
796.912—dc23
2011038522

In her forties, Erica Rand bought a pair of figure skates to vary her workout routine. Within a few years, the college professor was immersed in adult figure skating. Here, in short, incisive essays, she describes the pleasures to be found in the rink, as well as the exclusionary practices that make those pleasures less accessible to some than to others. Throughout the book, Rand situates herself as a queer femme, describing her mixed feelings about participating in a sport with heterosexual story lines and rigid standards for gender-appropriate costumes and moves. She chronicles her experiences competing in the Gay Games and at the annual U.S. Adult National Figure Skating Champion-ship, or "Adult Nationals." Aided by her comparative study of roller derby and women's hockey, including a brief attempt to play hockey herself, she addresses matters such as skate color conventions, judging systems, racial and sexual norms, transgender issues in sports, and the economics of athletic participation and risk taking. Mixing sharp critique with genuine appreciation and delight, Rand suggests ways to make figure skating more inclusive, while portraying the unlikely friendships facilitated by sports and the sheer elation of gliding on ice.

"*Red Nails, Black Skates* is a fabulous read, a smart and often hilarious account of one queer critic's journey deep into the heart of figure skating. The intricate interplay of gender, race, and class in skating culture makes it a perfect site for tackling the ways that antigay and sexist paradigms re-enforce one another, as well as anxieties about race and class. In this brilliantly written book, Erica Rand takes feminist sports studies to a new level, without sacrificing her own stories about the pleasures of figure skating and the lessons that she has learned as a skater."

—*Jennifer Doyle*, author of *Sex Objects: Art and the Dialectics of Desire* and the feminist soccer blog *From a Left Wing*

"Erica Rand brings us into the fascinating world of skating on ice. Her personal journey is riveting. In sharing it, she offers insight into the complexities of spending a lifetime immersed in her sport and tells many stories about figure skating that have not been told until now. A brilliant piece of work and a must-read."

—*Helen Carroll*, Sports Project Director, National Center for Lesbian Rights

ERICA RAND is Professor of Art and Visual Culture and of Women and Gender Stud-ies at Bates College. She is the author of *The Ellis Island Snow Globe* and *Barbie's Queer Accessories*, both also published by Duke University Press.

Duke University Press
Box 90660 Durham, NC 27708-0660
www.dukeupress.edu

ISBN 978-0-8223-5208-2